.

Mysteries of Judaism III
Common Sense Evaluations of Religious Thoughts

Mysteries OF Judaism III

Common Sense Evaluations
of Religious Thoughts

Israel Drazin

gefen גפן
publishing house בית הוצאה לאור
Est. 1981
JERUSALEM ◆ NEW YORK

Cover design: Leah Ben Avraham
Typesetting: Raphaël Freeman, Renana Typesetting

ISBN: 978-965-7023-10-5

1 3 5 7 9 8 6 4 2

Gefen Publishing House Ltd.
6 Hatzvi Street
Jerusalem 94386, Israel

972-2-538-0247
orders@gefenpublishing.com

Gefen Books
c/o 3PL Center
3003 Woodbridge Ave
Edison, NJ 08837
516-593-1234
orders@gefenpublishing.com

www.gefenpublishing.com

Printed in Israel

Library of Congress Control Number: 2019912351

Dedicated as usual
with love, to my wife Dina, my inspiration
who makes it possible for me to write
books and articles

Forty-six books by Israel Drazin

FOREWORD TO:

Maimonides' Hidden Torah Commentary, Genesis Book One
Maimonides' Hidden Torah Commentary, Genesis Book Two
Maimonides' Hidden Torah Commentary, Exodus Book One
Maimonides' Hidden Torah Commentary, Exodus Book Two
An Odyssey of Faith
Gentle Jewish wisdom

WITH CECIL B. CURREY

For God and Country

WITH STANLEY WAGNER

Understanding the Bible Text: Onkelos on the Torah: Genesis
Understanding the Bible Text: Onkelos on the Torah: Exodus
Understanding the Bible Text: Onkelos on the Torah: Leviticus
Understanding the Bible Text: Onkelos on the Torah: Numbers
Understanding the Bible Text: Onkelos on the Torah: Deuteronomy
Understanding Onkelos
Beyond the Bible Text
Iyunim Betargum (Hebrew)

WITH LEBA LIEDER

Can't Start Passover Without the Bread
Sailing on Moti's Ark on Succoth

AS DANIEL A. DIAMOND

Around The World in 123 Days
Crisis on Queen Victoria
Rational Religion

NOVEL

She Wanted to Be Jewish

Acknowledgments

Thanks to Darlene Jospe who edited this book and prepared the Index, Table of Contents, and the List of Sources, and to Ruth Pepperman of Gefen Publishing House who did the final editing of this book.

Contents

The Siddur

Secular Novels

Midrash

Jewish Practices

More on Maimonides

Introduction

This is my third book in my series that I call *Mysteries of Judaism* where my goal is to give readers an opportunity to understand better the source and content of sacred texts and practices. Although I am an observant, Orthodox Jew, my goal is to try and minimize the harm that zealots from various backgrounds use to define and describe Judaism as a whole, and hurt individual Jews by teaching false ideas, suggesting unnecessary behaviors, and by restricting Jews when the restrictions themselves are unnecessary.

My books respectfully urge readers to question accepted values and to challenge conventional "reality" in the light of higher ideals, to respond to the social requirements of our time, and to live a life based on the use of intelligence with a sense of commitment to all human beings. As in my other books, I emphasize the teachings of Maimonides.

In my first book in this series, I showed that none of the holy days are observed today as mandated in the Torah. I also explained why the rabbis had to change the way the days were celebrated and, in most instances, totally eliminate the biblical concept and develop a new one.

In *Mysteries of Judaism II*, I focused mostly on Jewish practices and showed how they changed, why they changed, and the value of the change, including even the concept as to when the day begins, for in the Bible, it began in the morning not at night.[1]

In this book, I focus primarily on ideas, and show that they too have changed.

The book is divided into nine topics:

---

1. This is the view of Rashi's grandson, the sage Rashbam.

BIBLE

Among other things, I discuss what the Torah states about life after death, the soul, the world to come, repentance, what if anything we must believe, changes that occurred in our concept of God, multiple violations of Torah laws by biblical persons and why this occurred, misunderstandings about the Ten Commandments, if the Torah is rational, divine involvement in miracles, prophecy and human activities, biblical and other ancient Jewish books that were neglected or rejected, humor in the Bible, portraying all biblical figures with their faults, and changing biblical laws and rabbinical customs.

SIDDUR

This section explains that the siddur is not what people think it is; there are mystical additions to the siddur, and different views about the value of prayer.

TALMUD

How to read the Talmud and the *Daf Yomi*.

PHILOSOPHY AND THEOLOGY

The stark difference between philosophy and theology; Judaism's first philosopher; discussions on sin; contacts with non-Jewish cultures; the untraditional elements in the biblical book Ecclesiastes; and the untraditional views of Orthodox thinkers such as Rashbam, Nachman Krochmal, J.B. Soloveitchik, David Hartman, Nathan Lopes Cardozo, and others.

SECULAR NOVELS

Discussions on the novels of Nobel Prize winning authors Hermann Hesse and Jose Saramago and others such as Ray Bradbury, Isaac Asimov, Alexander Pushkin, and Shakespeare that make us think about our current ideas and behaviors.

MIDRASH

Maimonides's view on why they were written and their value today.

JEWISH PRACTICES

Examination of practices such as kissing mezuzahs, the Torah and holy books; the impact of foreign cultures on Jewish practices and halakha; conversion; and intermarriage.

MYSTICISM AND ATHEISM

Analyses of mysticism and atheism, including the *Zohar*; Rabbi Kook's revolution; mystical views on immortality, resurrection, and the age of the universe; the values of secular culture; the views of Moshe Chaim Luzzatto and his *Mesillat Yesharim*, and of Arnold Ehrlich.

MORE ON MAIMONIDES

Although Maimonidean ideas pervade this volume, this section tells what most people do not know about him; punishing people despite repentance; false prophets who can still prophesy; Maimonides, Nietzsche, and Gersonides; Maimonides's views on faith and the biblical Akeidah story.

THE BIBLE

Why We See and Hear What We Do Not See or Hear

It is not surprising that many people find it hard to accept new ideas, and perhaps do not even have the ability to see and hear them. Scientists have recognized that there is a phenomenon called "cognitive dissonance." People tend to see, hear, read, taste, and feel things that they are convinced they know they are sensing, but they are wrong.

COGNITIVE DISSONANCE

Cognitive dissonance is a psychological phenomenon that most people experience. It is the mental and emotional discomfort and stress experienced by a person when a belief clashes with new evidence contradicting the previously held belief. When confronted with this situation, most people see the new evidence or interpret it as if it complies with their former belief, or else they reject the new evidence. Therefore, most people hold onto the religious teachings they were taught as children and are unable to see and hear the more mature ideas.

AN EXAMPLE

Leonard Bernstein's Young People's Concerts was one of the best shows on television in its time. He introduced the young and old to music, what it is, what it means, and how to enjoy it. In the 1958 hour-long film, the first in the series, he focused on "What Does Music Mean?" Then he explained that it is the combination of notes, just as speech is the combination of words. He made his point by clear, brilliant analyses, and by examining the music of Ravel, Rossini, Strauss, Beethoven, Mussorgsky, Tchaikovsky, and Weber.

He started by playing the William Tell Overture and asking his audience what they think about when they hear this music. Virtually everyone responded that it is music of the American wild west, and they think of The Lone Ranger. He then explained that we think that the overture is about a racing horse in the wild west because we were told this many times. But the Italian composer Gioachino Rossini, who wrote the opera in 1829 in which the overture appears, knew little or nothing about the American west and did not have this in mind at all. Rossini wrote it to portray a musical picture of life in the Swiss Alps: dawn, a storm, calm after the storm, a short three-minute march by Swiss soldiers. There are no horses in the opera or cavalry charges. We hear what we are told to hear, not what was intended.

To prove his point, he told a made-up story about a jail break, which he said could be understood as an interpretation of a piece of music. The story did interpret the music in one way, but the music's composer had something totally different in mind; it was not about a jail break, it was about the Spaniard Don Quixote and his servant Sancho Panza with Don Quixote thinking he is an ancient knight.

IT IS SO WITH THE BIBLE

As I listened to the lecture, I realized why so many devout people of all religions mistakenly see things in the Bible that are clearly not there. For example, as children, they were taught that the Bible was composed by God who writes clearly, and children must understand what God has written and obey. They are not taught that all good literature has ambiguities, obscurities, metaphors, and that some writings should be understood as parables. As a result, cognitive dissonance forces many of them to read the biblical text literally, not as it was intended to be read.

Does the Torah Mention
Life After Death?

The Bible says nothing about life after death. It does not mention heaven or hell as an abode after death. The Hebrew Bible's entire focus is on the betterment of life, human and non-human, on earth. The only rewards offered to those who need the carrot of physical rewards and the threatening stick of punishments are consequences that occur during a person's life on earth.

THE MEANING OF THE TERMS *SHEOL* AND *NEFESH*

The Bible speaks about the dead going to *sheol*, but, although the dictionary defines *sheol* as "the abode of the dead," *sheol* means nothing more than the grave. When Jacob wails that his beloved son Joseph's death will cause him to go down to *sheol* in Genesis 37:35, he means nothing more than that he feels that his depression will kill him.

The Bible also uses the term *nefesh*, which Modern Hebrew defines as "soul." However, the biblical Hebrew has only the connotation of "life," "a person," and "life force." When Leviticus 2:1 speaks of a *nefesh* offering a sacrifice, it is certainly not describing an out-of-body experience in which a soul somehow separates from the encasement of its body to travel to the temple to offer an animal sacrifice.

When Rachel was dying in Genesis 35:18 and Scripture says that her *nefesh* departed, it is not suggesting that her soul traveled to another world; it means that her "life" ended.

Ecclesiastes 12:7 expresses this biblical view: "For that which befalls people [literally, the son of men] befalls the beast, the same thing befalls them; as the one dies, so dies the other; they have the same breath; man has no advantage over the beast; for all is vanity. All go to one place; all return to the dust." On his death bed, King David says the same in 1 Kings 2:2, "I go the way of all the earth."

Most scholars recognize the true meaning of *sheol* and *nefesh*, but some scholars insist that "sometimes" *nefesh* does mean soul and that *sheol* is "sometimes" the afterworld of these souls. This is simply a case of forced reading, a disingenuous attempt to compel the text to express one's preconceived notion even when the notion is nowhere present.

THE MEANING OF *OLAM HABA*

The Hebrew term for the afterlife – not found in the Bible – is *olam haba*. Since most people today think that after death they or their souls will leave earth and go to another place, they translate *olam* as "world" or "place," and *haba* as "to come" or "the future." Thus, they understand the phrase to say that there is a site – usually thought of as heaven – that they or their souls will inhabit in the future, after death. They also think that the phrase is ancient and adds support to the idea that an afterlife exists.

However, as we said, the phrase *olam haba* is not in the Torah, and the single word *olam* in the Bible means "eternal." It only came to mean "world" in post-biblical Hebrew. Thus, and this is significant, we frequently do not know what an author means when he uses the phrase; he could be referring to a place or an eternal life in an unspecified area. It appears that Maimonides, for example, who states in his work *Chelek* that "heaven" is not an area, uses the term to mean "an everlasting existence." He felt that what had an everlasting existence was the human intelligence. Thus, the Torah does not discuss life after death and the terms *nefesh, sheol* and *olam haba* are not early scriptural indicators of an afterlife.

Now it should be stressed that the fact that the Bible does not mention an afterlife does not prove or even imply that an afterlife does not exist. All that can be said is that this is not a subject that the Bible addresses.

DOES DANIEL 12 REVEAL THE EXISTENCE OF LIFE AFTER DEATH WITH REWARD AND PUNISHMENT?

The biblical books preceding the book of Daniel, as we said, do not contain clear unambiguous statements about the existence of life after death. Although several chapters appear to refer to life after death, such as Ezekiel 36, these are speaking of the resurrection of the Jewish people after the nation is apparently destroyed. Is Daniel an exception?

Daniel 12:2 and 3 state:

And many of those who sleep in the dust of the earth shall awake, some to everlasting life, and some to shame and everlasting contempt. And those who are wise shall shine like the brightness of the firmament; and those who turn many to righteousness, like the stars forever and ever.

Daniel 12:13 states:

But go your way to the end; and you shall rest and shall stand in your allotted place at the end of the days.

Assuming for the moment that these verses are informing Daniel about life after death, what are they saying? The verses are not at all clear.

If "those who sleep in the dust" denotes the dead and "awake" means that they are restored to life, what is everlasting life? The term is obscure. Even commentators who believe that the verses announce a life after death recognize that "everlasting life" could mean a long life that ultimately ends in a second death.

Additionally, what is the meaning of "those who are wise" and those "who turn many to righteousness?" Whatever it means, it seems clear that it is not referring to those who were well behaved or those who observe Torah commandments. And in verse 13, what is Daniel's "allotted place" and when is the "end of days"?

AN ALTERNATIVE INTERPRETATION OF DANIEL

In view of these questions, many scholars are convinced that Daniel 12 is not referring to life after death. Daniel, according to these scholars, lived during a period – probably around the time of the Maccabean revolt against the Syrian Greeks – when life in Judea was very difficult and many misguided Judeans were seducing their co-religionists away from Judaism and toward the acceptance of pagan Hellenism.

Daniel's vision, expressed in this passage, is not addressing a personal afterlife, for this was not his concern, but the existence of the Judean nation; Daniel envisions that the dire situation will not continue. Many living anti-Hellenists will find the strength to rise, as if awakened from the dead, combat the pro-Hellenists, shame them, and still be able to live a long life in peace. Who are the anti-Hellenists? They are the wise people mentioned in the passage, scholars who taught their fellow Judeans the correct views of Judaism. They "will shine," be respected by, their co-religionists.

Daniel feels that he is being told to be patient. He is advised to "rest." He will be among the victors, where he belongs when the day of victory arrives: "in your allotted place at the end of the days."

This interpretation seems more reasonable and appropriate and relevant considering the historical context and the personal concerns of Daniel; the verses are not a revelation about a personal life after death, but the revival of Judaism that is under duress.

SUMMARY

There is no explicit biblical statement that life continues after a person dies. Rabbinical interpretations on Exodus 20:12, "Honor your father and mother so that your days may be long upon the land that the Lord your God gives you," does not refer to a reward in the afterlife. It is not the plain meaning of the verse. Indeed, the commentator Abraham ibn Ezra explains that it means that when people show kindness to their parents, they demonstrate to their children how they should treat them, and because of the kind treatment by their children they will have a longer and more pleasurable life.

There are other scriptural passages that seem to be speaking of life after death, such as Ezekiel 36 and Daniel 12, but a close reading of the verses show that they are speaking of the survival of the Judean nation.

The absence of the discussion of a life after death does not in and of itself prove that the Torah and ancient Jews did not accept the concept. The Torah, unlike the contemporary Egyptian culture, stressed, as it should, that the focus of people should be on life and not death.

Repentance is Not a Biblical Concept

Parts of Hosea 14, beginning with 14:2, are read as the haphtara (synagogue reading from the prophets) two or three times a year – with the portion of Vayeitzei, on Shabbat Shuva (the Shabbat between Rosh Hashanah and Yom Kippur), and sometimes with the portion Vayeilekh. This practice is based on the idea that a person can return to God by doing *teshuva* (repentance) – an idea that the rabbis felt the prophet Hosea was teaching when he wrote *Shuva Yisrael ad Hashem elokekha* (Return Israel to the Lord your God).[1] Hosea says in chapter 14 what he said several times in earlier chapters: stop worshiping idols and worship only God. According to the rabbis, repentance is accomplished by pointing out one's misdeeds during prayers to God.

THE ANCIENT VIEW OF REPENTANCE

The rabbis believed that Hosea was a descendant of Jacob's firstborn Reuben, who they say was the first of Jacob's sons to do *teshuva* for selling their brother Joseph. *Genesis Rabba* 84:18–19 states that God said: "'By your life, a descendant of yours will begin and open the gates of repentance.' Who was this? This was Hosea, who said, 'Return, Israel, unto the Lord your God.'"

As noted in my *Unusual Bible Interpretations: Hosea*[2] to 14:2, Hosea was not speaking about *teshuva*, and neither Hosea nor any other prophet who lived during his time or before ever mentions repentance.

---

1. Babylonian Talmud, *Yoma* 86a.
2. Rabbi Dr. Israel Drazin, *Unusual Bible Interpretations: Hosea* (Jerusalem: Gefen Publishing House, 2017).

In my book *Mysteries of Judaism*[3] I wrote:

Repentance, *teshuva* in Hebrew, is a practical endeavor.[4] Repentance doesn't magically absolve people of wrongs they committed. It's not abracadabra. Jewish repentance practices remind people to take practical measures to correct their mistakes. Maimonides put it this way:[5] *teshuva* is when a person decides to abandon his or her past misdeeds, resolves not to do them again, thinks how to correct them, and develops habits to assure they are not repeated.

Neither the term *teshuva* nor the concept of repentance as we know it today appear in the Torah. The ancients, Israelites and non-Israelites, believed that what one said, especially vows, or what one did cannot be erased. When an egg is broken, its shards cannot be reassembled. Misdeeds, they thought, are remedied only by punishment.[6]

Scholars suppose that the current idea that people can nullify misdeeds by doing *teshuva* developed in three stages.[7] It began around 722 BCE, centuries after King Solomon's death, when his kingdom split into two with Israel in the north and Judea in the south.[8] In that year, the Assyrians conquered the northern nation of Israel and exiled most Israelites from their land.[9] The Judeans living in the south who saw the cyclopean catastrophe were convinced that the disaster happened because of the misdeeds of the northern tribes, especially their abandonment of God and worship of idols.[10] They knew that they had done the same and searched

---

3. Rabbi Dr. Israel Drazin, *Mysteries of Judaism* (Jerusalem: Gefen Publishing House, 2014), 8–9.

4. Most people understand repentance and confessions as they do sacrifices, as pseudo-magical recitations that remove misdeeds – as if words recited during a synagogue service could somehow change the past, erase the slap a husband gave his wife, and restore a loving relationship. "I don't understand why you're still angry," the husband wails. "I did *teshuva* in the synagogue!" This isn't the way life works.

5. Moses Maimonides (Rambam). *Mishneh Torah, Hilkhot Teshuva*.

6. This concept is still reflected in the Talmudic view that death atones. Babylonian Talmud, *Shabbat* 32a, *Yoma* 86a, *Sanhedrin* 43b and 47a–b.

7. *Olam Hatanakh, Devarim* (Keter, 2002), 221–23.

8. Ten tribes in northern Israel and Transjordan revolted and formed their own nation after Solomon's son Rehoboam refused to reduce their taxes.

9. Some escaped to the south, to Judea, but the rest disappeared from history and are known today as "the ten lost tribes."

10. See Hosea 8:5–13. Hosea was an eighth-century BCE prophet in Israel.

for a way to save themselves, to nullify their wrongs without punishment. It was then that *teshuva* began to develop as an idea that repentance can erase prior misdeeds. It was further entrenched after 586 BCE when Judea itself was destroyed by the Babylonians and many Judeans were exiled to Babylon. The final stage began in 70 CE when the Second Temple was destroyed by Rome and Jews again felt that their misdeeds caused the destruction, and rabbis developed practices that they hoped would rid Jews of wrongs.

So it is no surprise that after sitting in a synagogue all day on Yom Kippur and even if one recites all the prayers and poems and beats one's heart, the magic fails, and the congregant reverts to past practices. The synagogue service does not clean people of past deeds and overcome long-held habits. The service is designed to prompt a person to realize that change is necessary, mistakes need to be corrected. How is this done? Just as Maimonides wrote: Understand that you did wrong, decide to correct the wrong, correct it, find a way to assure you do not repeat the wrong, such as developing new habits.

*   *   *

One might ask: doesn't the Torah itself say to offer a sacrifice as atonement for a misdeed? For example, Numbers 31:50 states, "we brought the Lord's offerings... to make atonement [the Hebrew is *lekhaper*, from the root *kh-p-r*] for ourselves before the Lord." Thus, it appears that "repentance" is mentioned frequently in the Hebrew Bible.

The root *kh-p-r* occurs 101 times in the Hebrew Bible. Both scholars and rabbis recognize that we do not know the basic meaning of *kh-p-r*. It is used for "cover up," as in Genesis 6:14; forms the basis for the word *khaporet* (a covering), twenty-one times as in Exodus 25:18; means "clean" in places such as Exodus 30:10; is translated as "atone" in verses such as Leviticus 4:20; and is also used for "ransom" thirteen times, as in Exodus 21:30.

The term *shuv* (return), from which the rabbis developed the word *teshuva*, is popularly translated today as "repentance." It is used often, for example, by the prophet Hosea and others, as in Hosea 14:2, "Return Israel to the Lord your God," which does not mean "repent your sins," as many believe, but rather the prophet was saying in 14:2, as he said frequently in earlier chapters, "return" to the proper worship of God, don't worship idols or give in to fetishes.

Additionally, and significantly, to address the question directly, the rabbis emphasized that sacrifices do not bring repentance or atonement without changes to new proper behavior. The sacrifices were designed to prompt the changed behavior.

So, as previously stated, the Torah does not speak of repentance as it is understood today.

The Concept of "Sin" is Not Jewish

When I first read Oscar Wilde's *The Picture of Dorian Gray* as a youngster it made a deep and lasting impression upon me and changed my way of thinking.[1] Oscar Wilde, an Irishman, was born in 1854 and died at an early age of 46 in 1900. He published the book in 1891 from an original short story of 1890, and the Gothic tale became a favorite to many. It was his only novel, and he achieved fame for it and for his many delightful plays, such as *The Importance of Being Earnest* (1895), which many critics consider to be a masterpiece. He was accused of being decadent and for being homosexual, which was reflected in the original short version, but played down in the full-fledged novel. He was imprisoned for the maximum term of two years for being homosexual, and then he left Ireland and England when he was released, never to return.

OSCAR WILDE'S STORY

I enjoyed reading *The Picture of Dorian Gray*, but what especially made an impression upon me was the concept of sin. In the novel, sin has a deleterious effect upon people. It is lethal to the body and soul. Like a poison, it harms both. In the book, Dorian Gray was a handsome man who prayed that he would not age, but that his portrait should age instead of him. This is what happened. He remained looking young despite growing old and despite the many sins he committed. Instead of affecting his looks, it only caused his portrait to become ugly. What impressed me was the idea that sin could affect people in this way. I thought about it and concluded that while most people today believe this, it is not true.

---

1. Oscar Wilde, "The Picture of Dorian Gray." *Lippincott's Monthly Magazine*, July 1890.

Do Jews Believe in the Existence
of Satan and Demons

Jews are no different than people of other religions. There is no subject that every Jew accepts. Even rabbis differ in what they think is right. Many Jews reject the notion of the existence of demons and even angels. They feel, like Maimonides, that there is no mention of demons in the Hebrew Bible and the term angel in the Bible is a metaphor for the laws of nature. Satan in the book of Job is not a demon, but simply an advocate for a differing opinion. Also, the story of Satan in Job is only a fable. Many others, like Rashi, are convinced that demons exist. The first group insists that God is all-powerful and needs no helpers. Those who accept the existence of angels and demons think that they serve a divine purpose. The following is a sample of both ideas.

RATIONALISTS REPUDIATE THE NOTION OF SATAN, ANGELS AND DEMONS

Rational Jewish thinkers like Saadiah Gaon, Abraham ibn Ezra and Maimonides insist that biblical, midrashic, and talmudic declarations that contradict reason, science, and philosophy must be interpreted in a rational manner.

Saadiah asserts that Satan in Scripture's Job is a human, a contemporary of Job, who despises Job. The "sons of God," also mentioned in Job, are members of a religious group. God, the book is telling us, does not interfere and allows Job's human enemies to torment him.

Ibn Ezra offers four possible explanations of Genesis 6, which speaks about *b'nei haElohim* marrying women. The *b'nei haElohim* are (1) children of nobles, (2) people of lofty character, (3) exalted descendants of Seth who yielded to lust and cohabitated with the ethically inferior descendants of Cain, or (4) people with astrological knowledge (ibn Ezra, like most people of his age, believed in the efficacy of astrology) who chose proper wives based on their superior knowledge.

Maimonides contends that since God is good, God created only good things. Thus, it is inconceivable that a Satan or evil heavenly beings exist. Additionally, in his *Guide of the Perplexed* 2:6 he states that the term "angel" does not refer to heavenly beings but denotes anything that implements the laws of nature, even rain and snow. In his *Mishneh Torah, Hilkhot Avodah Zarah* 11:16, he flatly denies the truth of the existence of angels and demons: "All of these things are lies and untruths with which the ancient idol worshippers deceived the people, to entice them to follow them. It is not fitting for Israel, who are a really wise nation, to be attracted by such vanities, or to suppose that they have any value.... Whoever believes in these things and their like and thinks that they are genuine and a kind of wisdom, but that the Torah forbids them [even though they work] belongs to the fools and the deficient in knowledge."

OTHERS, LIKE RASHI, RELYING ON MIDRASHIM, WERE CONVINCED THAT DEMONS EXIST

The eleventh century French Bible commentator Rashi (1040–1105), who explained Scripture with Midrashim that he felt fit into the plain meaning of the text, explains the story of Jacob and Joseph in *Genesis* 37:2 by paraphrasing the *Midrash Genesis Rabba* (edited in the beginning of the fifth century C.E.): "Jacob wanted to dwell in peace, but the troubles of Joseph sprang upon him. The righteous want to dwell in peace, but the Holy One Blessed Be He said, 'Isn't what is prepared for them in the world-to-come enough for the righteous, but they want to dwell in peace [also] in this world!'"

The Midrash itself uses stronger and more figurative language, "When the righteous wish to dwell in tranquility in this world, Satan comes and accuses them: 'They are not content with what is in store for them in the hereafter, but they wish to dwell at ease even in this world!' The proof [that the righteous are acting improperly] lies in the fact that the patriarch Jacob wanted to live at ease in this world, whereupon he was attacked by Joseph's Satan."

The position of this Midrash is that bad things happen to good people in this world. The reward for good behavior is given in the world-to-come. It is even improper to expect to live in peace. Satan in the Midrash could be understood as a metaphor for natural troubles. The Midrash is insisting that Jacob made a mistake in thinking that he could settle in Canaan with a life of ease. As the saying goes, "Man thinks, but God laughs!"[1]

RASHI RELYING ON THE TALMUD

Relying on the Babylonian Talmud, *Hagigah* 16a, Rashi writes in his commentary to Genesis 6:19 that Noah saved the demons in his ark along with his family and animals.

Regarding the golden calf, he elaborates on a view mentioned in the Babylonian Talmud, *Shabbat* 89a, and the *Midrash Exodus Rabba*. He argues that the Israelites were misled by the demon Satan, who scared the people by creating frightening turmoil in the heaven and anxiety-producing darkness, and who told the people that Moses was dead. He even showed them what he said was Moses's bier. The non-Israelite mixed multitude, which accompanied the Israelites during the exodus, were the first to be misled. They, in turn, enticed some, but not many, Israelites to join them. They threatened Aaron with death. Aaron tried many tricks to delay them from carrying out their plan to substitute a calf for God. However, Satan harried the people. He was assisted by magicians among the people, who produced the golden calf instantly though their magic.

RASHI'S INTERPRETATION OF THE AKEIDAH STORY

Rashi sees Satan being involved in everything that occurs in Genesis 22, the story of the Akeidah,[2] the binding of Isaac. Satan criticizes Abraham when he has a conversation with God: "Abraham has huge feasts but never offers you a single sacrifice." God responds that Abraham never ceases loving God. And, since Satan is speaking of sacrifices, God says that there is no doubt that Abraham would even sacrifice his son to God if God requested the offering. Thus the "test," according to Rashi and the rabbinic sources from which he derives his view, is a trial to see if God or Satan is correct about Abraham's love of God.

---

1. Maimonides explained in his essay called *Chelek* that people who believe that Midrashim state the truth are fools because Midrashim were composed as allegories and parables to help people understand truths even though the stories in the Midrashim are not true themselves.
2. Akeidah means "binding."

Continuing the theme of Satan's involvement, Rashi explains God's words at the end of the test, "Now I know that you are a God-fearing man," meaning, "Now I know what to respond to Satan and others who ask why I love you."

Rashi understands that Satan does not cease his malicious acts after the near-sacrifice. He elaborates that Satan entangles the ram in a thicket in a failed attempt to keep the ram out of Abraham's hands and stop him from showing love to God by sacrificing the ram.

THE *ZOHAR*

Scholars date the *Zohar*, the most significant book of Jewish mysticism, to around 1290 and names its author as Moses de Leon. The world of the *Zohar* is a universe constantly at war with the left, or "other" side, filled with demons and evil forces known as *kelipoth* (husks), with Samael, also known as Satan, looming large as a threatening and forceful diabolical leader. This is a dualistic world that cannot be reconciled with strict monotheism, the spirit of prophetic Judaism or simple reason.

Samael/Satan, the *Zohar* maintains, was repeatedly involved in Jewish history. He was among much else what the Bible called the snake in the Garden of Eden. He seduced Eve both intellectually, as Scripture states, and sexually, and Eve bore Cain from this union. He was also the "man" who wrestled with the patriarch Jacob in Genesis 32:25, and whom Jacob barely defeated. He later ruthlessly loaned Pharaoh six hundred chariots to enable him to pursue the Israelites whom God had just released from Egyptian bondage in Exodus 14:7.

THE TASHLICH CEREMONY IS A BRIBE TO SILENCE SATAN

The Tashlich ceremony preserves a superstitious belief held by Jewish masses of ancient times concerning water and the divine beings that dwell around it. The rite has been reinterpreted over time, modified slightly and rationalized, but its original superstitious and pagan origin is quite clear.[3]

The name Tashlich is derived from Micah 7:19 where the prophet homiletically

---

3. The rabbis were initially opposed to the superstitious practice, but later accepted it after they modified it somewhat because the people wanted to do it. This is a case of the tail wagging the dog, and is not a unique phenomenon.

and metaphorically states *v'tashlich,* "you will cast all your misdeeds into the depth of the sea." Many Jews took this metaphorical statement literally and the practice of Tashlich began in the Middle Ages.

The idea behind Tashlich is the recitation of certain prayers near a body of water, preferably a river, stream, or any body of water that contains fish. Jews toss breadcrumbs or other foods to the fish as a bribe, confident that the fish would take the food and deliver it for them to Satan, and the bribe would stop Satan from accusing them of past misdeeds before God.

PIRKEI DE-RABBI ELIEZER, DEMONS AND ANGELS

The Tashlich service was not the only ceremony that the masses felt they must observe to avoid having Satan harm them.

The eighth-century Midrash *Pirkei de-Rabbi Eliezer* is a rather unusual volume of biblical folk legends that many Jews insisted were true history. The author believed that the fate of the Jewish people, both collectively and individually, was determined on Yom Kippur by God during God's annual analysis of their behavior of the past year. He felt that God did not deliberate alone and could be persuaded by advice given to the deity by angels and demons. The author was also convinced that the chief demon, Satan, was corruptible and could be bribed to give a favorable report. He also thought that despite his angelic status, Satan was a dupe and could be fooled.

In part 46 of the 54 parts of the volume, the author informs his readers that many of the Yom Kippur practices were instituted to stop Satan from acting as an enemy advocate against the Jewish people, persuading God to punish the Jews for their past misdeeds.

Accordingly, like many of his co-religionists, the author states that the goat that Leviticus 16 says was sent to Azazel was, in fact, an annual bribe driven into the desert where Satan lived. The demon would smell it, take it, consume it, and, be satisfied with this inducement, and would reverse his usual evil demonic tactics and shift to the side of the Jews, acting as their advocate in his Yom Kippur discussions with God.

(The author of *Pirkei de-Rabbi Eliezer* and most of his audience were unbothered by the way in which he demeaned God. He portrayed the deity as an ignorant medieval prince who needed advice from both good and bad advisors, who was unable to differentiate his bad from his good ministers, and who was foolishly indirectly influenced by the bribe given to one of his advisors because he was too ignorant to see what was happening.)

If Satan was not persuaded by the bribe, the author informs his readers, the demon was fooled by the Jews acting as if they were angels and not human beings because, presumably, Satan would not dare say anything bad about angels. The masses believed that angels did not eat, were unable to bend their knees, stood straight at all times, and did not wear shoes. Thus, he writes, on Yom Kippur many Jews fasted, stood upright for all or at least most of the holiday service, and were barefoot, or at least did not wear leather shoes.

The Babylonian Talmud (*Yoma* 31b, 32b, and 35a) of several centuries earlier contains the same idea. It states that the biblical book Leviticus required the high priest to wear white on Yom Kippur when he entered the Holy of Holies to pray for forgiveness for the misdeeds of the Israelites. It relates that he was to be dressed like an angel. Jacob Z. Lauterbach explains, "The white garments were aimed to deceive Satan who, when seeing the High Priest dressed in white, would mistake him for an angel and not seek to harm him. The custom, still prevailing in the Synagogue, that the pious worshippers, and especially the reader and the leader of the service, wear a white robe ("sargenes" or "kittel") on the Day of Atonement also aims to make the worshippers appear like angels."[4]

Lauterbach also explains that the masses inconsistently thought that one of the reasons that the Bible told the high priest to enter the Holy of Holies with smoking incense was the belief that the smoke would drive the demon away and the high priest, whom Satan might recognize despite his disguise as an angel, would be protected from the demon.

Thus, four methods are used in dealing with Satan on the Day of Atonement. (1) He is bribed. (2) He is deceived by Jews disguising themselves as angels in order to ensure they are protected even if the bribe is unsuccessful. (3) To heighten the chances of success, the high priest prays to God on behalf of the people, disguised as an angel so that Satan does not harm him. (4) In the unlikely event that Satan is neither successfully bribed nor fooled, he is chased away from the Holy of Holies

---

4. Jacob Z. Lauterbach, *Rabbinic Essays* (Cincinnati: Hebrew Union College Press, 1951), 63.

using smoke while the high priest prays to God during the annual time that the deity is deliberating the fate of Jewry.

This was the primitive belief of many of the masses as recorded in the midrashic and talmudic literature. It was certainly not the understanding of rationalists such as Maimonides, who gave entirely different and more mature explanations for the practices.

THE ANCIENT UNEDUCATED JEW BELIEVED THAT GOD CONSULTS DEMONS

The idea that God consults with demons is based on the primitive notion of Jews and non-Jews that God does not make decisions without first consulting with angels and demons and that the angels and demons can persuade God (who needs help) to act contrary to the interests of humanity. This notion was supported by misreadings and misunderstandings of many biblical and post-biblical sources.

For example, these people took the first chapter of Job literally. The chapter tells of a *satan* having a discussion with God about Job and trying to persuade God (who can be persuaded) to punish him. The term *satan* in Job does not refer to the demon who was given the biblical name Satan many years after this book was composed. In the book, *satan* means adversary. Nevertheless, the average Jew saw the Job story as a depiction of the very thing he feared and wanted to avoid: the demon Satan acting as a prosecutor in the heavenly court, seeking to persuade God to punish him.

Jews found reinforcement in Midrashim such as *Genesis Rabba* 8:3, which comments upon Genesis 1:26, "And God said, 'Let us make man.'" The Midrash disregards the Bible's use of the "royal plural" of "us" and asks: "With whom did God take counsel? Rabbi Joshua ben Levi said: God took counsel with the works of heaven and earth, like a king who had two advisers without whose knowledge he did nothing whatsoever."

The Babylonian Talmud, *Sanhedrin* 38b, bolsters this view. It states: "God does not do anything without first consulting heavenly beings." These beings, the masses were convinced, were angels and demons.

WHY BLOW THE SHOFAR ON ROSH HASHANAH?

The original reason for blowing the shofar on the New Year, to frighten and expel satanic forces that may persuade an influenceable God that the Jew is a sinner and should be punished and perhaps even killed during the upcoming year, is explicitly reported in the Babylonian Talmud, *Rosh Hashanah* 16b. The Talmud states that the shofar is blown "to confound Satan" and to prevent him from approaching God and accusing Jewish people of past sins.

ANOTHER PRACTICE DESIGNED TO CONFUSE SATAN ON ROSH HASHANAH

It is a widespread Jewish custom to announce the date of the new moon at the morning synagogue service on the Shabbat before the onset of the new month. This takes place each month except for the Shabbat preceding Elul, the month which ends with the holiday of Rosh Hashanah. The commentators explain that the practice originated, like the shofar soundings, to confuse Satan. The fearful masses persuaded themselves that when they did not publicly announce the date of the new moon, Satan, whom they must have thought attended Shabbat services and paid attention to announcements, would not know on which date Elul would begin, and he would thus be kept from traveling to heaven and prosecuting Jews before the heavenly court.

THE KAPPAROT CEREMONY

The Kapparot ritual is not mentioned in the Bible or the Talmud. In ancient times, a rooster was slaughtered with the sacrificial formality of laying of hands so that it would be accepted by Satan as a suitable sacrifice/bribe.

Virtually all ancient sources recognize that the practice was originally designed, just as the Jewish masses understood the biblical Yom Kippur Azazel ceremony in Leviticus 16:8, as a bribe to Satan to keep him from accusing Jews for their misdeeds during the past year before God. The *Machzor Vitri*, composed by Simcha of Vitri, France, a student of Rashi (who died in the same year as his teacher, 1105), admits that the purpose of the Kapparot is the same as the scapegoat sent to Azazel; both are bribes for the devil. This was also the opinion of Yaakov Hayyim Zemach in *Nagid u'mitzvah*, Isaiah Horowitz in *Sh'lah*, and J.Z. Lauterbach in HUCA 11, "Tashlich."

Lauterbach writes: "The real significance of this ceremony was that it represented a revival of the old idea of bribing Satan or demons by offering to them a sacrifice as had been done in the times of the Temple [for the Bible mandated in Leviticus 16:8 that on Yom Hakippurim a goat was sent to Azazel]."

A rooster was chosen for the bribe because (1) it was an animal that was not allowed to be sacrificed to God, and therefore an appropriate sacrifice for a devil and (2) the masses thought that this bird resembled Satan: it had horns like Satan and its feet resembled the demon's feet.

TARGUM PSEUDO-JONATHAN

Onkelos was not the only Aramaic translation of the Pentateuch. Two other full translations have survived the ravages of the ages and are still in existence – *Targum Pseudo-Jonathan* and *Neophyti*. Both are not literal renderings of the biblical text. They are translations filled with midrashic material, much, but not all, of which is contained in the Talmuds and Midrashim. Many of its elaborations to the biblical texts are folk tales and superstitions. Among its many elaborations upon the biblical text are claims about Satan, such as the following in *Pseudo-Jonathan*:

1. The Targum sometimes personifies the *yetzer hara*, the evil inclination, not as a human emotion, but as a diabolical being unconnected to the human body, even the devil itself. The evil inclination is Satan who entered Eden, insinuating himself into human affairs at the onset of creation as the first couple is enjoying Paradise, enticing Eve to eat the forbidden fruit and precipitating the fall of God's first humans (Genesis 4:1).
2. Satan is dissatisfied with bringing destruction by speech alone. He has intercourse with Eve. She conceives and Cain is their child (Genesis 3:6).
3. This "evil inclination" Satan, is not even satisfied with degrading and destroying humans through seduction. In Genesis 22:20 he sinks to the depth of evil when he shocks the matriarch Sarah to death with the lie that her husband Abraham killed their son Isaac.
4. Satan is an expert in manipulating crowds. When Moses ascends Mount Sinai to bring the glory of the Law, the Decalogue, to the weak and susceptible erstwhile slaves, Satan takes advantage of their condition and misleads the masses to believe that Moses was killed on the mount. They accept the deception as truth and build a successor substitute leader, the golden calf (Exodus 32:1).
5. An amicable and convivial seducer, Satan entices some of the Israelites to dance. As Moses descends Mount Sinai, he sees Satan dancing among the multitude who worship the inanimate calf (Exodus 32:19).

6. Aaron defends the worshippers to his outraged brother. He pleads with Moses, saying that they are basically good people, but "the evil inclination led them astray" (Exodus 32:22).

7. Aaron also defends himself. He explains that all he did was toss gold into the fire, hoping it would melt, but "Satan entered it and the image of this calf emerged from it" (Exodus 32:24).

8. Satan leads his execrable life not only in the bodies of humans and in their outside daily affairs, but even in heaven, where he battles against Israelite interests. Feeling that God needs a reminder and that Jews should be punished for deeds committed by their ancestors, Satan ascends to heaven to remind God constantly of the Israelite worship of the golden calf (Leviticus 9:2) and the brothers' misdeed of the sale of Joseph (Leviticus 9:3). In fact, *Pseudo-Jonathan* is one of the sources that maintains that the New Year holiday's shofar sounding was instituted to confuse Satan so that he will not persist in making similar accusations during this holiday when God is judging the Jewish people (Numbers 10:10 and 29:1).

9. *Pseudo-Jonathan* notices that various kinds of animals were used as sacrifices. Why was the goat offered? The Targum answers in Leviticus 9:3, "Because Satan is similar to it, so that slander not stick to you concerning the goat kid that Jacob's sons killed [to spread upon Joseph's coat as proof that he had been killed]." The translator continues in 9:6, "Remove the evil inclination from your hearts, and immediately the glory of the Shekhina [the feeling of the divine presence] of the Lord will be revealed to you."

10. In the translation of Leviticus 9:2 the targumist explains that Moses told his brother Aaron to sacrifice "a bull calf for a sin offering lest Satan speaks with a slanderous tongue against you concerning the matter of the [golden] calf that you constructed at Horeb." The idea is also in the *Midrash Sifra*. It is unclear whether the Aramaic means that the sacrifice atones for the sin of the golden calf or, as the language seems to imply, it is a bribe given to Satan to stop him from reminding God of Aaron's misdeed.

TODAY

Even today, in the twenty-first century, a sizable percentage of people believe in these superstitions. The 2006 ArtScroll edition of Kings, for example, speaks about many Jews discarding their heritage so quickly and easily. It states that there are many factors that lead to this behavior and indicates that "one must add the Satan's powerful effort to drag Israel down from its noble calling."[5]

A personal note on the subject: Several years ago, while at the funeral of my brother-in-law in an ultra-Orthodox cemetery, I was suddenly hit by a rock and started to bleed. Apparently, it was the ritual at the cemetery to throw rocks around to scare off demons.

After thirty-one years in the military and with a rank of general, I was never injured. Yet I got injured twice, both in the context of a Jewish practice. The second time was while officiating at a civilian bar mitzvah, and when candies were thrown during the service in a congratulatory gesture, and to encourage the participation of the children, I was hit by a hard candy and bled.

---

5. ArtScroll. *The Prophets, I–II Kings* (New York: Mesorah Publications Ltd., 2006), 137.

The Torah Requires Orthopraxy
Not Orthodoxy

Jeffrey Radon's easy-to-read book *Reconciling A Contradictory Abraham* introduces readers to an orthoprax view of Judaism, an approach held by many ancient Jewish sages.[1] Orthopraxy is not a watered-down Judaism; it is arguably the correct form of Judaism. Radon is a practicing Jew.

WHAT IS ORTHOPRAXY?

Orthoprax Judaism stresses that the Torah contains no philosophy, no system of beliefs, and no requirement to have faith; it teaches people to behave properly. Orthoprax is a Greek-Latin word meaning "correct conduct." In contrast, the term orthodox, Greek-Latin for "correct beliefs," stresses that its adherents accept and act in accordance with certain prescribed beliefs. While the terms orthodox and orthoprax are used very often today, the Oxford English Dictionary reveals that they are recent terms, first used in 1851.

Radon recognizes that the term *emuna* in the Bible does not have the meaning "faith," or "belief," the definition given to the word in Modern Hebrew. He recognizes that the widespread translation of the biblical word in English as "faith" or "belief" is a mistranslation. The biblical term *emuna* means "holding firm, steadfast, being loyal." It is not a theological term but a behavioral one. Thus, for example, when Genesis 15:6 states about Abraham *v'he'e'min*, that is often erroneously translated "and he believed in God," the true meaning is he was loyal to God; the verse does not address his theology but his character and behavior.

---

1. Jeffrey Radon, *Reconciling A Contradictory Abrahan: On the Orthoprax and Anti-Theological Nature of the Hebrew Bible* (Jerusalem: Mazo Publishers, 2017).

The great revolution of the Hebrew Bible, Radon writes, is not monotheism, but that God demands that people act with proper behavior. The biblical prophet Micah summarized this in Micah 6:8: "He has told you, man, what is good and what the Lord demands of you: to do justice, to love lovingkindness, and to walk humbly with your God." The sages Hillel[2] and Rabbi Akiva gave the same idea without mentioning God: "What is hateful to you, do not do to others" (Hillel), and "Love your neighbor as yourself" (Rabbi Akiva).

While many Jews today think that the Torah requires orthodoxy, the term orthodoxy implies theological faith, which is not in the Torah or required by it and is a Christian-based notion. The Torah stresses good deeds primarily in a behavioral rather than ritual sense, and contains mitzvot, commands, referring to the biblical commands on how to act. According to orthopraxy, Jews can believe what they want if they behave properly and do not harm others. This is like the US Supreme Court definition of the "Free Exercise Clause" of the US Constitution. It does not restrict religious belief if there is no compelling reason to restrict it, meaning harm to others.

Additionally, orthodoxy tends to disparage and delegitimize fellow Jews who do not accept orthodox beliefs and causes hurt feelings and schisms; orthopraxy encourages and facilitates harmony and good relationships.

A QUESTION

But is it true that traditional Judaism focuses on behavior and not beliefs? Didn't the philosopher and codifier Maimonides list thirteen principles of Judaism? One needs to understand that Maimonides wrote in the introduction to his *Guide of the Perplexed* that he writes for two audiences, for the common people and for intellectuals. Many scholars have recognized that he composed the thirteen principles for the average Jew who needed such a set of beliefs, since they were faced and confused by sets of beliefs by Muslims and Christians. In any event, Maimonides was the first Jew to develop such a list, and beliefs, as previously stated, are not required by the Torah.[3]

---

2. Hillel was not called a rabbi because the institution of being a rabbi did not begin until around the time when the temple was destroyed in 70 CE.

3. Many scholars are convinced that Maimonides himself did not think that all thirteen beliefs that he wrote for the public were correct.

Did Jews Shift Their Understanding of God?

As is well-known, there are many ways that are used to interpret the Bible. There is even a tradition that there are seventy ways to do so. In biblical days seventy was a metaphorical figure indicating a large number. Besides recognizing that the Bible sometimes uses symbolic language, another way of interpreting the Bible is to recognize that both ideas and practices that are recorded in the Bible change.

SEVENTY IS A FIGURATIVE NUMBER

In regard to the number seventy, Exodus 1 for example states that seventy descendants of Jacob came to Egypt even though anyone counting the names will find that there were less than seventy.[1] So, too, the captivity in Babylon was said to be seventy years even though the exile was far shorter than seventy.[2] The Torah according to legend was given in seventy languages.[3] Stones were said to have been placed in the Jordan containing the Torah in seventy languages.[4] Seventy was considered old age.[5]

THE BIBLE SHOWS CHANGES IN HOW GOD IS UNDERSTOOD

This symbolic number aside, as previously stated, there are many ways that the

---

1. See also Babylonian Talmud, *Bava Batra* 123a–123b.
2. Babylonian Talmud, *Megillah* 11b–12a.
3. Babylonian Talmud, *Shabbat* 88b.
4. Babylonian Talmud, *Sotah* 35b.
5. Babylonian Talmud, *Moed Katan* 28a.

Torah can be interpreted. The thesis in the scholar James L. Kugel's book *The Great Shift, Encountering God in Biblical Time*[6] is that the Bible describes God in different and evolving ways, depending on when the biblical book or section was composed, and this shows a developing idea about what God is and how God functions, as well as what humans thought about themselves and their abilities.

For example, Genesis 3:8 states that Adam and Eve "heard the sound of the Lord God walking about the Garden [of Eden] at the breezy time of day." Kugel understands that this depiction of God is different than later ideas. God in Genesis 3:8 is not remote, "nor a deity who inhabits a special temple or shrine reserved for Him, along with a specially trained cadre of priests who serve Him in a state of ritual purity." God is depicted as being present in the same garden inhabited by the naked humans God created. Still later, Kugel writes, "God is generally just *elsewhere* and only on occasion crosses over into the world of human beings," unlike Genesis 3:8 where, "He is already there." (Emphasis by Kugel.)

Another development is a new view of what God wants. Kugel asks why Abel's sacrifice to God of meat gained divine favor while his brother Cain's gift of vegetables did not (Genesis 4:4–5); and he answers that the ancients, Jews and non-Jews, felt that God liked meat. He points out that the modern concept of a temple being a house of prayer is not the ancient idea; the Bible describes the sanctuary as a place where sacrifices were offered; prayer is not mentioned in association with sacrifices. The early idea about the gods was that the gods controlled nature and needed to be bribed; the ancients didn't think of the gods as the makers of laws. Later, after the temple was destroyed in 70 CE, the Jews ceased thinking that God wanted or needed sacrifices.

Kugel asserts that the early Hebrews changed from being convinced that there were many gods to the idea that there is only a single deity. The introductory sentence of the Decalogue, he writes, does not mean "there are no other gods except Me." Scholars recognize that the Hebrew should not be translated "except Me," but "in My presence" – "You can't worship Me and some other god or gods."

The ancients also did not think that God or gods were all-knowing and all-powerful; and this would explain why God asked Cain where his brother Abel

---

6. James L. Kugel. *The Great Shift, Encountering God in Biblical Time* (Boston: Houghton Mifflin Harcourt, 2017).

was (Genesis 4:9). Kugel also tells us that the ancient Hebrews thought that the Israelite God had power only in Israel, like the pagans who had a different deity for every location.

The greatest shift resulted from an understanding of human nature. Why, he queries, did prophecy cease? He explains that this was due to the developed sense of God as no longer being present on earth, a new sense of self and understanding of human capabilities, including knowledge that people can act to control their lives.

Did the Post-Moses Israelites
Know about the Torah?

Scholars reject the traditional teaching and suggest that the ancient Isra-elites knew nothing about the Torah until the time of King Josiah (649–609 BCE).[1] Among much else, it is significant that none of the biblical books before this time mention Moses's Torah; none of the Israelite leaders and prophets, who frequently criticize their nation for its faults, ever criticize them for violating Torah laws; some post-Moses practices are significantly different than those mentioned in Moses's Torah such as the levirate marriage of Ruth; and there is no indication in the Bible that the Israelites observed important holy days mentioned in the Torah such as the Sabbath and the Festival of Matzot that commemorated the exodus from Egyptian slavery. Joshua and the Israelites totally ignored the clear mandate in Numbers 33:50–56 that the Israelites must expel all Canaanites from Canaan lest they be a thorn upon them and entice them to worship idols. The Israelites not only failed to obey this divine command, there is no indication that they even considered it; it is as if they knew nothing about this Torah command. Instead, they allowed the Canaanites to remain in the country and took tribute from them, until the Canaanites grew strong, became a thorn upon them, and enticed many to worship idols.[2] The following are four examples.

1. See 11 Kings 22–23 and 11 Chronicles 34–35 for the history of the finding of part of the Torah.
2. Joshua 22:5 reports Joshua warning the Trans-Jordanian tribes to "heed the commandments and the Torah that Moses the servant of the Lord commanded you, to love the Lord your God, and to walk in his ways, and to keep his commandments, and to cling to him, and to serve him with all your heart and entire being." This could be a refutation of the idea that the Israelites knew

THE PROPHET MICAH

The eighth century BCE prophet Micah is an example of a prophet who apparently knew nothing about the Torah. The book of Micah contains seven chapters in which the prophet constantly criticizes both the southern nation of Judah and the northern nation of Israel for improper behavior and promises that they will be destroyed because of their acts. But despite the catalogue of wrongs, Micah never mentions that they violated the Torah of Moses or failed to observe the holidays, such as the Sabbath and the three festivals of Passover, Shavuot, and Sukkot, mentioned in it.

Micah lived at the same time as Amos, Hosea, Jonah, and first Isaiah, around the time of the destruction of the northern kingdom of Israel in 722 BCE. He berates the people for basic immorality: "They covet fields and seize them; and houses and take them away; they oppress a man and his household in this way, a man and his heritage" (2:2). "You cast out the women of my people from their pleasant houses; you take away my glory forever from their young children" (2:9). Micah castigates his people for lying, robbery, murder, bribery, priests and prophets charging for their teachings, merchants using deceitful weights, violence, and disrespect of parents and in-laws. In 4:2, he mentions that non-Israelites will ascend the mountain of the Lord and God will teach them the divine ways and laws, but he does not mention the Torah of Moses. In 4:6, he states that the Israelites "will walk in the name of the Lord our God for ever and ever," but does not say that they will observe the Torah of Moses.

In 6:4, Micah states that God sent Moses, Aaron, and Miriam to redeem the Israelites from Egyptian slavery, as if he did not know that the Torah states he sent only Moses and Aaron.[3] In 6:6–8, he responds to the people who desire to offer God a thousand rams and ten thousand rivers of oil, and their first-born sons to

---

nothing about the Torah: it mentions Moses's Torah and the words are like those in Deuteronomy 6. However, while the term Torah refers today to the Pentateuch or entire Bible or Jewish teachings, it simply means "teachings" when used in the Bible. Also, the wording, while similar, is not exact and may not be a quote. As well, scholars claim that the book of Deuteronomy was discovered and used during the reign of King Josiah when the book of Joshua was composed, so this language could have been inserted at that time.

3. The Targum invents a role for each. Moses to teach religion and law, Aaron to teach how to repent, and Miriam to give instruction to women.

atone for their transgressions. As in Hosea in 6:6, he tells his people that God does not want sacrifices but moral behavior and does not mention the Torah. "It has been told to you, man, what is good and what the Lord requires of you: only to act justly, and love mercy, and walk humbly with your God."

CITIES OF REFUGE

Despite Moses's Torah stating that cities of refuge must be established, there is no evidence that such cities were ever created, either in any of the biblical books or other literature. True, they are mentioned in Joshua 20, but since there is no indication they were ever made and in view of other evidence, scholars feel that this chapter was composed centuries after the time of Joshua and it reflects an ideal situation that was never realized.[4]

Cities of refuge are mentioned in Exodus 21:12–14, Numbers 35:9–34, and Deuteronomy 4:41–43; 19:1–13. Numbers and Deuteronomy give details about the cities. In early times, Israelite and non-Israelite communities allowed people who killed other people sanctuary if they took hold of the temple altar. Exodus 21:14 later restricted this practice to only unintentional killings.[5] The Torah established the concept of refuge cities to save the lives of people who negligently, but unintentionally killed others; there they would be safe from the revenge of the deceased's relatives, called "blood avengers."[6] As long as the manslayer resided in the city, he

---

4. See *Olam Hatanakh*'s treatment of Joshua 20. *Olam Hatanakh, Sifrei Chamad Yehoshua* (Jerusalem: Misrad Hachinuch Vehatarbut), notes that some of the cities assigned as cities of refuge and as Levite towns were not conquered by Israel until the time of King David, suggesting a late composition of the book Joshua.

5. This is discussed in the Babylonian Talmud, *Makkot* 12a, and Maimonides, *Mishneh Torah, Rotzei'ach* 5:12. See 1 Kings 1:50 and 2:28–30 for instances in which manslayers sought refuge at an altar. The Roman Catholic Church retains the concept of sanctuary at a church, but not a field altar. The concept that an altar is not so holy that it saves murderers fits in with Maimonides's concept that nothing has a holy essence; holiness depends on human behavior. See Menachem Kellner, *Maimonides' Confrontation with Mysticism* (Liverpool: Littman Library of Jewish Civilization, 2006).

6. Discussed in the Babylonian Talmud, *Makkot* 10a, and Tosephta *Makkot* 3. The rabbis added many details to this concept (see *Makkot* 13a and Maimonides, *Mishneh Torah, Rotzei'ach* 8), including designating the forty-two cities assigned to the Levites (Joshua 21 and 1 Chronicles 6) as additional cities of refuge, making a total of forty-eight.

was safe, but if he left the city, the "blood avenger" could kill him.[7] There were three Levite families and each was assigned two of the six refuge cities.[8]

There are two significant problems relating to cities of refuge. (1) There are differences between these two Torah sources, such as Deuteronomy stating that Moses said that the Israelites should choose the cities of refuge while Numbers has Moses name them, and Numbers states that there should be three such cities in Canaan while Deuteronomy 19 states six. (2) More significantly, both Torah sources differ with the book of Joshua, as if Joshua did not know about the Torah details.[9]

THE URIM AND THUMMIM

The Urim and Thummim is another example suggesting that post-Moses Israelites knew nothing about the Torah until the age of King Josiah. Exodus 28:30, Leviticus 8:8, Numbers 27:21, and Deuteronomy 33:8 speak about an Urim and Thummim that the high priest wore to communicate with God to secure divine guidance. While Moses was able to speak to God directly, God advises Moses to have Eleazar the priest use the Urim to communicate with God whenever Joshua and the Israelites "go out." Yet, there is no indication that either Joshua or Eleazar or any other post-Moses person used the Urim in the book of Joshua or any other biblical book.[10] It is possible that they did not take advantage of its power because

---

7. Numbers 35:27.

8. Although, as previously stated, Deuteronomy 19 seems to indicate that there are nine cities of refuge.

9. There is a detailed discussion of the many differences in *Olam Hatanakh*. For instance, among others: (1) The Torah does not require the manslayer to defend himself before the elders of the city of refuge before he is allowed entry, but Joshua 20:4 does so. (2) 20:6 seems to have conflicting times when the manslayer can leave the city: "until he stands before the community" and "the death of the high priest."

10. The Urim and Thummim were placed in the folds of the *choshen*, a garment worn by the high priest. It contained the name of God and was used by the high priest to consult with God on matters requiring divine guidance (Numbers 27:21). Scripture does not reveal exactly what it looked like, or of what materials it was made of, or exactly how it was used. There is a tradition that the letters on it (in Jacob's sons' names) would light up and the high priest, by means of divine inspiration, would interpret their message. The Babylonian Talmud, *Yoma* 73a–b, states that they are called Urim and Thummim because they bring light (Hebrew: *or*) and are perfect (Hebrew: *tam*). Although the Urim is mentioned six times in the Torah (Exodus 28:30, Leviticus 8:8, Numbers 27:21, 1 Samuel 28:6, Ezra 2:63, and Nehemiah 7:65), we have no evidence

it did not exist. The Urim is mentioned in Ezra 2:63 and Nehemiah 7:65 as a hope for the future, but it was not used at the time and these books were composed after the first temple period,[11] when scholars agree the Torah existed. The sole time it is mentioned earlier is in 1 Samuel 28:6 where it states that God did not answer King Saul by any means, not by dreams, the Urim, or prophets. This may be a late interpolation.

ALLOWING OR COMMANDING THE INSTITUTION OF A MONARCHY

Another seeming proof is Deuteronomy 17:14–20. It states that when Israelites settle in Canaan and desire to appoint a king, they may do so,[12] but the king is restricted in certain ways. Yet 1 Samuel 8 and 12 describe Israelites requesting the prophet Samuel to appoint a king for them, and he scolds them and says he is opposed to a monarchy. Why didn't the people respond by reminding him of Deuteronomy 17 or at least discuss whether the people are correct in petitioning for a king? Is it possible that neither they nor he knew anything about Deuteronomy 17?

WERE THE ISRAELITES ENSLAVED IN EGYPT?

Arnold Ehrlich was convinced that the early post-Moses Israelites knew nothing about Moses's Torah. He even questioned the history of the Israelite enslavement in Egypt.[13] He felt that he could support his view with: (1) None of the prophets, except Micah 6:5, mention the enslavement. (2) Micah 6:5 has a different version than the Five Books of Moses. It states that God sent Moses, Aaron, and Miriam to redeem the Israelites. The Five Books state that only Moses was sent, Aaron was only an assistant to Moses, and Miriam had no role in the redemption other than gathering the women to sing praises that the Israelites were saved at the Red

---

that it was ever used. Arguably, this does not prove that the authors of post-Pentateuch books knew nothing about the Urim or that the Israelites never used it because this is "an argument from silence."

11. The first temple was destroyed in 586 BCE. Ezra and Nehemiah's date are unknown, but probably around the fifth century BCE.

12. Maimonides (*Mishneh Torah, Hilkhot Melakhim* 1:1) understood that the Torah obligated the Israelites to appoint a king when they entered Canaan.

13. Arnold Bogumil Ehrlich, *Mikra Ki-Pheshuto* (*The Bible According to its Literal Meaning*), ed. Harry M. Orlinsky (New York: Ktav, 1901, 1969), Numbers 13–15.

Sea. (3) Scholars say that the song in Deuteronomy 32 is a very old composition. In this version, in 32:40, God found the Israelites in the desert. Thus, Ehrlich feels that the original Israelites were desert nomads who conquered parts of Canaan, settled it, forgot their origin after some generations, and invented a legend that they were saved by God from slavery and brought to Canaan.

More on the Post-Moses Era Not Knowing About Moses's Torah

As I previously stated,[1] scholars insist that there is no indication in the biblical books that the Israelites knew about Moses's Torah or observed the laws contained in it until the time of King Josiah (641–609 BCE). An example is the Mishkan which was a core element of the religious practices according to the Five Books of Moses but is not mentioned in post-Pentateuch books.

DID THE MISHKAN EXIST IN THE POST-MOSES ERA?

Exodus 25 begins an extensive description of the tabernacle that Moses built in the desert, a dwelling used for religious inspiration and sacrifices. The Torah emphasizes that the building, called Mishkan in Hebrew, based on the root *s-k-n* meaning "dwelling," and suggesting the divine dwelling place,[2] was directed by God who described precisely how it and the implements placed in it were to be constructed.[3] The careful description of the details of the Mishkan makes it clear beyond cavil that the Mishkan was a significant part of early Israelite history, the focus of Israelite worship. Yet there is only one possible, but debatable, mention of the Mishkan outside of the Five Books of Moses.

---

1. Rabbi Dr. Israel Drazin, *"Did the Generation of Post-Moses Israelites Know about the Torah?"* (Posted January 2014).
2. Exodus 25:8.
3. Exodus 25:9.

Arnold Ehrlich[4] and others argue that the authors of the subsequent biblical books, Joshua, Judges, Samuel, Kings, the prophets, and the others, knew nothing of the Mishkan and Moses's Five Books, and that various documents were composed, as Bible critics contend, around the time of the Second Temple and were assembled into the Five Books by Ezra in the fourth century BCE.

Ehrlich does not mention Joshua 22:19, the only source that has the word Mishkan. The Israelite leaders tell the tribes that remained in Transjordan to reconsider and settle in Canaan, "the land of the possession of the Lord where dwells the Mishkan of the Lord." In support of Ehrlich, this is most likely not a reference to Moses's tabernacle: the term Mishkan here could be a poetic repetition of *shakhan*, "dwells," which has the same root and precedes it, and should be translated, "where dwells the dwelling of the Lord," and means "you should settle in Canaan, God's land."

Ehrlich's observation about apparent ignorance of the Mishkan reflects the more disturbing problem that I mentioned in my earlier discussion. The Five Books of Moses have many laws, traditionally 613 commandments mandated by God. Yet there is no mention of Moses's Five Books or the divine commands in any of the subsequent biblical volumes until the seventh century BCE. This absence seems to verify the critique of the Bible critics. If Joshua, the judges, Samuel, and the other biblical figures such as the prophets knew of the Torah commands, why is there no mention of them? Since Jews feel that the commands are, or should be an integral part of their lives, why is there no incident describing any of the post-Moses Israelite leaders observing laws such as the Sabbath and keeping kosher? Why, for example, in the book of Ruth does Boaz go through a levirate marriage procedure that is different than the one mentioned in the Five Books? Why when prophets such as Amos, Hosea, and Micah and leaders such as Joshua and Samuel criticize the people for many wrongs the people committed focus on immoral acts and never mention that they failed to observe the Torah of Moses; and why are there some things in these books that are contrary to the Torah?

There are many dozens of examples that can be cited that seem to indicate that the post-Moses Israelites knew nothing about Moses's Torah. For example, I Samuel 2 raises this question: The priest Eli's sons committed many wrongs and a

---

4. Ehrlich, *Mikra Ki-Pheshuto*.

prophet, called *ish elohim,* appeared to Eli and goes into some detail in delineating the wrongs committed by his sons, yet he does not mention that they violated the law of the Torah regarding sacrifices which was their primary offense.[5]

Also, verse 2:18 states that Samuel wore a linen ephod. The Torah has only the high priest wear the ephod, not an ordinary priest and certainly not a non-priest.[6] The same problem exists in II Samuel 6:14 which states that King David donned an ephod. Neither Samuel nor David were priests.

Another of many examples from Samuel is that it describes Samuel sleeping "in the temple of the Lord where the ark of God was." The rabbis pointed out that this was not allowed and amended the text.[7] The Targum, for instance, states that he slept in the chamber of the Levites, and Gersonides wrote that he slept in an adjacent room, both saying what is contrary to the plain reading of I Samuel 3:3.

In I Samuel 8, to cite another of many examples, the people demanded that Samuel appoint a king to rule over them. Samuel did not want to do it and only agreed when God told him to accept the people's demand. Why didn't the people and God say to Samuel that the Torah explicitly allows the appointment of a king?

Why were the people surprised when a book of the Bible was discovered in the seventh century BCE which prompted King Josiah to reform the religious practices in Judea?[8] Was this, as Bible critics argue, when a part of the Five Books was developed?

---

5. Leviticus 7:34 which states that the priests' share was the breast and right thigh, and Leviticus 3:3ff which states that nothing should intervene between the giving of the offering and the burning of parts that are set aside for God. Eli's sons violated these laws.

6. Exodus 28:6ff is understood to say that only the high priest wore the ephod.

7. Babylonian Talmud, *Kiddushin* 78b and *Midrash Tanchuma Leviticus* 6:2.

8. A story told in II Kings 22–23 and II Chronicles 34–35.

Was the Biblical Joseph Autistic?

While the idea presented in Samuel J. Levine's book *Was Yosef on the Spectrum* that the biblical Joseph, son of Jacob, was autistic, having Asperger's Syndrome, may bother some people who prefer to think that Israel's ancient leaders had no imperfections,[1] they will still find much to learn and much to appreciate in this book. Readers will discover that Levine's analysis explains numerous seemingly strange behaviors by Joseph, who is called by his Hebrew name in this book, behaviors that stymied many scholars for generations. We can now better understand his strengths and weaknesses.

COMPARING JOSEPH'S BEHAVIOR WITH AUTISTIC PEOPLE

Levine shows more than a dozen examples of how Joseph's behavior closely resembles many of those common among individuals with forms of high-functioning autism called Asperger's Syndrome.

Samuel J. Levine is a professor of Law and Director of the Jewish Law Institute at Touro Law Center and has taught at four law schools. He studied at Yeshivat Kerem B'Yavneh. He does not present his thesis in a legal manner, but supports it with easy-to-read logic, sources such as the Talmud, Midrashim, classical Bible commentaries, and psychological studies.

Both people with autism spectrum disorders and Joseph have "social challenges

---

1. Contrary to what numerous people think, many rabbis recognized that none of the ancient Israelites were perfect. Nachmanides, for example, wrote that Abraham committed a great wrong when he lied and claimed that his wife Sarah was his sister so that Egyptians would not kill him when they kidnapped his wife. He also assumed that Jacob did wrong when he married two sisters, which is contrary to the law in the later promulgated Torah. See Rabbi Dr. Israel Drazin, *Nachmanides: An Unusual Thinker* (Jerusalem: Gefen Publishing House, 2017).

punctuated by an inability to read social clues, understand and anticipate the feelings and reactions of others, attachment to animals or inanimate objects in place of intellectual relationships, heightened intellectual capacity and creativity in narrow areas of interest, repetitive and inflexible behaviors, an obsessive and compulsive focus on a private way of perceiving the world, and a rigid and literal perspective on truth, ethics, and morality that sees virtue in extreme terms rather than allowing for nuance," Levine stresses "that this way of analyzing the story of Yosef should not be seen as casting Yosef in a negative light."

There are many clues that may lead readers of the Bible's story of Joseph to conclude that he was autistic. It is not any single behavior that leads to this conclusion, but the accumulation of many of his acts. We are first introduced to Joseph when he is caring for animals. Children on the spectrum, as previously stated, often feel more comfortable with animals than with people.

The commentator Rashi, relying on Midrashim, states that although he was seventeen years old, the Bible calls him a *naar*, a youth, because he acted childishly. Rashi adds that Joseph had been ostracized and marginalized by his half-brothers the sons of Leah because of his behavior, leading him to seek companionship with his less prominent half-brothers, sons of other wives. But even there he has trouble piloting his social environment. This is understandable. It is common for autistic children to possess advanced cognitive abilities, but still appear childish, immature, and socially inappropriate, leading them to be ostracized. Despite having an advanced intelligence, children on the spectrum may, as in the case of Joseph, be unable to understand the feelings of others.

Like other children on the spectrum, Joseph engages in attention-seeking behavior by repeatedly relating his dreams about his future to his family, totally oblivious to the feelings of those he is addressing.

When children on the spectrum are treated with hostility, as Joseph is, they turn to an authority figure for help. Joseph turns to his father Jacob with the misguided hope that reporting on the misbehavior of his brothers will resolve the situation. But he is unable to anticipate the ramifications of his actions. He cannot understand that telling tales about his brothers will exacerbate his alienation from them. Like others on the spectrum his obsessive need to tell the truth leads him to express his views regardless of other considerations.

Like other autistic children, he is unable to read social clues and respond by adjusting his behavior in a socially appropriate manner, in a way that would benefit him and others. Joseph is absorbed in himself and in his dreams. He sees nothing wrong or harmful in trying to bring his brothers and father into his own world.

Jacob sends Joseph to discover how his brothers are doing, and he gets lost. "It may not be surprising that Yosef is lost, given that children on the spectrum often have spatial and other sensory deficits, coupled with a degree of self-absorption leading them to be somewhat oblivious to their physical surroundings, all of which impact their sense of direction."

His brothers sell him as a slave. In Egypt, as a slave to Potiphar, Joseph continues the same type of behavior that infected his relationship with his brothers, his inability to anticipate and navigate social challenges, this time with Potiphar's seductive wife, leads him into trouble. "When Potiphar's wife looks at Yosef, she not only observes that he is a handsome young man. She also notices that he is engaged in childish, self-absorbed, and dreamlike activities, singling his inability to effectively navigate his surrounding, and his vulnerability to the attacks – or in her case, the advances – of others, particularly adults in positions of authority." Joseph is unable to read Potiphar's wife's intentions and to anticipate and handle her maneuvers. Joseph runs from Potiphar's wife without realizing that he should have snatched his coat – the evidence against him – from her hands.

He is imprisoned, and it is in prison that he can begin to utilize his advanced cognitive abilities in a way that will impress people around him. He interprets the dreams of two of Pharaoh's officials. "Yet, without missing a beat or allowing for a gradual and socially appropriate dialogue to develop, Yosef calls out his own desires, demands, and expectations, unable to picture the situation from someone else's perspective." It is no surprise that the official ignored Joseph's demand and only fulfilled it by chance two years later.

It is also possible that the official thought it inadvisable to plead with Pharaoh on behalf of someone with Joseph's disabilities. This may explain why the official later described Joseph to Pharaoh as a *naar*, as "a warning to Pharaoh, to be prepared to encounter possibly strange behavior – albeit coupled with brilliant insights."

It is no surprise that Pharaoh overlooked Joseph's disabilities because many leaders can identify the strengths in others and the contributions the person can bring to the country. Pharaoh tells Joseph that he heard that he can interpret dreams. Without waiting to hear the dream, Joseph curiously interrupts Pharaoh and contradicts him, "It lies beyond me. God will answer Pharaoh's peace." This response seems ill advised. It shows again Joseph exhibiting socially inappropriate behavior, not thinking how his actions impact others and even his own safety. Joseph should not have contradicted Pharaoh's generous remark. And Joseph who has still not heard the dream seems overconfident that God will answer Pharaoh. Also, mentioning God identifies Joseph as one of the Hebrews who were held in contempt by the Egyptians.

After interpreting the dreams, Joseph continues his unwise behavior. Unasked, he offers Pharaoh advice on a course of action Pharaoh should take for the next fourteen years. This was discourteous and downright reckless. Perhaps recognizing Joseph's disability and his perspicacity, Pharaoh gives Joseph dignified clothes (because people on the spectrum commonly have challenges about personal grooming – and this may also explain why Jacob gave him a coat), an honorable name, servants to help him, and a wife from a prominent family to protect him and help him navigate his social surroundings.

Joseph seems to have been able to channel his deficits during the ensuing years and achieve success. But when he encounters his brothers again, "Yosef returns to some of his old – and odd – behaviors" in the ways he treats his brothers and fails to consider their reactions and those of his father when he learns how the second-to-Pharaoh treated them. He also acts inappropriately when Jacob is near death and wants to bless Joseph's children; he attempts to intervene and have his father bless the children as he, Joseph, feels is appropriate. And when Jacob requests that Joseph swear that he will bury him in Canaan, Joseph refuses to take the oath, and responds tersely, "I will do as you have said," Jacob again requests Joseph to swear, and this time he complies.

Do these and other behaviors by Joseph suggest that he had Asperger's Syndrome? People may differ. Many, but not all, finding the evidence very persuasive. And if we are convinced that he did have the syndrome, this does not belittle him. It helps us understand the many strange and inexplicable things that Joseph did.

People Don't Know What Is in
the Ten Commandments

Catholics, Protestants, Muslims, and Jews are convinced that while they do not know much about their religion, they do know about the "Ten Commandments." This is not true, as the following examples show.[1]

THE TRUTH ABOUT THE DECALOGUE

There are not ten commandments. The oft-used term "Ten Commandments" is incorrect. Scholars and clerics know there are more than ten commandments in the Decalogue, although they differ as to how many there are. The correct term for the document, the one used by the Torah itself, is *aseret hadibrot* (ten statements). In Greek, "Decalogue" means the same. There are ten statements that contain between eleven and fifteen commands. We do not know when or why the erroneous title for this document was invented.

There are two versions of the Decalogue in the Bible. One is in Exodus 20:1–17 and one in Deuteronomy 5:4–21. There are a couple of dozen differences between the two versions in the wording and spelling, and Deuteronomy has some additional words.

Many people consider the first sentence beginning "I am the Lord your God" to be the first command even though no command is explicit in the words, and it appears as a separate command in the classic layout of the two tablets in synagogues, but others, such as the Masorites, discussed below, are convinced it is not a command at all, but God being introduced to the Israelites.[2]

---

1. Several times this number could be cited.
2. Maimonides, in his *Mishneh Torah* considered this introductory statement as a command to

There are different opinions among Jews as to how to divide the ten statements. The Masorites combined what many Jews today consider the first two statements into one and divided the last into two. Masorites lived during the second half of the first millennia. They were the Jewish scholars who determined the correct wording of the Torah and, among much else, the spacing of Torah sentences and paragraphs. The term Masorites derives from the Hebrew *masora* (tradition), and they were so called because they established or continued the Torah traditions. Their spacing of the Decalogue is the one found in the Torah scrolls used during the Torah reading in synagogues. Thus, it is rather remarkable that their view of the spacing of the Decalogue, the one in the Torah scrolls, is not accepted by many Jews.

The first (or second) command states that one should not have "any other gods (*elohim acheirim*) before me." It does not say, do not worship idols. Many scholars take the wording literally and are convinced that the early Israelites believed in the existence of many gods, and the Decalogue is mandating that the Israelites may not worship or seek help from the other gods, only *y-h-v-h*, who, as indicated in the first paragraph, took the Israelites out of Egypt.

This first or second statement can be divided into more than a single mandate: (1) serve no other gods except the God who brought the Israelites out of Egypt; (2) make no image of God; (3) Make no image of anything on earth, the heaven, or in the water; (4) do not bow down to them; and (5) do not serve them.

Another difficulty with the Decalogue is how to interpret the prohibitions. For example, one statement says that we may make no image of items on earth, in heaven, or in the water. Yet, contrary to this explicit prohibition in the Decalogue, ancient Jews had images in their synagogues and the rabbis allowed the making of and owning pictures and statues.

Similarly, another command states "Thou shalt not kill." Yet shortly after the giving of the Decalogue, the Israelites were commanded to kill the Midianites who seduced many Israelites to worship idols. Additionally, this command seems to prohibit self-defense and may even forbid killing animals for food.

One command states in Exodus "Do not take the name of God in vain," but

seek to "know about God" by studying what God created, the laws of nature. The King James translation of the Bible does not consider the introductory statement as a command.

in Deuteronomy it states "Do not utter the name falsely." Which is the true command? Many people go so far as to not even write the word "God," but write instead "G-d." Yet when they speak, they say "God." Is not writing the word "God" what the Decalogue commands? Is saying "God" a violation of the Decalogue?

Similarly, Exodus states that one should "remember" the Sabbath day to keep it holy. It does not state how the day should be remembered. In Deuteronomy, the command is changed to "observe," without saying how one should do so. Is "remember" or "observe" the true command?

Still another difficulty: in the last statement (or last two, according to the Masorites)[3] about coveting what does not belong to us, does this prohibit mental desires, or only the improper taking of another person's object? Coveting in Hebrew and English means desiring, wanting something that belongs to another person. It is part of human nature of most people to desire the splendor that others have. How can this natural reaction be proscribed? The rabbinical interpretation is that it disallows adultery and theft even though this is contrary to what is stated, because coveting is a mental process.[4]

These "difficulties" show that many Decalogue commands should not be taken literally but must be understood as interpreted in the oral tradition.

---

3. The ninth is coveting the neighbor's house and wife. The tenth is coveting his servants, animals and all his other possessions.

4. This raises the question of how this command differs from the injunction against theft.

What does the Decalogue Really Say?

Some Jewish philosophers and rabbis and non-Jews disagreed over what exactly the Bible was saying in the Ten Commandments. The philosopher Philo who lived during the beginning of the common era is an example.

PHILO'S UNIQUE INTERPRETATION OF THE DECALOGUE

The following are some of the many things that the philosopher Philo (20 BCE–50 CE) wrote about the Decalogue:[1]

1. Philo accepted the current understanding of the Decalogue, not the teaching of the Masorites and divided the first statement into two and combined the last two. He called the document The Ten Commandments and treated it as such even though there are clearly more than ten.
2. Like Saadiah Gaon (882–942), Philo considered the commands as "generic rules, comprehending nearly all offenses." In other words, one can see that any wrong committed by people can be subsumed under one of the general ten laws.[2]
3. God did not "speak" the commands because God is not anthropomorphic; God does not have vocal cords allowing speech. God created a miraculous sound that spoke the commands.
4. The Greek Septuagint translation had two distinct orders for the Decalogue, different than all other translations which parallel our Masoretic text. Our text

---

1. Rabbi Michael Leo Samuel, *Torah from Alexandria, Philo as A Biblical Commentator, Exodus* (New York: Kodesh Press, 2014).

2. Why did they consider the ten commands as ten categories? We do not know. It is possible that they thought since the Decalogue is described in the Torah as being promulgated in a miraculous manner, different than all other commands, it must have special significance.

is: You shall not murder...commit adultery...steal in Exodus 20 and Deuteronomy 5. The Septuagint changes the order in Exodus to commit adultery...
steal...murder, and in Deuteronomy to commit adultery...murder...steal.
Philo accepted the Septuagint order.

5. Philo states that the first four commands deal with relations between man
    and God. The fifth about honoring parents focuses on both honoring God
    and treating people properly. The remaining five are commands dealing with
    human relations. They begin with adultery (in the Septuagint and Philo order)
    because according to them this is the greatest of crimes.

6. The first law ("I am the Lord") "opposes the polytheistic doctrine and teaches
    that the world is ruled by one sole governor."

7. The second, forbidding making idols, is "in order that the only true God might
    be honored in truth and simplicity."[3] God does not need honor, but God
    desires to aid humans from going astray, to teach them to follow natural law.

8. The third prohibits the wrongful use of God's name. This restrains people
    from making unnecessary oaths.

9. The fourth about the Sabbath obligates people to work during the six other
    days of the week and to use the seventh day to contemplate how to improve
    oneself. It requires people to become self-reliant and not to rely on servants
    and animals, and to give servants rest so that they should not despair of better
    times that lay ahead. Contrary to the Greek society in which he lived, Philo
    felt that slavery is an affront to God and humanity.

10. The fifth requires honoring parents. This is both a human and divine-oriented
    command. People must learn how to reciprocate with service to those who
    have done them a service. The command teaches that we must reciprocate
    not only to parents, but to God, nature, and all people; to everything.

11. Philo's sixth law bars adultery. As previously noted, it is "the greatest of all
    violations of the law." It has as its source the love of pleasure that enervates
    the body and destroys the chance for proper improvement. It affects people
    and their families, the husband, the adulterer, and the wife and her children.

12. The seventh in Philo's order of Exodus 20 is murder, an act of sacrilege, for

---

3. This concept of worshiping God in a very simple manner stresses acting properly with fellow
humans rather than pompous grandiose religious observances.

humans are godlike and are supposed to be civilized and act with reason. Murder robs a person of the sacred gift given by God, life.

13. The eighth in his Exodus order is stealing. A thief is an enemy of the state and all that a state stands for. Stealing one object leads to other transgressions and develops habits that grow progressively worse.

14. The ninth, outlawing being a false witness, can produce "every kind of terrible danger." Such a person corrupts the truth, which is the most sacred treasure any of us can expect to own in life.

15. Philo understands that the tenth, the prohibition against "covetousness," bans improper desires, not deeds.[4] Covetous desires is the original passion from which all other mischiefs emanate. People need to learn to become obedient to the laws of moderation.

---

4. See Moses Maimonides, *Guide of the Perplexed* (Chicago: University of Chicago Press, 1974), 3:50 where Maimonides explains, like Philo, that people need to learn to control their desires. However, as a matter of halakha (law), Maimonides states (in *Mishneh Torah, Hilkhot Geneivah* 1:9) that the rabbis understood that it is the acts that the Torah forbids.

The Bible is Filled with Obscurities and Ambiguities

Quite a few years ago I read virtually all of the writings of the Argentinian author Jorge Luis Borges (1899–1986), and enjoyed his writings immensely. In 1982, a Columbian author Garcia Marquez (1927–2014) won the Nobel Prize in Literature (although my vote would have been for Borges). Both authors wrote tales with "magic realism," as did the Israeli author and Nobel Prize winner S.Y. Agnon. I had a professor who described magic realism as: it describes, for example, a man walking across a bridge and when he reaches the mid-point rises and flies the rest of the way. I found many ideas in Borges's books that helped me to understand the Bible better, especially his descriptions of good literature.

SOME BORGES QUOTES

I always remember the following three Borges quotes that I applied to the Bible. I was unable to find the source of these quotes, and I am citing them from memory, which may be faulty.

- "All good literature is filled with obscurities and ambiguities." Since the Bible is good, even superb literature, it must contain these elements.
- Since good literature contains obscure and ambiguous elements, readers read unstated events, dialogues, and explanations into what they are reading and: "Two people write a book, the author and the reader."
- "I think that the reader should enrich what he is reading. He should understand the text; he should change it into something else."

EXAMINING SOME OBSCURE AND AMBIGUOUS BIBLICAL INCIDENCES

I think that a good example of this kind of writing is the biblical view of women. Because the Bible descriptions are not clear, readers, including rabbis and scholars, have developed three conflicting evaluations. Some say the Bible disparages women, others that it portrays them favorably, and the majority acknowledge that they do not know. Additionally, many have used the obscurities in Scripture to disparage women. The following are some examples of this thinking, and of opacities and disparagements.

A sage in the Babylonian Talmud[1] lists seven female prophets: Sarah, Miriam, Deborah, Hannah, Abigail, Hulda, and Esther.[2] One opinion in the Talmud rates Sarah as a prophet superior to her husband Abraham. Many people read the Genesis tale and feel that the first female, Eve, was superior in intelligence and initiative to her passive husband Adam.

Yet, there were unfortunately many sages who read Judges chapters 4 and 5, the story of Deborah, and made disparaging views about women. For example, Don Isaac Abarbanel (1437–1508) asks: If Yael's husband made a treaty with Jabin, king of Canaan, how could Yael breach that treaty? His answer: Women are not bound by treaties; they must only do what their husbands tell them to do. Abarbanel also questions why Deborah, a judge and prophet, needs to sit under a tree. The Aramaic translation of Judges, *Targum Jonathan*,[3] answers that she dwelled in a house that was shaded by a tree. However, Abarbanel responds that she felt that it was inappropriate for a woman to be alone with a man in a house, so she arranged her meetings with men outside, under a tree. *Zohar* 3:19b reads: "Woe unto the generation whose leader [judge] is a woman." Several sources state:

---

1. *Megillah* 14a–b.

2. This view raises many questions. There is no indication in the Bible that the women other than Deborah and Hulda were prophets. And the Bible states that other women heard God – namely Eve (Genesis 3:13), Abraham's concubine Hagar (Genesis 16:17), and the mother of Samson (Judges 13:3). Why didn't the Talmudic sage include them? Did he exclude Hagar and Samson's mother because they heard God through an angel or because they and Eve only experienced a single prophecy? Did he exclude Eve and Hagar because they were not Israelites?
 What is the sage saying and why did he employ the oft-used number seven? We do not know. Is he arguing against those who minimized the value of women?

3. The date of composition of this translation is disputed with dates extending from the second to the ninth century CE.

"Prophetess though she [Deborah] was, she was yet subject to the frailties of her sex. Her self-consciousness was inordinate.... The result was that the prophetical spirit departed from her for a time while she was composing her song."[4]

EVE

Whether Adam's wife is pictured favorably or not has left experts with three conflicting views. The Bible says that Eve was created to be an *eizer khenegdo*. The two words literally mean "help" "against him." Is it suggesting that she was to be an equal, or a being that is somewhat an adversary?

Was her eating the forbidden fruit a wrongful act? Maimonides tells us in the second chapter of his *Guide of the Perplexed* that the story is a parable designed to teach a lesson about proper behavior.[5] God gave the command not to eat the fruit to Adam, not to Eve. We assume that Adam passed on the command to Eve, but the Bible does not say that he did so. Even if he did, was Eve showing initiative, being active, as people should be, while Adam, as previously stated, was passive. Yes, she was punished, but was the punishment for a wrongdoing, or was the Bible teaching that even praiseworthy acts have consequences and people need to be careful.

SARAH

The Bible states that Abraham's wife laughed when angels predicted that she would give birth to a son when she was old and past the child-bearing age. Was she acting reasonably or improperly? When Abraham took Sarah to Egypt because of the famine in Canaan, he knew that Sarah could be kidnapped, and protected himself from being killed by saying that Sarah was his sister. Did he do wrong, as Nachmanides insisted? And what about Sarah, why was she silent? Why didn't she refuse to accompany her husband? Why did she allow herself to be kidnapped? Was she violated when she was given to Pharaoh and placed in his harem? There

---

4. Babylonian Talmud, *Pesachim* 66b; Moshe de Leon, *Zohar* 3:21b–22a; *Midrash Genesis Rabba* 40:4; and others. Also see Louis Ginzberg, *The Legends of the Jews* (Cosimo Inc., 2006), Vol 4:36.
5. He notes that the fruit of the tree is called the fruit of good and evil, and not truth and falsehood, and states that the lesson of the parable is to go beyond the conventional ideas of doing what is good and avoiding what is bad. This is wrong. People should focus instead on avoiding traditional notions and use one's intelligence about what is true and false before deciding how to act.

is a Midrash that states the people were sure she was, and that Isaac was Pharaoh's son, and therefore God made Isaac look like Abraham to dispel this mistake.

REBECCA

Similar questions can be asked about the patriarch Isaac's wife, the matriarch Rebecca. Did she act improperly when she deceived her husband making him think that he was giving his blessing to Esau when he was blessing Jacob? And did she act improperly by making Jacob her accomplice?

LEAH

Did Leah do wrong when she made Jacob think he was marrying his beloved Rachel? And was Rachel complicit in the deception? If not, why didn't she warn Jacob? We do not know and can only speculate.

TAMAR

Jacob's son Judah married a Canaanite woman and had three sons with her. When they reached the appropriate age, he gave the oldest to a woman named Tamar.[6] When his first-born died, he gave his second son to her. When he also died, Judah thinking the third son would also die, of an unknown cause, did not give Tamar his third son.

Judah's wife died, and Tamar was seeking a way to get Judah's third son. She somehow knew that Judah would want the services of a prostitute and decided to seduce him. We have no idea why she thought that the seduction would accomplish the goal of gaining the third son or what other motivation she had. Judah did have sex with her without knowing she was his daughter-in-law. She bore a son who later became the ancestor of King David. The Torah does not tell us what happened to Judah, Tamar, and the third son. Furthermore, it does not reveal whether Tamar's behavior was wrong. Also, why does the Bible tell us that King David was the ultimate result of a sordid affair?

THE WIVES OF JOSEPH AND MOSES

Why does the Bible tell us that Jacob's son Joseph and the lawgiver Moses mar-

---

6. The story is in Genesis 28.

ried daughters of pagan priests? Each had two sons. Why doesn't the Bible tell us about these sons? Were they good people? Jacob blessed Joseph's sons and made them tribal leaders, but we do not know why. Scholars claim this tale was added long after the time of Moses to explain the existence of the two tribes at the later period, but this is pure speculation. What happened to Moses's sons is not recorded. Rabbis imagine that Moses's grandson was a priest at a temple of idol worshipers.[7]

YAEL

Chapters 4 and 5 of Judges are filled with unclear events. The judge Deborah agrees with the Israelite general Barak's condition that he will lead the army in defense against the Canaanite attack only if she joins with him, but the Bible does not reveal why Barak felt he needed her or her role in the battle. Also, she ridicules him by prophesying in a cryptic manner that a woman, not he, will get credit for the victory. Her prediction may refer to Deborah being praised, or to Yael who slew the enemy general Sisera after the battle. It is also doubtful if she is disparaging women generally or, if not, what the intent is of the ridicule.

After Barak and Deborah defeat the enemy forces, Sisera seeks shelter in the tent of Yael. She is called a Kenite, but it is unclear if the word means she was a non-Israelite, as some commentators think, or she was an Israelite living in Kenite territory.

Yael offers Sisera milk which makes him sleepy. When he falls asleep, she kills him, and is proclaimed a hero in Jewish tradition. It is unclear why she is a hero. Wouldn't it have been better and more moral to call the Israelite forces to come and capture him? True, she may not have had an opportunity or ability to do so, but the Bible is silent on this issue.

Why did Yael want to kill Sisera? Was she angry about something? Did she want revenge for something? Was it from a feeling of justice, or perhaps self-preservation? We do not know.

Another obscurity regards Yael's husband, Verse 4:12 states that Yael's husband left Judah's territory and apparently, but this is unclear, aligned his family with the

---

7. See Judges 18:30 and my commentary on the verse in: Rabbi Dr. Israel Drazin, *Unusual Bible Interpretations: Judges* (Jerusalem: Gefen Publishing House, 2015).

Canaanite enemy. In the story only Yael was in her tent; we can only speculate what happened to her husband.

Additionally, both Deborah and Yael were married, yet acted independent of their husbands. Was this bad?

BAT SHEBA

King David's relationship with Bat Sheba is unclear. Why was she bathing apparently naked in an area where the king could see her? What attracted David to her? Did he rape her? Why aren't Bat Sheba's thoughts and emotions mentioned here in the Bible? Why did David ignore the biblical prohibition against adultery? Why after having sex with her did he ignore her until she came to him revealing that she was pregnant? Did David want to marry her? What were her thoughts about marriage and about the man who killed her husband? If David wanted to marry her, why did he try repeatedly to get her husband to have sex with her so that he could claim that the pregnancy was a result of sex with the husband? Why does the Bible ignore her after she gave birth to Solomon until the death bed scene where she comes to David, prompted to do so by a prophet? Is there a hint here that he was not that interested in her? If so, why did he marry her? Was it to claim that her child resulted after his marriage and to hide his adulterous relationship with her? Why when he was on his death bed and was cold did he have a virgin sleep in his bed to make him warm. Bat Sheba was not young, but was she not warm?

THE MEDIUM OF EN DOR

Now let's take the opposite approach. In the former cases, the women were considered nice, or so it seemed. Let's now look at women that many think were bad. But were they as bad as people think?

When King Saul was convinced that he and his army were in trouble in his battle against the Philistines, he went to a medium, some translate her title as "witch," for her to bring the prophet Samuel from the dead to tell him the outcome of the war.[8] The medium treated him courteously, brought up Samuel from the dead, and after Saul spoke to Samuel and received bad news, the medium gave Saul food to eat. We have no idea if this was a trick, or miracle, or precisely what

---

8. The story is in 1 Samuel 28.

happened during the séance because the Bible does not tell us. True, the medium violated the Torah prohibition against sorcery and King Saul's own law on the subject, but was she bad?

ATHALIAH

Athaliah was the only woman in the Hebrew Bible who is reported to have reigned in the northern kingdom of Israel or the southern kingdom of Judah.[9] Her father was Ahab, the evil king of Israel, and her mother was Ahab's famed evil queen Jezebel. She married Jehoram, the son of Jehoshaphat the righteous king of Judah who, like all the kings of Judah were descendants of King David. Why the righteous king of Judah would condone a marriage with the daughter of two evil people, individuals who worshipped idols and persuaded their nation to do so as well, is obscure.

When Jehoram's father died, Jehoram became king, but he soon died. As we would expect, Athaliah led her husband to abandon the righteous ways of his father and to worship idols during the short time that he ruled. He was succeeded by his son Ahaziah who also died.

Athaliah then seized the throne and killed all of her children and other possible claimants to the throne, except for a single one-year-old child. The sister of King Ahaziah secretly took Athaliah's son Joash and hid him in the temple for six years. During the six years, from about 841 to about 835 BCE, while Athaliah ruled Judea, the priests educated Joash. When Joash was seven years old, the priest brought him out of hiding, killed Athaliah, and made Joash king.

This story is filled with obscurities. True, Athaliah murdered her own family to become the ruler of Judea, but Jehu who seized the throne from Ahab in the northern kingdom of Israel, and who was anointed king by the prophet Elisha, did a similar act. He killed the seventy sons of Ahab so that they could not take the kingdom from him. Other Israelite rulers did the same. This was the practice of the time among Israelites and non-Israelites. We recognize the practice as barbaric, but should Athaliah be castigated because she followed the well-accepted practice?

Why did a man of God, the prophet Elisha, crown Jehu as king because of a prophecy since he turned out to be a bad king, killing many, and worshipping the

---

9. Her story is in II Kings 11 and II Chronicles 22 and 23.

idol Baal? While the Bible is silent on this issue, we know that the Torah is replete with prophecies and virtually all of them were unfulfilled. Thus, for example, King Josiah and King Zedekiah were prophesied to have long life, but both are killed before they reach old age. Tosaphot notes this and states that a prophet does not foretell what will be, but what ought to be.[10] This phenomenon of unfulfilled prophecies is difficult for those who maintain the view that God directed the prophet to make the pronouncement. It is not difficult for Maimonides, ibn Ezra, ibn Caspi, Gersonides,[11] or others who consider prophecy a higher level of intelligence.

There are other unanswered questions in this biblical story. How did Athaliah manage to kill her children and relatives? Why did the Judeans let her get away with these murders? Was she protected by an armed force? If so, why didn't these soldiers aid her when the priest brought out Joash from hiding, made him king, and killed her? Why didn't the priests bring out Joash earlier? Why did they bring him out when he was only seven years old? Did they do so because they had taught him for six years and felt sure he would do as they wanted, especially because he was so young?

Also, should Athaliah be excused because she knew no better than what her parents, Ahab and Jezebel, taught her? Should people have the right to believe what they want and, if so, what is wrong with idol worship? Was God involved in saving the child Joash, the sole survivor of the line of King David? Yes, Athaliah was ambitious, but what is wrong with ambition, especially when her murders were the rule of the day?

IN CONCLUSION

There is no way to answer these questions because like much else in the Torah, many details are left to our imagination, all we can do is speculate, and speculations are not facts.

---

10. Tosaphot to *Yevamot* 50a. The Tosaphists were commentators to the Bible and Talmud who lived for the most part in Germany and France during the twelfth and thirteenth century. The first Tosaphists were the sons-in-law and grandsons of Rashi (Rabbi Solomon Yitzchaqi, 1040–1105).
11. Levi ben Gershom (Gersonides), *Milhamot Hashem* 6, 2, 10.

An Opinion about the Oral Torah

One of the fundamental principles of Orthodox Judaism is the belief that there is a Written and an Oral Torah, both of which were revealed by God to Moses. Quite a few Orthodox rabbis declare that if a Jew does not accept this teaching, the Jew is not Orthodox and is a rebel, an apikores – one who disputes the existence of God. These rabbis insist upon believing that the Oral Torah is divine even though it differs radically with what is stated explicitly in the Written Torah. If people insist that they will only observe what is in the Written Torah and dismiss the Oral Torah, they will be behaving totally different than other Jews. Once again I plan to show that Jews can accept the view that the Oral Torah is not divine, but rather an invention of the Pharisees and rabbis. They recognize that Judaism today is not Biblical Judaism, but rather a Rabbinical Judaism, and thus can observe the laws as explained by the rabbis and still be considered a good Jew, even an Orthodox Jew. Samuel David Luzzatto is a good example, as one can see from his writings.[1]

RABBI SAMUEL LUZZATTO

Samuel David Luzzatto (1800–1865), known as Shadal, was a brilliant Orthodox Jewish scholar, and the great-grandnephew of the equally famous Moshe Chaim Luzzatto (1707–1747) author of *Mesillat Yesharim*.[2] He was a devout believer in the divinity, unity, and antiquity of the Torah, but he read the Torah with an open mind and drew interpretations from many sources, Jewish and non-Jewish,

---

1. The facts stated herein are from Samuel David Luzzatto, *Shadal on Exodus, Samuel David Luzzatto's Interpretation of the Book of Shemot*, trans. and ed. Daniel A. Klein (Kodesh Press, 2015).
2. Discussed later in this book.

ancient and modern, and always focused on the plain simple meaning of the text, as he understood its *peshat*.

ORTHODOX, BUT A NON-KOSHER JEW

Shadal disliked Maimonides and philosophy, and preferred the commentary of Rashi, but not Rashi's midrashic interpretations. He recognized that while he considered himself Orthodox, he was not so "according to the ideas of the majority of the 'kosher' Jews." He rejected source criticism and emendation of the Bible text advocated by contemporary Bible critics. In view of this and in view of his rational interpretations, which we will see below, it is strange that he disliked Maimonides. It is possible, and this is one of the many fascinating questions that this scholar raises in the minds of readers, that he was convinced that Maimonides had gone too far and that he rejected the divinity of the Torah.

HALAKHA

Shadal was not averse to offering rational interpretations of halakha, the Torah's commands that differed from, and even opposed what halakha demanded, but he insisted that despite his interpretations, the halakha was controlling in practice.[3] The following are some of his ideas, including his understanding of the Oral Torah and his application of his understanding that the rabbis can change what is in the Written Torah to a law about women.

- God is present and involved in human affairs, performs miracles, but always includes the ways of nature in the miracles. For example, the ten plagues were natural events that occurred from time to time in Egypt, but God made them happen in a single year (Exodus 7:20).
- It is impossible that the Israelites entered Egypt as only seventy people, and left Egypt after 210 years numbering well over six hundred thousand. They must have been in Egypt for some four hundred years and the list of names

---

3. Maimonides did the same. For example, he explained in *Guide of the Perplexed* 3:48 that the three-time-stated command not to boil a kid in its mother's milk was ordained to avoid a pagan worship practice. Yet he included the rabbinic interpretation that one must not mix and eat dairy and meat products together. The commands are in Exodus 23:19, 34:26, and Deuteronomy 14:21, each using the same words.

were not consecutive generations, but rather other generations that are not listed between them (Exodus 6:20 and 12:40).

- The Israelites during the ancient period, like people of other nations, were very superstitious, and the purpose of the collection of a silver half-shekel for the Tabernacle was to alleviate their fear of the "evil eye" (Exodus 30:12).

- Mount Sinai is called the mountain of God, not because it was holy, but because the Decalogue would be revealed there (Exodus 3:1).

- The alien people who accompanied the Israelites when they exited Egypt were probably Egyptians who were married to Israelites and the flocks and herds that joined the exodus most likely belonged to them (Exodus 12:38).

- All of the Israelites heard all of the commands in the Decalogue because of a special miraculous voice that God created for this purpose (Exodus 20:1), or by means of a vision (Exodus 24:10).[4]

- The ancient Israelites were convinced that children are punished for the misdeeds of their parents, as indicated in Exodus 20:5, 34:7, Deuteronomy 5:9, Lamentations 5:7; but this view was changed in Jeremiah 31:28, Ezekiel 18:2, and Babylonian Talmud *Berakhot* 7a.

- Jewish tradition states that God has thirteen attributes (Exodus 34:6, Babylonian Talmud *Rosh Hashanah* 17b), but he notes that there is no consensus what they are. In fact, he lists a dozen different listings of the thirteen, and could have listed more.

THE ORAL LAW AND WOMEN

Two of Shadal's views are especially significant and may bother what Shadal called "kosher Jews." These views indicated that the Oral Law comprises commands developed by the rabbis, and that the rabbis changed the law concerning women's obligation to observe certain commandments.

Shadal does not accept the view that the Oral Law, also called the Oral Torah, was given to Moses at Sinai, or at any place or time. He contends, as do most scholars, that the Oral Law is comprised of rabbinic enactments. And he states

---

4. The *Midrash Mekhilta* and Babylonian Talmud *Makkot* 24a state the people only heard the first two commands. Shadal states that he understands that Maimonides wrote in *Guide of the Perplexed* 36 and 47 that God's speech was directed to Moses alone and it was a vision.

that the Torah itself orders, or permits, the rabbis to make changes, add rules, and delete what God decreed.

This permission is in Deuteronomy 17:11 which states that the Israelites should obey the decisions of the legal authorities of their time and "not stray to the right or to the left from the decision that they communicate to you."

Shadal explains that the rabbis made the changes due to deep wisdom, fear of God, and love of humanity, to alleviate social conditions, and, in some instances, to set up restrictive "fences" around the law to assure that the law itself would not be violated.

He recognizes that the rabbis use two terms *mi'd'oraita* (from the Torah), and *mi'd'rabbanan* (from the rabbis), to classify the origin of laws. But he tells readers that these terms should not be taken literally. A law is often called *mi'd'oraita* even though it is clearly not mentioned in the Torah, because the rabbis found an *asmakhta*, a peg upon which they could hang their decree.

THE RABBINICAL LAWS WERE IN THE SPIRIT OF THE WRITTEN TORAH

It is likely that Shadal felt that the rabbis did not consider their calling rabbinical enactments "biblical" because they were convinced that what they enacted was in the spirit of the Torah – the rules were wise and helpful, and the new post-temple era required them.

THE EXEMPTION GIVEN TO WOMEN REGARDING CERTAIN POSITIVE COMMANDMENTS

Shadal noted that there is no distinction made in the Torah regarding the observance of Torah commands; just as men are obligated to observe them, so are women. Yet the rabbis in post-biblical times decreed that women are not obligated to observe the Torah's positive commands that are time-bound, such as dwelling in a sukkah and using the four species on the holiday of Sukkot, or wearing tefillin since the observances are positive commands that occur at a specific time and are not always obligatory.[5]

---

5. The rabbis decreed that wearing tefillin is not required at night or on the Shabbat. Women must observe certain positive commands which have negative commands connected with them, such as the Shabbat, which is required in the Decalogue, but there are things which one may not do on the Shabbat.

Shadal supposed that when the Torah was revealed, women were treated fairly. But during the rabbinical period the rabbis noted that women were no longer treated as they should be and were obliged to do much work in their families. So, the rabbis, Shadal claims, having compassion upon women, lessened their religious burden by allowing them to ignore many biblical positive commands.[6]

MAIMONIDES

Shadal's strongly held conviction that the Torah and its commands are from God raises the question, if God gave these commands and God is all-knowing, why would he believe that the rabbis not only had the power to develop new laws, but to even annul what they desired?

A probable answer is that God gave commands that fit the generation when they were promulgated, but that God wanted the people to develop and change the laws. Examples of laws that needed to be changed are sacrifices, slavery, punishments of an "eye for an eye," the killing of a disobedient child, the murder of the inhabitants of an idol-worshipping town, and many more.

Although he disliked Maimonides, this idea that Jews can change even positive commandments is what Maimonides taught in his *Guide of the Perplexed* 3:32.

---

6. Shadal's view that women were treated fairly in ancient times is generally rejected. There is no proof that this is so. It is possible, as my friend Dr. Norman Wald wisely commented, that the Torah did not mention that women are obligated to observe the laws because they were treated as nonentities in the past. Later, when they were treated better, the rabbis understood that they were also obligated to observe the biblical commands, but they allowed them the dispensation.

Are Divine Commands Rational?

While there are famous Jews such as Nachmanides who are convinced that certain biblical commands are inscrutable and that even though we do not understand them, we must obey them, others like Maimonides and Abraham ibn Ezra were convinced that all the divine commands are rational, and people can, and indeed should understand them.[1]

THE VIEW OF IBN EZRA

In his commentary to Exodus 31:18 Abraham ibn Ezra (1089–1167) put it this way. He states that foolish people wonder what Moses did on the mountain for forty days and forty nights after the revelation of the Decalogue. These foolish people think that all that God wants of them is that they act as God instructs even if they do not understand the value of the command.

This, he wrote, is wrong. The Torah itself insists that Jews understand the reason for the commands. Deuteronomy 30:14 states that God's word should be "in your mouth and in your heart." Since the ancients considered the "heart" to mean the mind, it is clear that God wants people to understand the purpose of the divine commands.

---

1. Nachmanides, for example, argued that all the biblical commands have a mystical basis and can only be understood if they are explained by a teacher of mysticism who secured his knowledge from a teacher who himself received it by tradition from sages of long ago. Rabbi Joseph B. Soloveitchik, to site another example, said repeatedly in most of his writings that Jews must accept the Torah teachings on "faith" and must "surrender" themselves to God. Maimonides explained all the biblical commands in book 3 of his *Guide of the Perplexed*. Among much else, he wrote that the biblical commands have three purposes: to teach some lessons, to help people improve, and to improve society.

This is emphasized by the prophet Jeremiah. In 9:23, Jeremiah wrote: "Let him who glories glory in this, that he understands and knows me."

Ibn Ezra concludes that this explains why Moses was on the mountain for forty days and forty nights; it was during this time that God explained to him the purposes of the divine commands.

Is God Involved in Prophecy:
Heschel and Maimonides

The late Abraham Joshua Heschel (1907–1972) was one of the great Orthodox Jewish scholars, theologians, and philosophers of his generation. His books made a striking impression on many people, and many of his insights are eye opening. His book *The Prophets* is one of his classics.[1]

HESCHEL

Heschel tells us that he will not address the well-known question about prophets: Did God really speak to them? Did they communicate with God? Yet, I think he did not believe that God spoke to the prophets. I say this because his book is devoted to telling us about the passions that the prophets felt that encouraged, and even compelled them to speak.

Heschel's view of prophecy is radically different than that of Maimonides (1138–1204). The two seem to agree that prophecy is not a supernatural event, it is part of human nature. But they differ in whether the prophet is prompted to act by his emotions, or his intellect. Heschel mentions Maimonides in his book ten times, but only to disagree with him.

Heschel stressed the anguish of the sensitive prophets over what they saw. He considered this emotion a good thing and contended that their emotional reactions to what they saw around them prompted them to speak. Heschel not only contends that emotions are good and that it is an emotional reaction that compels prophets to speak, he also takes the biblical stories about God's reactions to the Israelites' behavior literally and states that God also has emotional reactions. God, he writes,

---

1. Abraham Joshua Heschel, *The Prophets* (New York: Harper Perennial Classics, 2001).

is "moved and affected by what happens in the world and acts accordingly. Events and human actions arouse in Him joy or sorrow, pleasure, or wrath...man's deeds may move Him, affect Him, grieve Him, or on the other hand, gladden and please Him." He writes that "the fundamental experience of the prophet is a fellowship with the feelings of God, a *sympathy with the divine pathos* (emphasis by Heschel)." God, according to Heschel, has these feelings because "His thoughts are about the world. He is involved in human history and is affected by human acts."

MAIMONIDES

While it seems to me that Heschel, raised as a Hassid, was influenced by Hassidic mystical thinking, Maimonides took the rational Aristotelian view that what is important is intellect and thinking, not emotions. Maimonides stressed that emotions must be controlled by the intellect, or they can be evil. He contended that it was not emotions that prompted prophets to speak but the higher level of understanding that the prophets had; his or her understanding that what was being done was wrong. They saw and understood what the general population did not understand.

Maimonides also rejected the idea that God could be affected by human behavior. He taught that God has no body and no emotions and all of the biblical descriptions of God having an emotional reaction refer not to God, but to the way the people perceive their own behavior. When the Bible states that God is angry, it does not mean that God suddenly changed and reacted with anger. It means that the people realized that the behavior was wrong and not what God wanted. A side effect of portraying God as having an emotional reaction is that it tends to frighten the general population who might think that God is angry at them, enough so that some might even change their evil deeds.

Thus, for example, Heschel, as well as Rashi and the Targum, understood that the prophet Hosea married a harlot and suffered extreme agony because of her adulterous behavior, and these emotions caused him to understand how the wavering of the Israelites and their abandonment of God, affected God. In contrast, rationalists such as Maimonides, Abraham ibn Ezra, and the Radak (Rabbi David Kimchi) interpreted the tale of Hosea's marriage to a prostitute as a parable that Hosea invented and used to dramatize his message, a message he developed intellectually.

Is God Involved in Human Activities?

I think that Maimonides would answer "no," while Nachmanides would reply with a resounding "yes." Some may say that the mystic Nachmanides (1189–1270) was more interested in heaven than in earth. Unlike Maimonides, who focused on a scientific study of the world, Nachmanides was concerned with the way in which Jews interact with God. Maimonides's view led him to see three people-oriented purposes for the Torah. In his *Guide of the Perplexed* 3:27–54, he states that God mandated the commandments (1) to teach people some ideas, (2) to improve the behavior of individuals and (3) to improve society. Nachmanides took a different approach. This can be seen in Nachmanides's discussion about Passover.

THE COMMANDMENT TO REMEMBER THE EXODUS FROM EGYPT

The Israelites were instructed in the Torah to remember, mention, and discuss the exodus from Egypt frequently. The rabbis understood that the Israelites were told, for example, to wear tefillin containing references to the exodus on each day except for the Sabbath, to place mezuzot containing biblical readings about the exodus on their doorposts, and to mention the exodus on every holiday in the Kiddush, the prayer over the wine recited at the beginning of the Shabbat and festive holiday meals. They were also instructed in the Decalogue to remember the Sabbath day because God ceased creating on that day and because of the exodus from Egypt. Thus, the exodus is recalled seven days a week.

MAIMONIDES'S UNDERSTANDING OF THE EXODUS'S SIGNIFICANCE FOR JEWS

Maimonides, as usual, sees a benefit for humans in the remembrance of the exodus. One benefit is that it prompts Jews to recall their history. In his *Guide of the Perplexed* 3:46, he explains that the Passover laws such as eating unleavened bread were instituted in Egypt "because they [the Israelites] could prepare it [their food] quickly... so that no one would be late in leaving Egypt with the main body of the people, and be thereby exposed to enemy attacks. These temporary commandments were then made permanent, so that we may remember what was done in those days."

In 3:43, he adds that Jews are told to observe the holiday of Passover because it is an opportunity for rejoicing, and people need joy.

Passover also educates Jews about the close connection between the laws of nature and divine law. Maimonides states that since Passover occurs in the spring, the association of the two reminds Jews of the important interrelationship between the laws of nature and biblical law. Torah law coaches people to use nature to live properly.

Maimonides writes that the "aim and object of the exodus from Egypt," was to bring the Israelites to Sinai where they were given the law. This lesson about the law is so significant that Passover is observed for seven days. "If the eating of unleavened bread on Passover were only commanded for a single day, we would never have noticed it, and its purpose would not be known." In other words, all of the reasons that Maimonides postulates for Passover; its observances, and why Jews were told to keep it in mind, are practical and people-oriented, and are designed to instill good ideas and improve individuals within a society.

WHAT IS NACHMANIDES'S VIEW?

What is the significance of Passover to Nachmanides? Why is it mentioned so many times in Jewish practices? Why is a father mandated to teach his children about the exodus? Why is it so important that a separate night was set aside to recall the exodus at a Seder meal?

Nachmanides discusses this subject in his commentary to Exodus 13:16, a verse that the rabbis interpret as a decree to don tefillin daily. After speaking about the exodus from Egypt, Scripture mandates: "And it shall be a sign upon your hand, and frontlets between your eyes; for by strength of hand the Lord brought us forth out of Egypt."

Nachmanides writes: "And now I will tell you a basic principle underlying many biblical commands." He identifies several kinds of individuals who have wrong-headed convictions. The first group denies the basic principle that God created the world. (The Greek philosopher Aristotle, for example, taught that the world existed forever and coexisted with God.) The second are people who refuse to recognize that God knows what occurs to humans. The third group is comprised of those who may think that God knows about people but denies that God pays attention to them. God, they assert, cares for humans as much as humans care for fish. They look at them and may even admire them and take delight in them but take no notice of their individual lives. Just as it is ridiculous to imagine people rewarding and punishing fish for their behavior, so, too, these people say, God neither rewards nor punishes.

Many scholars are convinced that Maimonides denies the existence of miracles. All agree that he at least minimizes them. But Nachmanides was convinced, strongly and unyieldingly, that God is constantly involved in the world, as an eagle watching its young, performing miracles lovingly for humans daily. He felt, as the saying goes, that no leaf falls from a tree unless God wills it and causes it to fall.

Nachmanides was persuaded that two kinds of miracles exist. The first, like the Passover plagues, are open and evident to all. Others are hidden and do not show God's involvement, like the falling leaf, winter snow and rain, even the shining sun. This belief in miracles was so significant and fundamental to Nachmanides that he proclaimed, "From [belief in] large perceptible miracles one [comes to believe] in hidden miracles, which are the very foundation of the entire Torah. A person has no share in the Torah of Moses our teacher until he believes that all that occurs is the result of miracles, not the laws of nature.... Everything happens by divine decree."

Nachmanides was convinced that the three above-stated erroneous convictions are rebutted and destroyed by the open miracles of Passover, which demonstrate what he considered the basic principle of Judaism: the daily involvement of God in world affairs and the existence of hidden and open miracles.

According to Nachmanides, when Jews ponder the exodus from Egypt – as they are told to do daily – and the miracles that preceded the exodus and made it possible, they realize that the three notions are wrong. The performance of the Egyptian miracles reveals: (1) There is a God who is involved in this world and who is constantly creating through miracles (and if God creates miracles, God certainly could have created the world); (2) God knows what is occurring to humans (for how else would God know of Israel's need for help?); (3) God punishes those who act improperly (such as the Egyptians); and (4) If a miracle is predicted by a prophet, as it was by Moses, it also shows the truthfulness of prophecy, that God lovingly reveals divine secrets to prophets. These perceptions, according to Nachmanides, are derived from the Passover epic and are basic to the understanding of Judaism.

Since, he continues, God does not repeat open miracles in every generation to teach scoffers the truth of the divine relationship with humanity, God instructed Jews to make a variety of visible signs to remind them daily of the profound and basic lesson of the exodus. This is the reason that the Passover Seder is celebrated, and the exodus is written in mezuzot on doorposts and in tefillin set upon a person's head and arm. A multitude of other practices are mandated for the same purpose: to recall the basic principle of the Torah, God's daily involvement with the world.

In short, Nachmanides offers a unique interpretation as to why so many Jewish practices are associated in one way or another with the exodus from Egypt. According to him, the miracles of the exodus teach the basic principles of Judaism: there is a God who created the universe, knows all that occurs, is involved daily in earthly affairs, performs open and secret miracles, helps the worthy, punishes wrongdoers, and communicates messages to prophets.

Can We Rely on Divine Miracles?

It should be clear from the prior essay that Maimonides would answer "no," while Nachmanides would say "yes." The following is an example of the Maimonidean thinking.

DID JOSHUA EXPERIENCE A MIRACLE?

Joshua 8 tells an unusual tale. Joshua assumed leadership of the Israelites upon Moses's death. He led them across the Jordan River into the promised land Canaan. He conducted them in several successful conflicts against the Canaanite inhabitants but lost a crucial battle. He was now worried and was unsure whether he could be successful in future wars.

The biblical book Joshua states that he has a friendly and reassuring conversation with God who, like a wise military advisor, details a strategic plan with tactical details of how to defeat the Canaanites in the city Ai. Joshua listens intently but, curiously, modifies the divine plan. Although God promised him a victory, he amasses an enormous fighting force, more than God suggested, and thereby showed that he did not rely on the deity's assurances. Although he lost his first battle against Ai, with his now larger fighting force, Joshua wins the battle against Ai during the second try. But this story raises many questions, such as: Since God assured Joshua of victory, why did he go beyond the specific divine order to lay one ambush and, instead, set two ambushes? Why did he organize an armed force of such a large number of troops, sixty thousand according to a rabbinic tradition? Why couldn't he simply send a small platoon of soldiers against the city of Ai since God assured him of success no matter how many soldiers he drafted for the battle? If God had decided to aid Joshua in giving him a victory, why was a battle – in which Israelites must have been killed – necessary?

DO NOT RELY ON MIRACLES

Commenting on this story, Yehuda Kiel[1] states that Joshua increased his fighting force because of the talmudic principle "one should not rely on a miracle."

The *Encyclopedia Talmudit*[2] (*Talmudic Encyclopedia*) explains that this is a command that the Jerusalem Talmud, *Yoma* 1:4, bases on Deuteronomy 6:16, "You should not try the Lord your God."

At first blush, Kiel's explanation of Joshua's behavior does not appear to be correct. The examples cited by the *Encyclopedia Talmudit* are not of situations in which God instructed someone how to act and assured him or her of a result. The talmudic principle states that a person should not put him or herself in a dangerous situation and rely on God to save him or her with a miracle. For example, one should not put one's friend in danger relying on the fact that he is a great and pious man and is worthy of a miracle. Similarly, even though there is another rabbinic principle that a person who is doing a good deed, a mitzvah, will not be harmed, he or she should not do the good deed in a dangerous area expecting to be saved by a miracle.

The principle of "one should not rely on a miracle" does not appear to be relevant to Joshua since he was not relying on a miracle; rather, he was following God's explicit tactics and assurances.

GOD PROMISED NOTHING

These difficulties disappear once we accept Maimonides's interpretation in his *Guide of the Perplexed* 2:48. Maimonides explains that the Bible frequently states that God takes a specific action when it only means that God is the ultimate cause of the occurrence since God created the laws of nature. What the Bible describes as God's act is something that occurred naturally through the laws of nature that God had created; God was not involved in the specific incident.

Additionally, Maimonides considered prophecy a higher level of intelligence and not the word of God. As he states in 2:44: when the Bible indicates that a person prophesies it means that "he finds *in himself* the cause that moves him to

1. Yehuda Kiel, *Daat Mikra, Sefer Yehoshua* (Jerusalem: Mossad Harav Kook, 1994).
2. *Encyclopedia Talmudit* (*Talmudic Encyclopedia*) (Jerusalem: Yad Harav Herzog, 1982), 1:679–681.

do something good and grand; e.g., to deliver a congregation of good men from the hands of evil-doers" (emphasis added).

Furthermore, Maimonides did not believe that God interferes with the laws of nature and readjusts the world from time to time with miracles. In his *Guide of the Perplexed* 1:11, for example, he states that God is "the stable one who undergoes no manner of change ... *nor a change in His relation to what is other than Himself*" (emphasis added). In 2:29, he states that what people think of as "miracles" are parts of nature that are preprogrammed into the world at the time of creation, not periodic readjustments. In 1:67, he explains that "on the seventh day [of creation] the state of things became lasting and established just as it is at present." In 2:10, he writes that "angels" who are mentioned in the Bible as participants in some "miracles" are nothing more than normal preexisting forces of nature, not supernatural beings.

Maimonides recognizes that God is good, God's creation is good, and God is all-knowing. For a person to imagine that God is like an incompetent workman who must repeatedly return to his job to reprogram and readjust his errors is a denial of God's competence, God's knowledge, and the goodness of the divine creation. God knew all that could occur and took it into consideration at the time of creation. As James Arthur Diamond[3] explains, "In truth, any events befalling man result from his own misadventures and have nothing to do with God's intervention in human affairs." People should not rely on miracles because they will not happen.

EXPLANATION OF JOSHUA 8

When we examine the story from this non-miraculous perspective, we see the following: Joshua evaluated the impending battle against the fortified city of Ai, inspected the battle area, and considered the psychology of his enemy. After a careful review, he felt certain (described in the Bible metaphorically as God's assurance) that he could defeat the Ai forces if he would undertake a deceptive tactic. He knew that he must not rely on a miracle (as stated by Yehuda Kiel in his commentary on *Sefer Yehoshua* and by Maimonides). He organized a suffi-

---

3. James Arthur Diamond, *Maimonides and Hermeneutics of Concealment: Deciphering Scripture and Midrash in the Guide of the Perplexed* (New York: SUNY Press, 2002), 94.

ciently large force, twenty times the number of his first failed attack, set troops in advantageous positions, and used a subterfuge that led the enemy into a trap because of its mistaken belief that the Israelites were retreating in terror as they did during the initial failed assault against their city. Joshua did not change God's instruction; he changed his initial thoughts because he felt additional forces would better assure success.

SUMMARY

Joshua 8, like many biblical episodes, describes a war in which Scripture states that God advised Joshua how to act and assured him of victory. If one accepts the story literally, understanding that God interfered with nature and was involved on the Israelite side, many questions are raised. However, understanding that the statement of God's involvement is only a figurative way of describing the laws of nature which God created, helps the reader realize that it was Joshua who developed the strategy and tactics, and all questions are answered.

A Neglected Biblical Book

Chronicles is neglected by most people, even clergy, because it is radically different than the other books of the Bible. Chronicles tells the stories contained in other biblical books but makes many changes in the tales. There are many incidences included in other biblical books that are omitted in Chronicles, new ones are inserted, the spelling is different in many places, and the overall goal of the book is not the same as the earlier books. For example, probably as an attempt to extol David, the book does not say that David's reign in Hebron for seven years only embraced Judah, as narrated in the book of Kings, but says he ruled over all of Israel for forty years, seven from Hebron and thirty-three from Jerusalem. Unable to reconcile the many differences, most people ignore this book or, at best, look at parts of it.

WHO WROTE CHRONICLES AND WHY?

It should be clear that Chronicles is a human product. It may have been divinely inspired but clearly God would not have wanted one version of a tale told in one book with a different version in another. The books of Kings and Chronicles were composed by different authors with diverse goals, even unlike theology. Kings, like the rest of the Bible portrays Israel's ancestors in both complementary and negative ways. It shows readers that the biblical heroes, like all humans have faults, but can nevertheless rise to greatness. Chronicles omits most negative statements and descriptions, as if to say that biblical personages never made mistakes.

SOME FACTS ABOUT CHRONICLES

- Chronicles I and II, were originally a single book, but as with Samuel and

Kings, the Christians divided it into two simply because the books were too long to be held in a single scroll. Jews accepted the Christian suggestion.

- Chronicles together with the books of Ezra and Nehemiah tells the story of the Jews' ancestors from Adam down to the fourth century BCE. The first book of Chronicles goes through chapter 29 with the death of King David. The second, containing thirty-six chapters goes to the decree of Cyrus around 538 BCE when the Judeans, as they were called at the time, were allowed by the king to return to Judea, the name of the country at that time because the land allotted to the Judeans was small and comprised mostly the area previously assigned to the tribe of Judah.

- We do not know when Chronicles was composed, or whether it is the work of a single individual or a group, although it seems certain that the book is not the work of a single individual or written at a single time. Scholars contend that the book was written sometime during Israel's Persian period between around 538–333 BCE. We also do not know what sources the author or authors or editor or editors used. The earlier books of the Bible were examined, but multiple changes were made in that material.

- The chronicler(s) wrote Chronicles with at least two purposes in mind. The first, which is the chief purpose, is to demonstrate by its version of history that the true Israel is the history of Judah. To accomplish this purpose, the chronicler(s) focuses on the kingdom of Judah, and the vicissitudes of the Northern Kingdom of Israel are almost entirely ignored. Additionally, to extol Judah, Chronicles omits episodes contained in Samuel and Kings that reflect badly on Judah, such as King David taking Bat Sheba and the murder of her husband and his troop.

- The second purpose is a presentation of the meaning and purpose of the Jewish history. It is stressed by the chronicler(s) that Jerusalem is the only legitimate place of worship, not the two temples that existed in the northern kingdom of Israel (nor the individuals assigned to the temple tasks in the northern nation), and that the priests and Levites who descended from Jacob's son Levi, are the only proper personnel to function there. This is supported by giving the genealogy of the Levites and priests.

- A third purpose was added in the books of Ezra and Nehemiah which many scholars contend was also composed by the chronicler(s), where it is stressed that strict observance of the Torah and exclusivism are of utmost importance to the survival of Judaism. Ezra and Nehemiah emphasized this by insisting that the Judeans of their generation dismiss their non-Judean wives.

SOME ADDITIONAL EXAMPLES OF CHANGES MADE IN CHRONICLES

Several further examples of how the chronicler(s) attempted to extol the ancient Judeans are:

- Solomon does not have a dream where God tells him that he will be wise, as told in 1 Kings 3; instead Chronicles exalts Solomon by having God appear to Solomon directly.
- The famed tale of the two prostitutes appearing to Solomon with each claiming that a live baby belongs to her is omitted from Chronicles. This may have been done to show that Solomon had no dealings with prostitutes or, more likely, because the chronicler(s) realized, as did the Talmud, that Solomon's reliance upon one prostitute saying that the child should be given to the other woman, is no proof that she is the real mother. She may have said this because of the stirrings of her conscience and wanting to return the child to its true parent. The Talmud resolves the problem of how Solomon knew the true mother by having God tell him so.
- Wanting to show Solomon in a favorable light, Chronicles omits Solomon's defection from God, his building of temples for idol worship, his catering to foreign women, the disaffection to his rule by Hadad and Rezon and their rebellions, and the dissatisfaction of Jeroboam and his rebellion, which was supported by the prophet Ahijah who proclaimed that Solomon acted improperly.

All these changes from the prior biblical books, the unrealistic suggestion that Israel's ancestors did no wrong, and the difficulty in deciding how to reconcile the two versions of Israel's history with the idea that God dictated or inspired the book, led many to ignore it.

The Book the Rabbis Loved
but Rejected from the Bible

There were ancient books that had good ideas, but Judaism did not include them as parts of the Bible. One of these books is "The Wisdom of Ben Sira." We do not know why this book was not placed in the canon.[1]

THE WISDOM OF BEN SIRA

"The Wisdom of Ben Sira" was composed around the year 180 BCE by Yeshua ben (son of) Eleazar ben (son of) Sira, about a decade before the 167 BCE onset of the events leading to the Chanukah story. It is a book that the rabbis did not include in the Hebrew Bible despite respecting it immensely and quoting from it some eighty-two times with approval in the Talmud and other rabbinical writings.[2] The author Yeshua is called after his grandfather Sira.[3] His book is also called "Ecclesiasticus." It is included in the Catholic Bible, but not the Hebrew Scriptures nor the Protestant New Testament. It comprises fifty-one chapters and is the longest volume in the Catholic Bible. It is part of what scholars call the Wisdom Literature

---

1. The question is also asked in an opposite fashion. For example, why was Esther included in the Bible despite Esther failing to show any observances of the divine Torah commands while the book Judith was excluded despite Judith following many Jewish practices. See Rabbi Dr. Israel Drazin, *Unusual Bible Interpretations: Ruth, Esther, and Judith* (Jerusalem: Gefen Publishing House, 2016), where this issue is discussed.

2. Such as in Babylonian Talmud, *Hagigah* 12a, Babylonian Talmud, *Niddah* 12b, and Jerusalem Talmud, *Berakhot* 11c.

3. As was done with Jesus, whose name was most likely Yeshua or the fuller version Yehoshua, which is Joshua in English. Christians prefer to use the Greek version of the name to diminish the Jewish origin. So, in Christian commentaries on the Ben Sira book Yeshua is called Jesus.

of Israel, together with Job, Proverbs, Kohelet (Ecclesiastes), the apocryphal[4] Wisdom of Solomon, and some of the Psalms that are called Wisdom Psalms because of what they teach.

GENERAL CONTENT

The Ben Sira book is pragmatic, not theological, and reflects the traditional Jewish mentality of the Hellenistic world of second century BCE Jerusalem where Ben Sira lived. The author was a teacher in Jerusalem, and his book, generally written in poetry, addresses subjects such as showing proper honor to one's father and mother and the beneficial results of that behavior, humility, almsgiving, true and false friendships, proper behavior to neighbors, advice concerning wicked and virtuous women, the use of wealth, as well as many other subjects such as malice, anger, vengeance, loans, eating, wine, servants.

LIFE AFTER DEATH AND WOMEN

Significantly, Ben Sira did not believe in life after death. According to him all rewards and punishments occur during the lifetime of the actor.[5] He also had the terrible ideas about women rampant in his age, and which have not been totally resolved even in the twenty-first century.[6]

WISDOM

But of most interest to many are his views about wisdom and the fear and love of God, which Ben Sira felt were related to each other and to wisdom. Ancient Jews believed that the world was created with wisdom. Proverbs 8:22 has wisdom say: "The Lord begot me as the firstborn of the ways, the forerunner of his prodigies

---

4. The term "Apocrypha" describes the fifteen books or parts of books composed before the common era (BCE) that Roman Catholics, Orthodox, and Eastern churches accept, wholly or partially, as canonical scripture but Protestants and Jews do not.

5. This is also the view of the author of the biblical book Ecclesiastes, Kohelet in Hebrew, where the author states that the end of humans is the same as the end of dogs.

6. There are statements such as "There is scarce any evil like that in a woman" (32:19). "In a woman was wrongdoing beginning: on her account we all die" (25:24). "My son, keep a close watch on your daughter, lest she make you a sport of your enemies" (49:11). "Give no woman power over you" (9:2).

of long ago."[7] Ben Sira reflects this view at the start of his book in 1:4, "Before all things wisdom was created, and prudent understanding from all eternity." In his autobiographical poem, in 51:13–14, he stresses the importance of wisdom: "When I was young and innocent I kept seeking wisdom. She came to me in her beauty, and until the end I will cultivate her."

What is wisdom? In 6:18–37, Ben Sira encourages his readers to strive for wisdom, as he said he did. He identifies wisdom with the Law: people can obtain wisdom by fearing and loving God and keeping the divine commandments. "The whole of wisdom is fear of the Lord; complete wisdom is the fulfillment of the Law" (19:20). By so doing, people are living the divine wisdom, which is revealed in the Law, and which gives many benefits.

Curiously, while he disparages women, Ben Sira personifies wisdom as did the author of Proverbs as a woman; as a female teacher (4:11–19), mother and wife (14:20–15:8), and lover to be wooed (51:13–21).

FEAR AND LOVE OF GOD

Ben Sira equates fear and love of God with wisdom; all three are the same. What does he mean?

Although he does not explain this, I understand "fear" and "love" of God suggesting a high degree of respect for nature that God created. He is saying seek wisdom by doing two things. First, obey the Law, and by Law he means the Torah, for the Torah contains wisdom, and wisdom brings personal and social benefits. This is also the view of Maimonides who in his *Guide of the Perplexed* 3:28 described three purposes of the Torah: to teach some truths and to aid people in improving themselves and society. Second, by the words "fear" and "love"[8] he is suggesting, as did Maimonides, that we need to study the universe that God created or formed because it reveals even more than the Torah how we can improve ourselves and others.

---

7. This probably means that there is wisdom in all that was created or formed.

8. The expressions "fear of God" and "wisdom" are the key words of the book. The first, or its equivalent, occurs about sixty times in the volume, only the book of Psalms has a larger number of occurrences, seventy-nine. Wisdom is repeated about fifty-five times. The opening two chapters, which gives the theme to the book, uses the word seventeen times, eleven in the first chapter alone.

Another Rejected Book

"The Wisdom of Solomon," as previously stated, is one of the books that scholars call Wisdom Literature. Two of these ancient books were not included in the Hebrew Bible. While not included, "The Wisdom of Ben Sira" was highly respected by the ancient rabbis, as shown by their many quotes in the Talmud, but "The Wisdom of Solomon" did not even receive this acclaim.

THE WISDOM OF SOLOMON

The Wisdom of Solomon is a book written in Greek by a learned Hellenized Jew of Alexandria, Egypt. David Winston offers us an excellent translation of The Wisdom of Solomon, in the *Anchor Bible* series of Bible commentaries.[1] It contains a comprehensive introduction of ninety-three pages, a smaller introduction before each section of the book's nineteen chapters, extensive clarifying notes on each section of the chapters, and twenty-seven pages of several indexes. He pinpoints the date of the book's composition as being during the reign of the Roman ruler Caligula, 37–41 CE.

STRESSING WISDOM

The book strongly urges its readers to engage in wisdom. It is composed in three parts: (1) Stating that wisdom's gift is immortality. (2) The nature of wisdom and Solomon's search for her (wisdom is seen as feminine). (3) A comparison between the Israelites in Egyptian slavery who were engaged in wisdom and the Egyptians.

---

1. David Winston, "The Wisdom of Solomon," in *Anchor Bible* (New York: Doubleday, 1979).

Much of what is in this book is not in the Bible. In the first part, among much else, the author expresses his view that humans will have immortality, but can lose it by abandoning wisdom. He says that the suffering that just people experience on earth is just a brief trial in the immortal destiny of righteous souls which will bring them peace and future glorification after death.

In the second part, he describes Solomon as recognizing that humans are unable to gain wisdom by their own efforts and that he could not gain wisdom unless God graciously bestowed her on him. The author continues by giving examples of how wisdom saved people in history from Adam though the Israelite's exodus from Egypt.

In the third part, he argues that Israel benefited by acts like the plagues by which Egypt was punished. For example, the Nile water turned to blood, but Israel obtained water from a desert rock. In this third part, in 11:17, the author, like Aristotle in his *Physics*, Plato in *Timaeus*, Philo in *Special Laws* 1.328–329, and possibly Maimonides in his *Guide of the Perplexed* 2:13, contends that contrary to the current view of most Jews God did not create the world out of nothing, but "out of formless matter."

WISDOM IS A FEMALE FIGURE

The author of this book did not invent the female figure wisdom. She appears in Proverbs and 1:20ff and 8:22ff, and Job 28:12ff. In Proverbs 8:30 God is said to have created her at the beginning of creation.

A PROBLEM WITH THIS BOOK AND SOME OTHER WISDOM BOOKS

A basic question is: should we take the statements about wisdom literally, that she is a being separate from God. This, as the contention that the Shekhina, a being that is not mentioned in the Bible, is a separate being that is held by many Jews, is problematical. It assumes a divine being other than God and seems to be a polytheistic notion.

Winston tells us that the term "wisdom" is a "hypostasis," meaning one of the "aspects" of God, one of the ways we describe how God interacts with humans, that God granted humans wisdom.

I think this is correct. But I would add that at times the term denotes the wisdom of the laws of nature that God created. This why Proverbs 8 (and Ben Sira 1:4

and 24:9) states that wisdom was created at the beginning of creation, meaning the laws of nature were placed in the world from the very beginning. Humans can only be successful if they understand science, meaning the laws of nature, how the world functions, and act according to this wisdom; not by prayer.[2]

WHY WAS THE BOOK NOT INCLUDED IN THE JEWISH CANON?

We do not know. It may be because of some of its content, but this is unlikely because some biblical books contain ideas that are contrary to current mainstream thinking. It is more likely that it was not considered for inclusion because it was not a very ancient book.

Yet, the book was not discarded. Many ancient books were lost, but not this one. Apparently, it was considered an important book, and it seems to reflect the thinking of the upper-class Jew just prior to the onset of the common era.

---

2. The word science comes from the Latin word "scientia," which means knowledge.

Does the Bible Contain Humor?

Many people will find it hard to accept the notion that there is humor in the Bible. Failing to recognize this, they take statements meant to be humorous or ironic literally and fail to realize what the Bible wants readers to know.

THE STORY OF THE BEHAVIORS OF KING SOLOMON IS A GOOD EXAMPLE

In his sixth "Young People's Concert: Humor in Music," Leonard Bernstein tells viewers that many very good pleasant pieces of music contain humor. He proves this by examining parts of musical compositions by Haydn, Mahler, Mozart, and Shostakovich. He tells us what it is in music that can make it funny.

Bernstein tells us that the same experiences that make jokes funny, make music funny. Humor requires a twist, a shock, something unexpected, something surprising, incongruous, and illogical. There are different kinds of humor. Wit, for example, is a surprising statement. Satire is making fun of something or someone, but unlike wit, it does not introduce anything new. Parody caricatures something simply for the fun of it. There is also good humor that does not attempt to ridicule or be illogical; it is designed to make a person feel good.

As I listened to Bernstein, I thought how unfortunate it is that many people do not see that there are many instances in the Bible where scripture is humorous. It tells us something ironic, something that people should not take seriously – although many do. For example: It seems clear to me that the story of Balaam's ass speaking to him was meant to be funny. The Bible could have made its point that Balaam was acting like an ass in another way, rather than painting an illogical picture.

In my book *The Authentic King Solomon*, I point out the frequent use of irony in Solomon's story. Every time when the Bible tells us that Solomon was wise, and it does so many times, protesting too much, it always follows these statements by describing how Solomon acted unwisely. It seems that the biblical author wanted to mock the king who foolishly laid the groundwork of high taxation followed by his son Rehoboam that led to the division of the kingdom that Solomon's father united.

The rabbis in the Talmud recognized this. For example, while most people fail to see the humor in the way in which Solomon decided the case in the story of the trial of the two prostitutes by suggesting that the baby be cut in two with each complainant receiving half a child, the rabbis recognized that the statement by one of the two women – do not kill the baby, give it to the other woman – does not prove she is the child's true parent. She may have said this simply because she did not want her child who would interfere with her acts of prostitution. The rabbis suggested that if the story were true, Solomon made his decision because God spoke to him at that time and told him who was the child's mother. The story of the visit of the queen of Sheba is another example. The Bible tells us that she came to ask Solomon riddles. This makes no sense. If Solomon was truly wise, she should have asked important questions, not played games. The rabbis suggested that her riddles were very clever and imagine some examples. The Bible also uses other women to mock Solomon. It states that he loved many foreign women, and then ridicules him by stating that he had seven hundred wives and three hundred concubines, using the oft-used numbers seven and three.

The Value of Reading Tanakh

Rabbi Hayyim Angel is one of my favorite authors who writes on the Bible. He is enjoyed by other readers and scholars as well. His book *Keys to the Palace* contains twenty essays and virtually all were accepted by and published previously by well-respected magazines.[1] I always look forward to reading each of his new books and articles. I like the way that he focuses upon what the Bible is saying, what is called in Hebrew, the *peshat*.

WHAT IS *PESHAT*?

Many commentators and even scholars who interpret the Bible seek to discover a message in the biblical verse, which they frequently find in ingenious ways through such things as missing letters in words, redundancies, interpretations of events that are only imaginative (called *derash* and Midrash), but not explicit in the passage itself. This is good. It has an important teaching, even moral purpose, but it does not tell us what the Torah itself is saying. This is the method used by most pulpit rabbis in their sermons with the result that the congregants do not learn what the Torah really says.

The ancient rabbis, in my opinion, recognized this problem and addressed it with a strong recommendation. Although they were the authors of Midrash, wrote books containing it, and used it to teach Jews proper behavior, they wanted Jews to know what the Bible states, not just the lessons they ingeniously derived from passages and words. They created the law that Jews should read the weekly Torah portion twice in its original Hebrew and once in the Aramaic translation of *Targum Onkelos*. They did not require fellow Jews to read their Midrash. They did so

---

1. Rabbi Hayyim Angel, *Keys to the Palace, Exploring the Religious Value of Reading Tanakh* (Kodesh Press, 2017).

not only because *Onkelos* was written in Aramaic, the language the people spoke at the time, but because *Onkelos* contained the *peshat* the plain non-midrashic meaning of the Five Books of Moses.[2]

RABBI ANGEL'S CONTRIBUTION

Rabbi Angel concentrates on the words of the Torah and the context in which the words appear. He uses Midrash when the Midrash examines what the Torah explicitly states, when it helps clarify the passage. He recognizes that the Bible means what it says, not what people imagine or want to teach. He should be commended and thanked for his approach to Torah.

Rabbi Angel devotes seven of the twenty essays in this book to discussing the more mature and sophisticated way the Torah is studied today. The seven are followed by thirteen that focus on specific interesting texts. In the seven, he tells readers about the growing circle of religious scholars, with Israel's Yeshivat Har Etzion at the vanguard of the enterprise. Their method is to understand that Oral Law and traditional commentary are central to the way we understand the revealed word of God and that it is vital to study biblical passages in their literary and historical context.

In the past, religious schools did not teach Tanakh because there are inconsistencies in the books, biblical figures performing acts contrary to the dictates of the Torah, and other problems. Modern religious Bible scholars address these problems. For example, many critical scholars propose that different sections of the Five Books of Moses were composed by close to a half dozen different authors and editors, each with a different agenda and each using his own writing style. Rabbi Angel tells readers in the first seven chapters how these problems are addressed by religious scholars today. The problems are not dismissed or somehow covered over. Angel surveys the approaches offered by religious scholars, which thoughtfully engage in the interaction between tradition and contemporary scholarship.

Many issues are addressed in these seven chapters. There is the authorship of

---

2. I prove in my book *Nachmanides: The Unusual Thinker*, that all the sages prior to Nachmanides understood that *Onkelos* was offering readers the *peshat*, with changes to remove anthropomorphic and anthropopathic depictions of God, showing Israelite ancestors in a favorable light, and some similar reasons. Nachmanides was the first scholar who mistakenly believed that *Targum Onkelos* contains *derash*.

the Torah and other biblical books, the reliability of the Masoretic Text, archaeology and the historicity of the Torah narratives, comparisons between the
Torah and ancient Near Eastern texts, the preponderance of contradictions in
both narrative and legal sections of the Torah, and the different wordings in the
Masoretic Text. Further addressed are the quotes by the sages in the Talmud and
Midrashim, whether the world was created in six days some six thousand years
ago, if Maimonides is correct that all angelic encounters mentioned in the Torah
were visions and not actual reality, the wrongs committed by biblical heroes, and
much more.

Among Rabbi Angel's discussions in the remaining thirteen chapters, is a
thorough analysis of the story of the binding of Isaac in Genesis 22. His analysis
includes the views of Maimonides, Immanuel Kant, Yeshayahu Leibowitz, Moshe
Halbertal, Soren Kierkegaard, David Shatz, and others. Among the questions he
addresses is why did Abraham try to save the inhabitants of Sodom, but remained
silent and acquiescent when he understood that God told him to kill his son?

Similarly, he addresses how we should understand Jacob's deception of his
father Isaac in Genesis 27 when he misled his father to give him the blessing Isaac
wanted to give to Esau. Again, the views of many scholars are examined.

Among the other incisive analyses in the thirteen chapters, he compares
the story of the Garden of Eden and the various Jacob narratives such as: the
contradiction between the prophet Nathan's prophecy of the eternal reign of the
Davidic dynasty in one verse and the conditional formulation in another, the
current view that there is life after death, and why there is no explicit reference
to it in the Tanakh.

In short, Rabbi Hayyim Angel has made a significant contribution to Jewish
thought in this volume and has done it interestingly and well.

Saving the Honor of Some Biblical Characters

Many people who read the Hebrew Bible recognize that it does not try to conceal the faults of even the most significant people, such as the patriarchs Abraham, Isaac, and Jacob, and its most famous kings like King David and King Solomon. It most likely did so to show us that every human makes mistakes and that even people who make mistakes can be great. Yet, since the public needs heroes without blemishes, there are rabbis who try to cover up the wrongs that the biblical heroes committed.

TARGUM ONKELOS

The Aramaic translation of the Five Books of Moses called *Targum Onkelos*, for example, made 104 changes in the translation to improve or alleviate seemingly disparaging comments about biblical figures. The many changes were made in the translation since the Aramaic translation was composed for the average Jew who was unable to understand Hebrew during the early fifth century when the translation was composed.[1]

OTHER BIBLICAL BOOKS

Targum Onkelos was not composed for the other biblical books, but commentators of these other books also felt that the reputations of the Israelite ancestors must be protected. For example, although the book of Samuel clearly states that King

---

1. See my book *Nachmanides, an Unusual Thinker*, where I show that *Targum Onkelos* was composed at this time. See also Rabbi Dr. Israel Drazin, *Onkelos on the Torah, Genesis* (Jerusalem: Ktav Publishing House), 2006, Introduction.

David committed adultery with Bat Sheba and had her husband murdered so that he could take her as his wife,[2] the Babylonian Talmud, *Shabbat* 56a, states that David did no wrong. It offers various reasons why David acted properly, including that Bat Sheba and Uriah were divorced and that Uriah deserved death because he did not obey David's order to go home.

Others recognize that David acted improperly, but still attempt to describe him as guiltless. The famed Bible commentator from Portugal Don Isaac Abarbanel (1437–1508) recognizes that scripture clearly states that David did wrong and asks how the Talmud could say that David did no wrong. He attempts to justify the Talmud in a manner many would find unsatisfactory. He writes,[3] "Since he repented and received his punishment, with this [punishment] his wrong was erased."

---

2. See Rabbi Dr. Israel Drazin, *The Tragedies of King David* (Jerusalem: Gefen Publishing House, 2018), where I detail the many tragic consequences that flowed from these acts.
3. Rabbi Don Isaac Abarbanel, *Perush Abarbanel* (Abarbanel's Commentary) (New York: Seforim Torah Vada'at, 1955).

Changing the Biblical Law

On November 8, 1949, *The Sun* newspaper in Baltimore, Maryland, published an article about my dad, Rabbi Dr. Nathan Drazin entitled "Biblical, Talmudic Law Seen Justifying Dog Experiments." The article failed to mention whether my dad felt this law should be changed. The following is the article with a few changes followed by my comment.

THE BIBLICAL AND TALMUDIC LAW

Biblical and Talmudic law supports medical men seeking stray dogs for experimental purposes according to Rabbi Dr. Nathan Drazin.

Such laws, declared Rabbi Drazin, would seemingly be against the stand of the Society of Prevention of Cruelty to Animals. He was the rabbi at the Shaarei Tfiloh Congregation and has made extensive study of Jewish law.

He noted that medical students must obtain experience somewhere and it would hardly be moral for their first operation to be on a human being. When medical schools use animals to discover ways of alleviating human sufferings they are justified by Jewish law by the biblical book Genesis, which gave humans domination over the fish of the sea, fowl of the air, and every living thing the moves upon the earth.

It certainly seems that a man giving his life and energy to mitigate human suffering should not be criticized for causing needless pain to animals.

Even the SPCA kills animals after a certain length of time with what it terms a merciful death. Their justification for the killing is that occasionally a stray dog bites a child, even though they have no proof that this dog they are killing is harmful.

They do this despite the fact that the killing of the dog does not save a human life, or alleviate human suffering. "I am not sure that Jewish law of Bible or Talmud would condone such needless destruction."

"In Exodus 23:5, humans are commanded to assist in unburdening even an ass of an enemy. In Deuteronomy 11:15, humans are admonished to provide fodder for his cattle before eating the food himself, according to the talmudic interpretation of the verse. Deuteronomy 22:10, forbids plowing with an ox and ass together.

"The rabbi explained that one reason for this is that the ass is pained when seeing the ox chewing his cud because he believes that the ox has received fodder denied to the ass.

"Also, Deuteronomy 25:4 forbids the muzzling of an ox that treads corn, appreciating the fact that the ox will see the food and smell it, yet is pained because he is muzzled and cannot eat it.

"Yet, despite concern for the pain of animals, the Bible 'permits killing them for food.' Furthermore, the Talmud, in Mishnah *Sanhedrin* 4:5, emphasizes the importance of saving human life. It states that 'the saving of one life is equivalent to saving a world, considering the descendants of one man.'"

DAD IS CERTAINLY CORRECT

The ancient laws in the Bible and Talmud, despite seeming contradictory statements, certainly allow using dogs and other animals in experiments to help create a better, less painful, and longer human life. On the one hand, they stress being careful about causing animals pain. A person must even chase away a mother bird before taking its eggs. Yet humans can kill the mother bird and eat her.

This situation is like the biblical laws of slavery which the Bible clearly dislikes. The Bible developed many laws that assure that slaves are treated humanely yet allows the ancient practice of slavery to continue with these modifications until people realize that slavery is wrong. Likewise, the primitive practice of sacrifices was "allowed," but, as Maimonides states,[1] they were curtailed in many ways. These abridgements were made to teach the people to cease slavery and sacrifices.

Dad must have said the same thing about animal experiments, but the reporter did not get the entire speech.

---

1. *Guide of the Perplexed* 3:32 where Maimonides states that God neither needs, nor wants sacrifices, and he quotes prophets who he felt said the same thing.

Changing Customs

Jews, like people of other religions and cultures, developed practices they considered essential to a proper life, but after a while changed them or ceased them entirely. This is natural. In each instance, the custom began among the people. Not everyone accepted it. It began with a few men and women and then spread as others saw individuals they respected doing the acts, but just as it began, it slowly ceased with perhaps just a few people continuing the routine or ritual, thinking it a law. A good example in Judaism is its rules about bread, milk, and wine.[1]

THE CUSTOM

Sometime during the early Middle Ages, the custom arose to not eat or drink *yayin nesech* (non-Jewish wine), bread, and milk.[2] The reason given for the wine prohibition was that generally non-Jews used their wine in one way or another for idol worship and drinking non-Jewish wine may lead to socialization with non-Jews and intermarriage.[3]

When non-Jews ceased worshiping idols, the rationale for the prohibition of *yayin nesech* no longer applied, but many Jews changed the prohibition to *stam yeinam*, "any [non-Jewish] wine," for all of their wine, and continued the practice.

---

1. See Daniel Sperber, *Minhagei Yisrael* (Jerusalem: Mossad Harav Kook, 1995), book 4, 277; Marc B. Shapiro, *Changing the Immutable: How Orthodox Judaism Rewrites its History* (Liverpool: The Littman Library of Jewish Civilization, 2005), pages 81–82, 95–99; Haym Soloveitchik, *Yeinam: Principles and Pressures: Jewish Trade in Gentile Wine in the Middle Ages* (Tel Aviv, 2003); and other books mentioned in these volumes.

2. Shulchan Arukh, *Yoreh De'ah* 123.

3. The intermarriage rationale is problematical since non-Jewish whiskeys and beers are allowed even though they too could lead to socialization.

Some went so far as to prohibit wine, even if produced by Jews; if it was touched by a non-Jew, made by Jews that a non-Jew saw even through glass, Jewish wine made or touched by a Sabbath violator, and even whiskey that was fermented in a wine cask. Others go so far to prohibit Jews having any benefit whatsoever from *stam yeinam*.

Non-Jewish wine touched by a non-Jew, that was *mevushal* (boiled), was allowed because it was felt that idol worshippers would not use this changed wine in idol worship.[4]

Today, most Jews do not insist on the extended version of this practice, eating only Jewish made bread and milk, although there are many who go so far as to declare that any foods cooked by a non-Jewish maid is rendered not kosher.

Many Orthodox Jews observe the *stam yeinam* restriction today (despite the opinion by many prominent rabbis listed in the Shapiro and other books, and despite the rationale that allows non-Jewish whiskeys and beers) raising questions about the rationale for the prohibition.[5]

CONCLUSION

The history of the bread and milk prohibitions being allowed by many Jews today show that ancient customs can be modified and even discarded. But the history of non-Jewish wine demonstrates how an ancient custom, which many call a law, was modified with increasing stringencies.

---

4. Many wines in Israel are not *mevushal*, although they are made *mevushal* when shipped overseas. As a result, the same wine tastes good in Israel and not as good outside Israel.

5. Whiskey and beer were not included in *stam yeinam* because they were not included in *yayin nesech*, and because ancient Jews thought that idol worshipers used wine in their observances, but not other alcohol beverages.

THE SIDDUR

The Siddur is Not What Most People Think

Contrary to what most people think, the siddur and machzor are not books containing a single view of Judaism. Additionally, much of what is in them are not prayers seeking help. The siddur and machzor are anthologies of diverse, even conflicting views, composed and collected and inserted into the collections by various people during different times with various world views. Some "prayers" even have beliefs that most readers reject such as the Musaph service for Shabbat which prays for the restoration of sacrifices, the Anim Zemirot song which describes God wearing tefillin, and the paragraph in the Shalom Aleichem song for Friday night which prays for angels to act as intermediaries who take our prayers to God.

WHAT ARE THE SIDDUR AND MACHZOR?

Siddurs are books containing prayers, extracts from the Bible, and other writings used at synagogue services and at home daily and on the Sabbath. Since including the services for the various holidays would make the books overly large, these services were placed in a separate set of books called machzors. The word siddur means arrangement. It refers to the order of the services and the instructions frequently inserted that tell when the contents are recited. The term machzor means cycle. It refers to the cycle of holidays that appear at certain set times.

THE FRIDAY NIGHT SERVICE

The Friday night service called Kabalat Shabbat and its well-known song "Lecha Dodi" is a good example of a service, which many Jews enjoy that was inserted into the siddur by mystics and has mystical, non-rational, even magical intents.

The Kabalat Shabbat service is made up of seven psalms from the biblical Book of Psalms and a couple of original compositions, one being "Lecha Dodi." The Kabalat Shabbat service was inserted before the general Maariv (evening) service. The mystics were also convinced that God is made up of ten parts called *sefirot*. Each *sefirah* (the singular of the plural form *sefirot*), "performs a distinctive function." The *sefirot* became disjointed, separated, causing God to be no longer whole. Humans can aid God to be rejoined by performing acts on earth as "sympathetic magic," a performance on earth that causes a similar act in heaven, such as pouring water from a jug on the temple altar, which would cause rain to fall.[1] When God is rejoined, the messianic age will begin.

Mystics developed the Kabalat Shabbat service to cause the rejoining of the *sefirot* which would cause the coming of the ultimate Shabbat of the messianic age by sympathetic magic.[2]

THE ORIGIN OF KABALAT SHABBAT

The practice of Kabalat Shabbat began in the mid-sixteenth century in the city of Safad, Israel, by three mystics. Moses Cordovero (1522–1570) who originated the idea to read seven psalms,[3] Isaac Luria, known as Ha'ari and as Arizal (1534–1572) who accepted the practice in part when he suggested deleting the first four psalms, and Shlomo Alkabetz (1500–1576) who composed "Lecha Dodi" and placed it into the service.[4]

---

1. The American Indians also believed in sympathetic magic when they danced up and down they were convinced that this could cause the rain to fall.

2. The practice to turn toward the door of the synagogue, or to the east according to some customs, is not to welcome the Shabbat as most people think, it is an act of sympathetic magic: if we welcome the messianic age here on earth, it will cause the heaven to do the same. This is also why the mystics suggested opening the door for the prophet Elijah during the Passover Seder and setting a cup of wine on the table for him; if we do so, it will cause him to come and bring the messiah with him.

3. All of these Psalms 95–99 tell of a setting up of a divine kingdom on earth. They all anticipate the event with joy. The sixth psalm, number 29, "from early times was associated with the Sabbath." In verse 10, it sings "of the Lord enthroned as King forever." The seventh psalm, which combines psalms 92 and 93 is "A psalm, a song for the Sabbath day," which also speaks of God reigning forever. Joseph H. Hertz, *Daily Prayer Book* (New York: Bloch Publishing Company, 1948). It seems clear that Cordovero selected these psalms because they suggested the messianic age to him.

4. Regarding the dates and practices, see for example, Rabbi Yehoshua Cohen, *Siddur Eizur*

"Lecha Dodi" is not a song celebrating the onset of the Shabbat. It is about combining the ten *sefirot*, the ten parts of God, and the word Shabbat is used to indicate the messianic age that occurs when God is combined again. The refrain "Come my beloved against the bride to receive the Shabbat" means "Come *sefira teferet* toward the female *sefira malkhut* so that the messianic age can begin."

THIS RAISES SOME QUESTIONS

Why were items inserted into the siddur and machzor with outdated theology, views that most Jews reject? Does God hear prayers? What is the value of reading what is in the siddur and machzor?

Most of the items inserted into the siddur and machzor were placed there because the people who placed them, mostly mystics, believed in what is stated. We have no proof that God hears prayers. And if God does hear them, we do not know if God supplies what we request. However, even if we have a negative view regarding the contents and the idea of divine intervention to satisfy our wants, reading the prayers can be very valuable.

THE PURPOSE OF PRAYERS

The Hebrew word for prayers has the root *p-l-l* which means judge. The Hebrew for "to pray" is *l'hitpaleil*, which is reflective, meaning it refers back to the person and literally means "to judge oneself." Thus, prayer is a time when a Jew reads certain ancient selections from various sources and is encouraged to think about what is read, judge oneself, and use the knowledge obtained to improve.

For example, reading about the sacrifices brought in the ancient temple during the Shabbat Musaph service should prompt us to think about Jewish history, about our relationship with God, what God wants of us, what sacrifices were designed to accomplish, can and should this goal be accomplished today, how ideas change, and much more.

Eliyahu K'minhag Rabbenu Hagra (Jerusalem: Machon Kerem Eliyahu, 5771). For the origin and purpose of *Lecha Dodi*, see for example, *Lecha Dodi Likrat Kala* (Jerusalem: Yisod Shalom, 5762). The later volume contains the commentary *Al Chaftzei Hachayim*.

More Examples of Mystical
Additions to the Siddur

There are multiple examples of additions by mystics to the siddur and machzor and to the practices concerning how and when the prayers are said. The following are a few examples.

ADDITIONS TO THE SHEMA

The several sections from the Torah, which the siddur and machzor call the Shema are recited in the morning and evening service. Based on the view of the mystical book *Zohar*,[1] mystics felt that the total number of words should total 248 the traditional number of positive commands in the Torah.[2] Since the words in the several sections do not add up to 248, the mystics developed a system to reach this total, depending on whether an individual is reading the Shema, or it is part of a service conducted with a chazan – a cantor, who generally keeps the synagogue attendees praying in unison by reciting the end of the prayers out loud.[3]

If a person is reading the Shema without a chazan being present, the individual should add the words *el melech n'eeman* at the beginning of the Shema and add

---

1. Scholars date the *Zohar* to around 1290 and state it was composed by Moses de Leon, while many mystics claim it was composed by Simeon bar Yochai around 130 CE.
2. In the third century CE, Rabbi Simlai invented the notion that there are 613 commandments, 365 negative commands and 248 positive ones. This is recorded in the Babylonian Talmud *Makkot* 23b. The Talmud states *derash rabe Simlai*, Rabbi Simlai delivered a sermon. He developed the sermon to emphasize that a Jew should observe the biblical commands with all the bones in the body (248) every day of the year (365). The sages recognized that this number was incorrect, but the idea caught on with the people, and even Maimonides helped by listing and explaining all 613 commands that the consensus of rabbis felt were explicit, or implicit in the Torah.
3. Cohen, *Siddur Eizur Eliyahu K'minhag Rabbenu Hagra*, 38–40.

a fourth word *emet* at the end.[4] The three words are not added when there is a chazan.

When there is a chazan who ends the prayers, the chazan reads the last words of the Shema without adding *emet* silently and then adds *Adonai eloheikhem emet* loud.

There are two problems with this practice besides the idea that Jews should add to the wording of biblical passages. First, while the individual adds four words, the chazan only adds three. The three added by the chazan and heard by the congregation is a substitution for the omission of *el melech n'eeman*. But by only adding three words, the chazan does not reach the desired goal (the congregants added four words). Secondly, and more significantly, the total number of words in the Shema read by individuals, counting the additional four is 247, not 248.

THE TWO LOAVES OF BREAD AT THE SHABBAT MEAL

A reasonable explanation why many Jews set the Shabbat table with a white table cloth, place two loves on the table, and cover the two loaves with a decorated white cover is that it reminds the family of the miracle of the manna that fed the Israelites during the forty years in the desert. No manna fell on the Shabbat. On Fridays, two portions fell, one for Friday, and one for Saturday, which are recalled with the two loaves. The manna fell on white dew and was covered with white dew, recalled by the white table cloth and the covering of the loaves.

Many mystics insist that both loaves should be cut. Non-mystics cut just one. Since they ate three meals on the Shabbat, Friday night, Shabbat noon, and the *seudah shelishit,* the additional third meal in honor of the Shabbat, and wanted to start the meal with whole loaves, they needed six loaves.

THE KIDDUSH OVER WINE DURING THE DAY OF SHABBAT

The ancient practice was to simply say the one sentence prayer before drinking the wine for the Kiddush of Shabbat day.[5] Isaac Luria instituted the practice to say additional words before the blessing.[6] While the rabbis stated that one must

---

4. The word *emet* is the first word in the following prayer.
5. Babylonian Talmud, *Shabbat* 106a.
6. Cohen, *Siddur Eizur Eliyahu K'minhag Rabbenu Hagra,* 251.

drink a sizable amount of the wine, and while the general rule is that one must say a *beracha achrona*, a blessing after drinking wine, one does not do so after this Kiddush. This is strange since it appears that the drinking of wine is not part of the meal and should not be included in the blessing after the entire meal. This also seems so since after the drinking of the wine, the family washes for the start of the meal and the meal is introduced by the blessing over the loaves of bread. Why is there no *beracha achrona*?

I think that despite appearances, the drinking of the wine is an integral part of the meal. We drink wine at the Shabbat meals to add to the joy of the Shabbat day and the meal.

Different Views about the Siddur

Not only do the siddur and machzor contain widely different views, but rabbis interpret what is in them, the laws concerning them, and how the prayers should be practiced in different ways. Rabbi Eliezer Melamed's book *Laws of Prayers*[1] is an example of items that some people would accept while not accepting other views that he states. Rabbi Eliezer Melamed (born in 1961) is an Orthodox rabbi and Rosh Yeshiva of Yeshivat Har Bracha.

THE BOOK

This book, called in its Hebrew original *Peninei Halacha*, translated as *"Pearls of the Law"* or *"Legal Pearls,"* is an easy-to-read, 413-page book that informs readers of the laws of prayer from the perspective of Rabbi Eliezer Melamed. The book is comprehensive. There are twenty-six sections, and each has between three and fourteen chapters. They address subjects such as the fundamentals of prayer (ten chapters), the *minyan* (prayer group of at least ten male Jews – ten), the place of prayer (eleven), the prayer leader and the mourner's Kaddish (eight), preparing for prayer (eleven), washing hands in the morning (nine), and many sections addressing specific payers, such as the Maariv prayer (nine). He identifies which practices are customs, and which are considered biblical and rabbinical enactments.

GOD NEEDS PRAYERS

According to the rabbi, God needs prayers and "without prayer, the world would cease to exist."

---

1. Rabbi Eliezer Melamed, *Laws of Prayers* (Maggid Press, 2011).

PRAYERS ARE ANSWERED

He is certain that "prayers do not return unanswered." A "person must exert himself greatly in prayer, and not assume that since he is praying, *HaKadosh Baruch Hu* [the Holy One Blessed is He – God] must fulfill his request. Rather, he should continue praying, knowing that *HaKadosh Baruch Hu* hears his prayers and that his prayers are most certainly doing some good, although how much, and in what way, are unknown."

WOMEN SHOULD NOT BE ALLOWED TO SAY KADDISH BECAUSE OF ANCIENT PRACTICES

Although there is a tendency today among modern-Orthodox Jews to allow women to say Kaddish, the mourner's prayer, he feels that we must object to women saying Kaddish so as not to undermine the power of *minhagim* (the way that the prayer was recited in ancient times).

HE ACCEPTS MYSTICISM

He accepts kabalistic notions, what rational thinkers would consider superstitions, such as *ruach ra'ah*, which he defines as an "evil spirit" that "rests upon one's hands after sleep and is likely to damage these organs. Only after a person washes his hand three times alternately will the *ruach ra'ah* disappear and, subsequently, the danger caused by touching any of his bodily orifices will be eliminated."[2]

HE UTILIZES THE ZOHAR

He spends several pages discussing the "evil spirit," quoting the thirteenth century mystical book *Zohar*, which he and others think was composed in the second century, and he gives minute directions on how to hold the washing cup and which hand to wash first. Children, he writes, should be taught to wash as soon as they "reach the age of understanding."

OTHER PROHIBITIONS

Other strictures include the prohibition to eat even a light meal a half hour before stars begin to appear and men should say the evening prayers when the stars appear.

---

2. This rule is in Joseph Karo's *Shulchan Arukh*, but not in Maimonides *Mishneh Torah*.

Jews should recite two psalms, 91 and 3, before going to sleep because they are "useful in warding off the evil spirits."

A "man [is forbidden] to sleep while lying on his back." The rabbi does not explain this prohibition and neither does his source. It appears that the practice was instituted out of respect for God, not to face the sexual organ (which God created) towards the deity. But, in a seeming inconsistency, one may read while lying on his back.

A LENIENCY

Rabbi Melamed is not always strict. He notes that some rabbis insist that women should cover their heads while praying. But he explains that the female head covering is a custom and it is acceptable for women not to follow the custom.

In contrast, while he recognizes that the current practice of many Orthodox men is to wear a yarmulke (head covering) all day is also just a custom; he feels that "in a synagogue [the obligation] is greater [and a head covering should be worn by men in synagogues], for it is rooted in law and not just a custom."[3]

---

3. He apparently means that while it originated as a custom, it became a law. This may appear to be strange. In simple English, all it is saying is, true like other customs, this one was also a custom, but we decided to turn it into a law. Why say about women it is just a custom, but with men we turned it into a law? What right do we have to do this? Isn't there an inconsistency? This inconsistency reminds me of the difference between fusing "all ready" into "already" and "all together" into "altogether," but refusing to fuse "all right" into "alright." "The difference may lie in the fact that already and altogether became single words back in the Middle Ages, whereas alright has only been around for a little more than a century and was called by language critics as a misspelling." American Heritage Dictionaries, *100 Words Almost Everyone Confuses & Misuses* (Boston: Houghton Mifflin Harcourt, 2004).

THE TALMUD

The Value of the *Daf Yomi*

Since sometime between 600 and 900 CE, after the Babylonian Talmud was finally edited, an idea arose that it is meritorious to study the Babylonian Talmud, thus many people began to do so frequently even on a daily basis.

THE PROBLEM

However, there is a problem with those who study the Talmud. Most of these people do not really understand what is being read. The Talmud is comprised of various opinions about a particular subject and generally does not disclose the reasons and relevance for the different opinions, why the Talmud states what it states, explain the different versions in other parts of the Babylonian and Jerusalem Talmuds, Mishna, Midrashim, or in the Tosephta. Nor does it explain how it differs with the literal reading of the Torah, what is the final ruling, and why the ruling is made – in short, they do not advance intellectually by the study.

This problem is increased by the well-meaning current practice of *daf yomi*. Many Jews have accepted the practice which requires them to read a *daf*, two pages of the Babylonian Talmud daily, and complete all of the books of the Talmud in just over seven years. Many synagogues have rabbis teaching the *daf*. Generally, only an hour is allotted to the study, an insufficient time to analyze the text. While this is a good practice, the participants get little out of it because of the lack of time to explain what the Talmud is saying, why it is doing so, what other sources say on the subject, the sociological and historical conditions that prompted the talmudic discussion, and more.

THE SOLUTION

The relatively new series of books on the Talmud in Hebrew by *Talmud Ha-Igud* (The Society for the Interpretation of the Talmud) "in which scholars immerse themselves in the ambitious project to apply the disciplines of academic scholarship to the Talmud Bavli [Babylonian Talmud], extend and perhaps deepen Talmudic inquiry begun a thousand years ago." The quotes are from Rabbi Dr. Shamma Friedman's preface to Babylonian Talmud *Eruvin* chapter X. Professor Friedman, the editor of the series, is a highly respected scholar, the winner of the Israel Prize.

Rather than a superficial reading of the Talmud, the authors of each volume explore the meaning of what is said in the Talmud by, among much else, comparing what is said to other ancient sources addressing the same subject. "The Society's unique format includes separating the chapter into discreet *sugyot* [the Hebrew plural of *sugya*, a unit of discussion] which are numbered and named, and assigning distinguishable typefaces to each of the major formal building blocks of the *sugya*: dicta of Tannaim, Amoraim, and the anonymous editorial voice [of the Talmud]."

For example, volume four of the series on the tenth chapter of *Eruvin* by Aviad A. Stollman addresses eleven *dafs* (pages), 95–105, and identifies forty *sugyot*. Where the Talmud has only eleven pages, volume four has 459 in Hebrew with an additional thirty pages in English where the author explains each of the forty *sugyot*.

In short, rather than reading the Talmud as a religious experience without understanding what is read, the series by The Society for the Interpretation of the Talmud makes it possible for the first time to understand what is being read.

PHILOSOPHY AND THEOLOGY

The Difference between
Theology and Philosophy

Theology and philosophy are radically different as they focus on separate things, causing people to think and act in unlike ways. Theology stresses the importance of the truthfulness of religion, its laws, customs, and ideas. Philosophy emphasizes the importance of logic, science, and common sense.

THEOLOGY

People who put theology first feel that the Bible and religious ideas are correct and seek to understand what they were taught by looking at science without changing the religious idea. They begin with their understanding of what the Bible is teaching and try to support it by their logic. Saadiah Gaon (882–942) is an example. The Torah states in many places, such as in Exodus 16:7–10 and 24:17 that the *kavod* (glory or presence) of God appeared to the Israelites. However, the Torah is obscure about what it is that the Israelites saw on these occasions. The biblical *kavod* was later called Shekhina.

Saadiah focused on the Bible saying that the *kavod* "appeared" and felt that he had to explain what physically appeared. In his *Beliefs and Opinions* 2:10, he recognized that people cannot see God, but he could not change what the Torah states. So, he explained that the *kavod* is a light that God created and caused to appear to the Israelites.

The problem with his view is that an appearance of light would not impact the people as the Bible states – that they felt the presence of God. If, on the other hand, the light had certain divine powers that the people could see, Saadiah's idea borders on polytheism.

PHILOSOPHY

Philosophy, in contrast, starts with logic and seeks to understand the Torah. Maimonides recognized that God never appeared to anyone physically, nor did God ever create a substitute to appear. He suggested that there is no being called *kavod* and Shekhina. When the Torah and later rabbis spoke of the *kavod* and Shekhina, they were speaking of a human feeling of the presence of God.[1]

---

1. In my books on the Aramaic translation *Targum Onkelos*, I argued that the targumist understood Shekhina, depending on what the verse states, as a feeling that God is present on earth or in heaven (transcendental).

Judaism's First non-Biblical Philosopher

Scholars recognized long ago that the Bible has Wisdom Books, books that contain philosophy. They are Proverbs, Job, Ecclesiastes (also called Kohelet), and Ben Sira (also called Sirach and Ecclesiasticus) and the Wisdom of Solomon. Only the first three are in the Jewish and Protestant Bibles. The Catholic Bible includes many writings not in these two Bibles, including the last two Wisdom Books. The philosophical writings of Philo are the first post-biblical philosophical works that still exist today, although there were other post-biblical philosophical writers before him.

PHILO

Until recently, it was Harry Wolfson's 1962–1968 two-volume work *Philo* that was considered the authoritative book on Philo of Alexandria, Egypt (about 20 BCE to about 50 CE). Today, because of the wealth of scholarly material contained in his five volumes and their presentation in a very readable manner, Rabbi Michael Leo Samuel's books can now be considered the authoritative work on the great Greek Jewish philosopher.

Because only Philo's philosophical writings still exist from the early philosophical writings after the Bible was codified, Philo is considered the first post-biblical philosopher. He was the first Jewish philosopher who contributed anything new to Jewish-Greek philosophy. His philosophy incorporated the somewhat mystical views of the ancient Greek philosopher Plato (about 428 to about 348 BCE). An estimate of forty books that he wrote still exist. They do not offer a systematic philosophy; they are a collection of sermons.

Philo was convinced that the Bible should be understood on two levels. The first level contains its literal or plain meaning; words mean what they say. The second, his contribution, is an underlying allegorical layer, which requires that the alert, more intelligent reader go beyond the obvious and delve deeper into the text. Philo used allegory to interpret virtually everything in Scripture, including names, dates, numbers, and events. Maimonides also understood that parts of the Bible contain allegory and even parables, but he did not identify as many allegories as Philo.

Rabbi Samuel has made a huge, necessary contribution to the thinking and understanding of all people, Jews and non-Jews, concerning the Bible, by collecting the commentaries of Philo from Philo's many sources and arranging them systematically, according to the Bible chapters. Rabbi Samuel tells us what Philo states and compares Philo's views with what others say: other ancient and modern philosophers, ancient Greeks and Romans, the Babylonian and Jerusalem Talmuds, Midrashim, *Zohar*, and others.

The following are some examples of Rabbi Samuel's contribution to understanding Philo, the Bible, and philosophy.

Among much else, in his Exodus book, Rabbi Samuel discusses Philo's views on telling the truth, how Philo, the rabbis, and Christians treated the issue in the Bible that states that God hardened Pharaoh's heart, the different order of the Ten Commandments in the third century BCE Greek translation called the Septuagint, Philo's thinking about the Ten Commandments and how it differs with the thinking of many people today, his view of the prohibition of not cooking meat and milk together, and his remarkable ideas about sacrifices. He also addresses such subjects as "You shalt not let a witch live" (Exodus 22:18), where the Septuagint interprets the Hebrew *machasheifa* (witch), as *pharmakous*, from which the common English word "pharmacist" comes. Philo explained that the pharmacon was really a drug dealer in Late Antiquity. Rabbi Samuel reveals that Greco-Roman society had a drug culture – much like we have today – and Philo regarded drug-dealers as a serious threat to any civilized society.

Among a wealth of fascinating material in Rabbi Samuel's Leviticus book, to offer other examples, we read about Philo's condemnation of pedophilia, the spiritual significance of circumcision, the role of ritual and its effect on ethics, the meaning of Abraham's near sacrifice of his son Isaac (the Akeidah), why salt was offered as a sacrifice, if Aaron had personal excellence, if a sinful priest could function in the temple (likewise the synagogue today), the symbolism of kosher foods, and the symbolism of circumcision. More examples are Philo's defense of the Holy of Holies that he explained when he met the Roman Caesar Caligula, the role of the high priest, why we fast on Yom Kippur, why one shouldn't marry sisters, what it means to love a neighbor, the prohibition against castrating animals, the meaning of the various holidays and the Sabbath, his warning to never reject wisdom, the concept of the equality of all people, how forgiveness works, defining ethics, Philo's thoughts on prenatal life, the unwritten law, and much more.

The Truth about Sin

There is no concept of "sin" in the Hebrew Bible as a distorting stain upon the soul that creates a sense of guilt requiring a kind of supernatural atonement process involving a ritual and the intercession of a priest and a sacrifice of some sort, as the concept is understood today. To the contrary, wrong behavior is seen in a rational, natural way.

THE ORIGIN OF SIN

Professor Paula Fredriksen of Boston University wrote *Sin: The Early History of an Idea*.[1] Her book is scholarly and informative. She explains that the Hebrew Bible speaks of three categories of wrongs that are not synonyms. There is *chet*, the misstep, literally meaning "missing the mark," as if one were shooting an arrow and hitting the outer rims of the target and missing its center. The Bible mentions it thirty-four times. The second, *pesha*, occurring ninety-three times, is a conscious rebellious act such as taking revenge, stealing, and murder. The third, *avon*, cited in 233 instances, is an error, an unintentional act that nevertheless has harmful consequences.

HOW SHOULD PEOPLE REACT TO MISDEEDS AND MISTAKES?

Understood in this natural way, it should be clear that the misdeed is something that shouldn't provoke passive feelings of guilt and prayerful recitations; individuals should recognize what they did wrong, think why they did the wrong, take actions that remedy the consequences, and assure that there will be no repetition.

---

1. Paula Fredriksen, *Sin: The Early History of an Idea* (Princeton: Princeton University Press, 2012).

CHRISTIAN VIEW

Jesus, according to Professor Fredriksen, retained this ancient understanding. The Gospels do not report him requiring special unnatural methods of atonement. "Jesus of Nazareth announced the good news that God was about to redeem the world. Some 350 years later (but not before that time), the church taught that the far greater part of humanity was eternally condemned." Even John the Baptizer did not believe that baptism removed wrong behavior. Fredriksen quotes Josephus who lived during this time.

In *Antiquities* 18:116–19, Josephus writes, "The immersion was for the purification of the flesh once the soul had previously been cleansed through right conduct."[2] "Jesus never intended to change any biblical concepts or laws, not even the smallest biblical letter. Jesus," Fredriksen writes, "defined living rightly as living according to the Torah."

PAUL INSTITUTED A CHANGE IN THINKING

Contrary to the thinking of some other scholars Fredriksen states that Paul, who did not know Jesus and who brought his understanding of Jesus's message to non-Jews, also wrote that Jesus taught that converts to Judaism must obey the Torah. Paul was an observant Jew. He wrote in Philemon 3:6, "As to righteousness under the Law, I am blameless." In Romans 7:21–31, he said, "Do we overthrow the law by this faith? Of course not! On the contrary, we uphold the law." He, like Jesus, attended the temple and he made no statement that contradicted the three-part biblical understanding of wrong behavior.

Paul's main message, the primary message of the Torah, was "to turn away from idols." "Paul opposes circumcision for gentiles-in-Christ" since they were not converting to Judaism, only accepting the teachings of Jesus, but if the convert wanted to become fully Jewish – for Christianity at the time was a branch of Judaism – circumcision was necessary even as it is required of all other Jews. Fredriksen writes, "The God of Jesus and of Paul had been, emphatically, the God of Abraham, Isaac, and Jacob; the God of Jewish history; the God of Israel."

---

2. Uniquely, only John, which differs with the other Gospels in many ways, and which was composed some seventy years after Jesus's death, reports that Jesus immersed penitent sinners.

OTHER EARLY CHRISTIANS AGREED

The second century Christian thinkers agreed. Valentinus (around 130) defined "sin" in his *The Gospel of Truth* as "a function of ignorance," "error," a mistake. Marcion (around 140) and Justin Martyr (around 150) agreed. As Justin Martyr wrote in *Dialogue with Trypho* 141, sin is when someone does something "contrary to right reason." As Fredriksen explains, "For Justin as for the Jewish tradition that he draws on, the paradigmatic pagan sin is the worship of false gods and their images – a theme strongly present in Paul's letters as well."

AUGUSTINE INSTITUTED THE CHANGE

When then did Christianity change? It did so with Augustine (354–430). Contrary to Jewish teachings that God is good and God's creations are good, as stated in Genesis 1, Augustine taught that people are born with the stain of sin. "According to Augustine, humanity left to its own devices [without God's mercy] can only sin."

Rather than seeing the story of Adam and Eve as an allegory, Augustine accepted the tale as historical reality and gave it a new interpretation. Adam was the originator of sin. Augustine believed that "Adam had all humanity in some special way 'in' him. His sin was 'our' sin and 'we' sinned when he sinned...." In this way, according to Augustine, God's justice... "fell on all humanity equally.... After Adam the will is defective: a person now functions with a sort of diminished capacity, unable if unassisted by grace to achieve the good...." After Adam, Augustine urged, "all humanity, is condemned; indeed, condemnation is all anyone deserves." In his *City of God* 13:23, he wrote, the "inheritance of sin and death [is] conveyed to us by birth." All people of all faiths are "part of *massa damnata* [the massive damnation], justly condemned because of Adam's sin."

AUGUSTINE'S NEW IDEA

God, according to Augustine's new radical view, saves only a small part of humanity, not all, and we have no idea why God selects some people and abandons others to hell because of Adam's sin. "Augustine's god, justly angry at sin, redeems only a small number of people, just enough to show his mercy." God is no longer the creator of what is good, but is emotional, angry, and vindictive. Yet, Augustine adds, somehow in an unknowable way that despite punishing innocent people, God is just.

THE ACCEPTANCE OF AUGUSTINE'S NEW IDEA

Many Christians, and many Jews who live in a Christian culture have absorbed Christian ideas, forgotten the biblical concept of wrong behavior (the concept taught also by Jesus), and call Augustine's invention of "original sin" a mystery that is an integral part of religion. But, as Professor Fredriksen has shown, it is only a mystery because it is inexplicable, and it is not basic to religion.

The Philosopher Nachman Krochmal

Guiding the Perplexed of the Modern Age by Jay M. Harris[1] is an in-depth, well-organized study of an important nineteenth-century Jewish scholar and philosopher, Nachman Krochmal. Harris is Assistant Professor of Jewish Studies at Harvard University. His book *Guide for the Perplexed of Our Time* made pioneering contributions in the areas of Jewish religion and history. This book, which addresses the various attacks against Orthodox Judaism, shows how an Orthodox Jew can accept biblical criticism and remain an Orthodox Jew and observe its practices.

NACHMAN KROCHMAL

Krochmal (1785–1840) lived in Galicia, Austrian Empire, which is now Ukraine. His book was published after his death in 1851 by the preeminent German scholar Leopold Zunz (1794–1886), a man often considered the greatest Jewish scholar of the 19th century. He began in 1819 the movement called *Wissenchaft des Judentum*, "Science of Judaism," which stressed the analysis of Jewish literature and culture with the tools of modern scholarship.

KROCHMAL AND MAIMONIDES

Krochmal was persuaded that the twelfth-century philosopher Maimonides was correct and that his book on philosophy *Guide of the Perplexed*, was a significant contribution to humanity. He became inspired to write his own updated version to reconcile Judaism with modern secular knowledge. He did so by tracing Judaism through its manifestations in history, literature, and religious philosophy. He

---

1. Jay M. Harris, *Guiding the Perplexed of the Modern Age* (New York: New York University Press, 1991).

wrote: "We are delighted, how great is our lot, for the word of God and the true Torah are with us, and it [the Torah] need not fear scholarly investigation from any perspective."[2]

THE THREE-STAGE CYCLE

Krochmal states that in the natural course of events, nations go through three stages: (1) the period of blossoming and birth of the national spirit, (2) the nation matures for a long or short time with strength, (3) the nation, as all natural organisms, incorporates the cause of their degeneration and death, and these destructive elements grow and spread, diminishing the nation until it disappears entirely. The Jewish nation, he admitted, is also subject to this natural order, but "the general spiritual essence within us will shield us from the fate of those who vanish.... The three-period cycles which we have mentioned were duplicated and triplicated with us... [but] there always emerged a new and reviving spirit; and if we fell, we arose and were fortified, and did not abandon God."[3] The philosopher Hegel claims that the train of history has passed Jews, but Krochmal asserts that "Jews are the conductors of that train; it is they alone who are capable of leading humanity to its promised land."[4] In essence, Jews are subject to the natural course of events, but "their spiritual essence remains beyond time."[5]

MODERN SCHOLARSHIP

Krochmal was convinced that almost all conclusions of modern scholarship about the Bible should not be considered challenging to rabbinic tradition. The rabbis knew what modern scholars found in and about the Bible. But they felt that they must hold their understandings from the masses for fear they might be misled by these insights.[6]

ISAIAH

For example, although the biblical book Isaiah appears to be about a single Isaiah,

---

2. Maimonides, *Guide of the Perplexed*, 143–144.
3. Ibid., 40–41.
4. Harris, *Guiding the Perplexed of the Modern Age*, 128.
5. Ibid. 135.
6. Maimonides, *Guide of the Perplexed*, 242.

Krochmal recognized that the last twenty-seven chapters of the book of Isaiah were by a second prophet. He offers proof that the ancient rabbis knew the lateness of the second half of Isaiah. He states that "if we moderns can discern the lateness of the book we must then suspect that the rabbis were also aware of this fact."[7] The rabbis were certainly not unsophisticated Bible scholars.

PSALMS

Krochmal also felt that the ancient sages knew that "a number of Psalms are products of the second century BCE, not compositions by King David."[8]

KOHELET

He applied the same reasoning to the biblical book Kohelet, saying it is obvious that Solomon did not compose this book. "In implausibly attributing the book to Hezekiah, the rabbis were furtively indicating that they knew full well that Kohelet was not of Solomonic origin."[9] He wrote that the ancient Greek Jews called Kohelet "Ecclesiastes," which means a member of the "assembly," to indicate that the author was a member of the Great Assembly, and not Solomon.

Krochmal recognized the significant dispute between the rational Maimonides and the mystic Nachmanides. Maimonides argued that laws derived from hermeneutic principles but not explicit in the Torah are rabbinic. Nachmanides claimed that the talmudic rabbis considered them Torahitic.

HISTORY AND MIDRASH

Krochmal agreed with Maimonides that the "historical" claims of the Talmud were never meant to be taken seriously as history. Maimonides and Nachmanides similarly differed regarding Midrashim. Maimonides taught that any one accepting them as true facts is a fool.[10] Nachmanides accepted them as true despite many

---

7. Harris, *Guiding the Perplexed of the Modern Age*, 173.
8. Ibid., 179–180.
9. Ibid., 174. Harris adds, "Now it is impossible that the words of Solomon (d. 920 BCE) could have survived all those generations in oral form until Hezekiah (late eighth century) finally wrote them down."
10. Maimonides, *Chelek*.

of them being outrageous. Krochmal wrote: "It never dawned on the rabbis that such stories, taught for homiletical purposes, were to be accepted as true."[11]

TORAH LAWS

He considered the laws contained in the Torah as outlines of the basic contours of the legal system, but "the halakha must necessarily have undergone development, rooted in the needs and desires of a living community."[12] In essence, the Torah was fluid, to develop over time. Even many Torah words were changed.[13]

TRADITIONAL PRACTICES

Harris states that Krochmal "developed a historical form of hermeneutics in which traditional claims are always taken seriously, but not literally."[14] Yet, despite his open mind to many Jewish traditions, "None of this was to lead to an abandonment of traditional practice, but to a renewed intellectual – indeed, modern – commitment to it."[15]

---

11. Maimonides, *Guide of the Perplexed*, 211.
12. Harris, *Guiding the Perplexed of the Modern Age*, 229.
13. Such as the *Tekunei Soferim*, "the embellishments of the Soferim."
14. Harris, *Guiding the Perplexed of the Modern Age*, 322.
15. Ibid., 314.

21 Lessons for the 21st Century

In *21 Lessons for the 21st Century*,[1] Yuval Noah Harari gives us an important book. He has a PhD in history from the University of Oxford, has a deep understanding of human behavior, and states his views clearly and vividly. His prior two books on the past and future of humanity, *Sapiens: A Brief History of Humankind* and *Homo Deus: A Brief History of Tomorrow*, were highly acclaimed, became global bestsellers, more than twelve million copies were sold, and the books were translated into more than forty-five languages.

DR. HARARI'S FIRST BOOK

In his first book, about the human past, he examined how an insignificant ape, one of about a half dozen species that inhabited the earth a hundred thousand years ago, became the ruler of the earth. Why did these foraging beings create cities? How did they develop ideas such as gods, human rights, families, and laws, and allow themselves to be enslaved by bureaucracy? Have humans become happier and wiser since they became civilized?

HIS SECOND BOOK

In the second book, he explored the long-term future of life and what the ultimate destiny of intelligence and consciousness might be. He notes that today more people die from eating too much than by eating too little; die from old age rather than diseases, and commit suicide instead of being killed by soldiers, criminals, and terrorists combined. But where do humans go from here? Can society influence the future? Will machines shape future thoughts and actions? These two books as well as this one are filled with need-to-know, easy-to-read information.

---

1. Yuval Noah Harari, *21 Lessons for the 21st Century* (New York: Spiegel & Grau; Penguin Random House, 2018).

THIS VOLUME

In this volume, Dr. Harari looks at the present, twenty-one challenges facing the world, the deep meaning and consequences of these events, and the choices that need to be made. It is an urgent book. It raises issues that are pertinent to human survival. We learn about artificial intelligence, the fact that data algorithms are more reliable than humans, that we have begun to rely on computers for our decisions, and that we need to better understand and use our minds before algorithms make up our minds for us. Artificial intelligence has already created cars that drive in a safer mode, causing far fewer deaths than human drivers. Computers understand us better than we understand ourselves. They advise us about our health. In the future, they will most likely advise us what profession or job is best for us and whom to marry, and thereby cut down the current 50 percent divorce rate. Computers can offer people many advantages, but there are also dangers. Harari warns us about the sale of personal information about us that is controlling us in many ways, frequently prompting us to act contrary to our best interest. We need to regulate data and our right to privacy.

CURRENT PROBLEMS

Harari tells us about many other current problems. Traditional religions, for example, are irrelevant to modern technical and policy problems and part of the modern problems. We need to better decide how a state should deal with terrorism, that present-day terrorism is mostly theater, and our harsh reactions to terror deaths that are far fewer than deaths caused by automobile accidents, is playing into the hands of terrorists and furthering their agenda. We must address the problems that wealth is concentrated in the hands of a small elite, privacy is being lost, and so are jobs and free choice. There are also the problems of immigration, nationalism, liberty, equality, and the quest for meaning and community in the twenty-first century.

FUTURE NEED

Harari shows us why we need to develop new social and economic models as soon as possible, and that despite the critical need to address these issues, humankind is far from understanding the issues, their impact, and reaching any consensus on them, thus we must act now and resume control of our lives.

The Views of Rabbi Joseph B. Soloveitchik

Many books have been published which are commentaries on various subjects, including the Bible, Siddur, and Haggadah, which are based on teachings of Rabbi Soloveitchik. These books were not written by the rabbi. They are collections of his sayings that the authors of the books found in various sources, edited and used as the rabbi's commentary. The book, *Megillat Esther Mesorat Harav*,[1] which can be translated as "The scroll of Esther according to the traditions of the rabbi," contains such commentaries on the biblical book Esther.

THE CONTENTS OF THE BOOK

The book has the entire synagogue service for the holiday of Purim, including the Maariv service that only occurs on Saturday nights, with commentary from Rabbi Soloveitchik's sources, as well as seventeen short essays which explain aspects of Purim and the book of Esther with the rabbi's views.

There is much in this easy-to-read book that will delight a variety of readers. My own favorite is Rabbi Soloveitchik's recognition that Purim was instituted as a holiday by common people, not rabbis nor Jewish leaders, and it was only after the people instituted the practice that the rabbis accepted it, which I also think is correct. This is what the book itself says.

Rabbi Soloveitchik recognizes that God's name is not mentioned in the book of Esther and all activities that are described are done by humans, but contends

---

1. Rabbi Joseph B. Soloveitchik, *Megillat Esther Mesorat Harav* (Jerusalem: Koren Publishers, 2018).

that although God deliberately hides the divine presence here and in life generally, God controls events and spreads protective care over people.

FIVE ITEMS THAT INFLUENCED RABBI SOLOVEITCHIK

Faith

To understand the writings of Rabbi Soloveitchik, one needs to realize that he was influenced by at least five sources. The first was Soren Kierkegaard who developed the idea that was later called "The Leap of Faith." Although the concept of faith is not explicit in the Hebrew Bible, the Tanakh, Rabbi Soloveitchik makes it a central core of his thinking and writings. True, the word *emunah*, exists in the Tanakh and it has the current meaning of "faith," yet in the Bible the word means "firmly." It addresses action, not a mind-set. Moses's hand was weakened as he signaled the troops led by Joshua against Amalek, and again when two people came and held his hand up for him, they were held *emunah*, firmly. Faith plays no significant part in Rabbi Soloveitchik's commentary on Esther because of his idea that the story shows how humans acted without relying on God, who is not explicitly mentioned in the book.

Mysticism

Secondly, he was influenced by his early teacher who was a Hassid. Thus, his writings focus on somewhat otherworldly mystical ideas. In this commentary, for example, he states that Esther was not a conventional beauty. She had charm, and this charm was the result of God entering her body.

Sermons

Third, again probably because of the influence of Hassidim, his writings are sermons, attempts to find meaning in what seems to be what he calls an arbitrary universe. He does not offer rational interpretations of the biblical texts, but rather somewhat mystical sermons about them. If one wants to find out what the Bible is saying, one must look elsewhere. This commentary is filled with such sermons, especially concerning what we can learn about acting with proper behavior today.

The dialectics of Hegel

The fourth is the theory of dialectics by Friedrich Hegel who contended that life is filled with multiple contradictions, and that two contradictions can be combined in what is called a synthesis. Rabbi Soloveitchik agreed with the idea that life is filled with contradiction and states this often in many of his writings, but disagreed with the idea of a synthesis. He felt that the contradictions are part of nature; this is good, and people need to learn how to deal with the conflict. Humans, according to Rabbi Soloveitchik, are always "burdened with an inner contradiction." The best-known example is his view that the book of Genesis 1 and 2, speaks about two kinds of Adam, each having a different personality. We see many examples of dialectics in this commentary where Rabbi Soloveitchik sees conflicting ideas and states that it is part of human nature to have such conflicts. One is his view that the book of Esther depicts melancholy and a cry of distress arising from fear and insecurity, and a hymn of joy and celebration marking Purim as a holiday.

Men and women have different makeups and duties

The fifth is his sometimes unique understanding of the Torah. For example, he contends that "Judaism has never discriminated against women." Both Mordechai and Esther "appear as actors on the historical stage.... Both...were created in the image of God; both were endowed with dignity and majesty; both possessed great talent." But, despite these words, he felt that the female and male talents are different, and that each has a different role in life and in Judaism. There are "basic differences of the sexes, not only physiologically, but psychically and spiritually as well. A historical masculine role cannot be assigned to woman, and vice versa, a feminine task must not be imposed upon man." Women are superior to men "in two areas: the area of applied, practical thinking and the area of prayer. The first intellectual judgment, the intuitive flash, the primordial revelation of truth belongs to man. However, when it comes to implementation, the woman is the master."

EXAMPLES OF THE RABBI'S VIEWS

Some examples of Rabbi Soloveitchik's methodology can be seen in "*Rabbi Joseph B. Soloveitchik on Pesach, Sefirat ha-Omer and Shavu'ot.*"[2] It is the second volume in a series of books put out by The Rabbi Soloveitchik Library presenting the thoughts of Rabbi J.B. Soloveitchik. The book addresses eleven issues concerning laws relating to Passover, the Counting of the Omer, the debate between the Sadducees and

---

2. David Shapiro, *Rabbi Joseph B. Soloveitchik on Pesach, Sefirat Ha-Omer and Shavu'ot*, ed. Jacob J. Schacter (Jerusalem: Urim Publication, Jerusalem, 2005).

Pharisees concerning the date of the holiday of Shavuot, and concludes with three of the eleven chapters focusing on the first four commands on the Decalogue. Much of the book is sermonic where the rabbi interprets laws in ways that tell readers how to act. He sometimes relies on mystical texts such as the *Zohar*.

SOME OF THE MANY ISSUES DISCUSSED

Why can Jews claim reparations from Germans for the brutal treatment of Jews during the Holocaust, but blacks are not entitled to reparations from the American white community for their enslavement? He says the difference is that the German's introduced the idea to make reparations to the Jews; in contrast, the whites in the US made no such gesture.

Why did God introduce himself as the deity which brought the Israelites out of Egypt, and not as the creator of the universe? God, according to the rabbi, wanted to address the Jews alone, and therefore focused on what God did for them.

His unique view that the Decalogue is not made up of ten commandments, but a single command that branches out into ten aspects. The basic command is that Jews must "surrender to divine authority." This "basic command" is the primary focus in all of the rabbi's writings, "total surrender."

Contrary to many Orthodox male Jews who contend that they are obligated to wear tzitzit and show them publicly, he felt that a man does not have to wear tzitzit if he does not wear a garment that has four corners. Similarly, if one lives in a house with no doorframe, he is not obligated to observe the mitzvah of mezuzah.

The word *Elohim* denotes power. It denotes "God Who abides in every natural phenomenon: in the flowering of the bush, in the far distance separating us from the stars, and even in my own flexible muscle... God's Will is embedded in every element of nature, through orderliness and causality rather than through miracles... *Elokim* means God Who controls the cosmic dynamics." The rabbi contends that *Elohim* "is thus immanent; He is readily discernible in the natural world in which we live. On the other hand, the name *Havayah* (*y-h-v-h*) represents God in His transcendence." This idea is unclear. Does the rabbi mean that God is manipulating nature constantly, which is the view of Nachmanides?

His disagreement with Maimonides who felt that all of the biblical commands are rational and could be understood logically. The rabbi connects this view with his idea of "total surrender": we must not search for a rational reason for God's commands, just obey.

Living in the Past

In *The God Who Hates Lies, Confronting & Rethinking Jewish Tradition,*
David Hartman with Charlie Buckholtz,[1] Rabbi Dr. David Hartman
(1931–2013), a champion of Adaptive Judaism, expresses his dislike of the
views of Rabbi Joseph B. Soloveitchik (1903–1993), the former Dean of
Yeshiva University. Hartman was a noted Orthodox rabbi and the founder
of the Shalom Hartman Institute in Jerusalem, which helps Jews confront
modernity. Hartman was a student of Rabbi Soloveitchik and agreed with
him until he saw the harm that his teacher's worldview imposed upon
Judaism.

RABBI JOSEPH B. SOLOVEITCHIK'S VIEW

Rabbi Soloveitchik insisted that Jews must obey all biblical and rabbinical commands, no matter how difficult, painful, or unreasonable they may appear, and
without any change because of modern situations and human needs. What is
important is total surrender to God, "self-denial, even the complete negation of
the self." Thus, for example, he insisted that Jews may not resolve the *agunah*[2]
and other harsh laws.

Ancient rabbis understood that the Torah allowed only men to initiate marriages and divorces. Women have no role in marriage and divorce other than to
accept their husband's actions. Thus, husbands can refuse to give wives divorces
unless they pay them hundreds of thousands of dollars, or spitefully refuse to grant

---

1. David Hartman with Charlie Bukholtz, *The God Who Hates Lies, Confronting & Rethinking
Jewish Tradition,* (Woodstock: Jewish Lights, 2011).
2. The ancient law that only allows men to perform divorces. As a result, when a husband refuses
to give his wife a divorce, she remains "chained" to her husband, *agunah* means chained.

divorces under any circumstance, and the women are chained to their husbands forever. Women are unable to remarry without the Jewish divorce, but Jewish law allows husbands under certain conditions to remarry and be unhurt by their outrageous behavior.

Some rabbis wanted to help these mistreated married women without changing the ancient law, but by annulling the marriage. Their idea was that the marriage was a mistake. Had the woman known before she married the insensible man that he was such an abuser she would never have married him. This procedure makes sense and it compassionately saves an *agunah* from a life of loneliness and allows her to marry again. But Rabbi Soloveitchik was so highly respected by rabbis that he was able to persuade the Orthodox Rabbinical Council of America to reject the idea.

Why?

Rabbi Soloveitchik reminded the rabbis of an ancient psychological statement in the Talmud, "It is better for a woman to stay married [even to a terrible mistreating husband] than to live alone." If this view made sense at all, it only did so in the past when women were totally under the power of men; when they needed a husband to protect them and provide for them. Although this situation does not exist today, and although most women today would prefer to live alone rather than live with an abusive husband, Rabbi Soloveitchik insisted that ancient practices and mindsets do not change. The ancient rabbis understood human nature, he insisted, and we dare not alter what they decreed.

RABBI HARTMAN'S VIEW

Rabbi Hartman, in this volume and in *From Defender to Critic*,[3] expresses his outrage that Soloveitchik refused to allow the means to resolve this offense and insisted that women were created as a servile helper to men. He wonders how anyone can "worship a God who considered half of the Jewish community to be not fully human." Even more disturbing is that many women have been brainwashed by rabbis such as Soloveitchik to believe such notions.

Soloveitchik, he writes, worships halakha, the Jewish legal system, instead of

---

3. David Hartman, *From Defender to Critic: The Search for a New Jewish Self* (Woodstock: Jewish Lights, 2012).

God. The Torah teaches love of neighbor and stresses love of a stranger thirty-six times, but Soloveitchik worships halakha. Soloveitchik teaches that the further Jews are removed from Mount Sinai the weaker their intellect is and the less they understand the truth. Thus, Jews may not reject the views of ancient rabbis, and must unthinkingly accept their decrees.

This thinking led to many human tragedies beside the *agunah*. A Russian immigrant who always thought he was Jewish and followed Jewish law, served in the Israeli army as a commander and was killed defending Israel, but was not allowed to be buried in a Jewish cemetery because a rabbi discovered that his grandmother wasn't Jewish. A middle-aged Jewish man, a Kohen, a descendant of the priestly line, was refused permission to marry the woman he loved, who had long ago converted to Judaism out of love for the religion, because of the ancient rule that a Kohen cannot marry a convert. Women are still excluded from many Jewish practices.

Hartman writes that Maimonides, unlike the rabbis who worship halakha, taught: "Halakha plays an important, but secondary, role in the religious process." Halakha is not the goal; it is the means to attain the goal of individual and social growth. Maimonides stressed that God placed eyes in the front of faces to encourage people to look forward, not behind. Humans must assume "the role of interpreting God's law for our time and place," and stop hurting people.

Jewish Law Needs to Change

Conservatism in politics and religion has captured the thinking in many countries today. This, like most things in life, can be good, but it can go to an extreme. Unfortunately, it affected Judaism terribly and prompted Rabbi Dr. Nathan Lopes Cardozo to write *Jewish Law as Rebellion, A Plea for Religious Authenticity and Halachic Courage.*[1] He suggests that rabbis need to change radically or be replaced.

RABBI DR. NATHAN LOPES CARDOZO

Nathan Lopes Cardozo is a Dutch-Israeli rabbi, philosopher, and scholar. He is the author of more than a dozen thoughtful books in which he addresses the all-to-many crises among Jews. Former Chief Rabbi Jonathan Sacks called him a man with a wide intellectual horizon, unafraid to confront challenges. His books are fascinating and are often, as this one, thought-provoking calls to action.

RABBIS CONSIDERING THEMSELVES DECIDERS OF JEWISH BEHAVIOR

In this book, among much else, he focuses on rabbis who call themselves *Posek haDor*, deciders for the generation, who teach *daas Torah*, the truth of the Torah. They portray themselves as supreme decision makers of Jewish law. The very language they use signifies arrogance and ignorance of Judaism, and this makes a farce of their idea. They fail to recognize that since ancient times, Judaism recognized that there are differences of opinion about Jewish law, and this is reflected in the Talmud which contains various opinions about many laws. Their insistence of using the out-of-date Ashkenazi pronunciation *daas* instead of the Modern

---

1. Rabbi Dr. Nathan Lopes Cardozo, *Jewish Law as Rebellion, A Plea for Religious Authenticity and Halachic Courage* (Jerusalem: Urim Publications, 2018).

Hebrew *daat*, dramatizes how they prefer to live in, and even speak the language of ancient times. Cardozo stresses that their view of Judaism and life generally is static and confining. He encourages rabbis to return to authentic religiosity.

The Israeli Chief Rabbinate, for example, refuses to recognize the conversion process of most Orthodox rabbis who live outside of Israel relegating the procedure to themselves alone, refusing to admit that conversion is not a biblical procedure, was invented most probably in the second century BCE, and can be changed. Similarly, they refuse to allow many women abandoned by their husbands to be divorced by a court because of an outdated psychological view "a woman would prefer to live even with an abuser than to live alone." Even children in high school would recognize that this psychology no longer exists.

WHAT MUST BE DONE

These *Posek haDor* rabbis must understand that times have changed, which may well mean that God demands different decisions from those in the past. Cardozo quotes Abraham Joshua Heschel who wrote: "Indeed, the essence of observance has, at times, become encrusted with so many customs and conventions that the jewel was lost in the setting. Outward compliance with the externalities of the law took the place of the engagement of the whole person to the living God."[2]

They must learn how to make Judaism exciting, ennobling, and relevant to the twenty-first century, how to deal with secular Jews and non-Jews, and with the problem of *hareidi* Jews not participating in defense of their country in the military. They must also try to bring religion and science together.

Cordozo writes: "We should be very thankful that we witness the disintegration of rabbinic authority in our days. Nothing can be worse for Judaism and the Jewish people than having rabbis admired as great spiritual halakhic leaders when for the most part they are not."

---

2. Abraham Joshua Heschel, *God in Search of Man: A Philosophy of Judaism* (New York: Farrar, Straus and Giroux, 1976), 326.

Must We Obey Rabbinical Mandates?

Why do people feel that they should listen to their clergy? There is nothing in the Hebrew Bible, New Testament, or Koran that says that its adherents must obey rabbis, priests, and imams. In fact, Judaism didn't have rabbis until around the year 70 of the Common Era after the Second Temple was destroyed by the Romans.

WHAT IS A RABBI AND WHEN DID RABBIS BEGIN TO EXIST?

No man before that time had this title. Those who think that Jesus was a rabbi are mistaken. The Torah gives the responsibility to teach the Israelites to the tribe of Levy. Later, the priests assumed this role. When the temple was destroyed, priests lost their function and Judaism continued to be a people who focused on observing the practices in the Torah, but not people who offered sacrifices. Anyone could teach Torah. Men who were recognized by their teachers to be adept at teaching Torah were called rabbis.

My father, Rabbi Dr. Nathan Drazin, pointed out in his book *History of Jewish Education* that: "Education has always been the pride and the cherished ideal of the Jewish people. In the words of Simon the Just, in the third century BCE (recorded in *Pirkei Avot* 1:2), Torah is the first of the three pillars upon which the entire world was founded." He reveals that the "Jewish school system went through three stages: first, the founding of academies for higher learning, later, establishing secondary schools for adolescents, and, lastly providing universal elementary schools." The first stage began about 300 BCE. The final reform of free elementary schools for all boys was "put into effect about the year 64 CE." In short, unlike ancient cultures that assigned religious responsibility to priests and kept religious knowledge restricted to this class, Judaism felt that all people should be educated and use their minds to solve life's questions. Rabbis are teachers, no more, no less. Jews are encouraged not to abandon their thoughts to others.

There were, apparently, religious leaders other than Levites and priests before the year 70. These included prophets who are mentioned in the Torah, who were usually ignored by most of the people. Also, *Mishnah Pirkei Avot*, composed around 200 CE, states that during the second temple period, between 516 BCE until 70 CE, there were "men of the great assembly" and "*zugot.*" However, there are many conflicting opinions about these men; and although tradition states that they were religious leaders, scholars say that we really don't know what their function was or what the general public thought of them.

In the beginning of the eighteenth century, Hassidic Jews developed the practice of relying on rabbis, who they called rebbes, to distinguish them from non-Hassidic rabbis. Extremely Orthodox Jews today have adopted this Hassidic practice. They turn to a rabbi whom they consider all-wise and an authority figure, and ask him every kind of questions, such as should I marry this girl, should I take this job, should I settle in Israel? But this innovation is contrary to the history of Judaism. To repeat, the authority given to today's rabbis is not biblical and it is not even based on ancient laws or even practices. Its origin is today's Judaism of all branches adopting the eighteenth-century notion of the rebbe.

Rabbis are human beings who completed a course of study. Many of them have only a limited secular education. Each has his own approach based on his education, intelligence, and life experiences and each has opinions that differ with those of other rabbis. How, then, should Jews relate to their rabbis? They should select a rabbi as they select physicians, looking for a person who is competent. They should evaluate everything the rabbi tells them and not accept what he says simply because he is a rabbi. They should consider the sources that the rabbi uses for his decision, and then make up their own mind how to behave. As with physicians, it sometimes pays to get a second opinion.

Why did people accept the opinions of rabbis? The answer is simple. These men had no authority, but enough Jews complied with what they said so their rulings became the law.

For example, when the temple was destroyed, and many Jews wanted to continue the sacrifices without a temple, the rabbis said that sacrifices should be discontinued. Why was this ruling accepted? Simply because many people agreed with them.

The same principle applies today. When a rabbi gives a ruling, it becomes mandatory only for people who adopt it. When a rabbi's decision differs with those of other rabbis, (which will occur because rabbis are only human) people need to decide which view they will accept.

I visited a synagogue where the rabbi had a long beard and wore a large black yarmulke. He delivered an astounding sermon. He spoke about his strong conviction that Jews must have faith in God and rely upon this faith.[1] He described a situation where a man fell over an extremely deep cliff. He was able to hold on to a tree branch half way down the cliff. He could not climb up. If the branch broke he would fall very far, a distance of more than several floors if this was a house.

The rabbi asked his congregation: "In this situation, should you hang on to the branch and keep calling out for help? Or should you let go of the branch and have faith that God will save you?" He then gave his message. "A true Jew would let go. He would have faith that God will save him." I was astounded. I left the synagogue certain that I had heard wrong.

About a year or two later, I happened to return to this synagogue, and heard the rabbi repeat the same sermon with the same admonition that I had heard before. Now I was certain that this rabbi was teaching his congregants something that I thought people should not do.[2]

Can failure to accept rabbinical mandates lead to religious anarchy? Absolutely. Therefore, wise people will recognize that different views exist in Judaism and respect each other. They will accept a decision when they feel it is necessary, even though it is contrary to their worldview, to help assure Judaism's survival. Thus, for example, as discussed previously, Orthodox rabbis disallow women from giving divorces based on an interpretation of a few biblical words with no explicit disallowance in the Torah, a practice that has resulted in thousands of women being chained to husbands they loath. Orthodox Jews who dislike this ruling accept the ruling and don't allow women to initiate divorces because this

---

1. The definition of faith, a concept that is not even hinted at in the Torah, is the accepting as true an idea that science, the senses, and logic state is untrue.

2. This is a true story. I really experienced it. While the rabbi gave only the cliff as his example twice, he could have given other examples of how he felt people should act. For example: when you come to a street with much traffic and you want to cross despite the red light telling you to wait, you should ignore the light and the traffic, have faith that God will protect you, and cross the street into the traffic. This he would emphasize, is what God demands!

would cause children born of a marriage following such a divorce to be considered illegitimate by many Jews, and thus affect the children's ability to marry fellow Jews. They would also not abandon Orthodox Judaism because of this ruling but work within the system of Orthodox law to change it.

SECULAR NOVELS

Was Abel and not Cain the Real Villain?

Many novelists explore ideas about humans and the world and develop ideas that should prompt us to rethink preconceived notions, and to develop more common-sense ideas. In his superb novel *Demian*, published in 1919, the 1946 Nobel Prize winning author Hermann Hesse (1877–1962), despite the biblical text clearly stating that Cain criminally murdered his brother Abel, suggested that it is possible to interpret the biblical story of Genesis 4 differently hinting that Abel was the brother who acted improperly.

THE 1919 NOVEL

Hesse's *Demian* is not as great a work as his *Magister Ludi*, his last novel, which is considered his greatest achievement, and is a marvelous work of art. Yet, after reading *Demian*, Thomas Mann, who won the Nobel Prize for Literature in 1929, argued for years that Hesse should also be a recipient.

The novel portrays how a ten-year-old boy Emil Sinclair from a well-to-do religious German family learnt to understand himself as he grew older and came to know the importance of life. We read about a larger and older bully who tormented Sinclair and blackmailed him until Sinclair met a strange young man, Demian, who saved him from the bully and began to teach him about life.

During the decade that followed, Demian taught Sinclair that people are obliged to learn to understand themselves and act based on this knowledge, a basic human requirement that most people cannot do because they are naturally passive. Demian also introduced Sinclair to his understanding of the Hebrew Bible and New Testament. One of Demian's views concerned the Cain and Abel story and the meaning of the Mark of Cain.

Demian explained that the Mark of Cain is a symbolic way of saying that people could see intelligence showing on Cain's face and on others who are exceptionally intelligent, such as Demian. The biblical story is suggesting that people are frightened by men and women who carry this mark and prefer to avoid them. If this is impossible the lesser intelligent people, such as Abel, harass those who carry the mark. Thus, Cain killed his brother in self-defense, and therefore Cain was never punished for his act.

The novel depicts how Sinclair goes through various stages as he grows older, including a phase where he indulges in drink, where he is impressed by a beautiful woman, where he meets a man with good intelligence who is unable to apply what he knows. Soon, Sinclair realizes that he is carrying the Mark of Cain.

THE FIRST ACCOUNT EXTOLLING CAIN

Hesse was, of course, not the first person to praise Cain. During the second century, the Cainites, also called Cainians, had a similar, but not identical view about Cain. They were mentioned by Tertullian and Irenaeus as a relatively small Gnostic and Antinomian sect existing in the eastern Roman Empire. One of their religious texts was the Gospel of Judas. Just as they praised Cain, they argued that Judas was the best of Jesus's disciples and only he knew the truth. They believed that the god mentioned in the Hebrew Bible and New Testament was the demiurge, who was not the supreme deity, but a heavenly being who is subordinate to the supreme God, and that this subordinate god and not the supreme God controls the material world and is antagonistic to all that is spiritual and good. The demiurge was antagonistic to Cain, whom the Cainites venerated, and included the false account of his encounter with Abel in his Hebrew Bible to defame him.

Whether you agree with them or not, and I do not, their ideas should prompt us to think. What did Abel do wrong? Why was Cain not punished? What was the Mark he carried? Why was it needed?

Cain by Jose Saramago

Jose Saramago (1922–2010), a Portuguese writer, won the Nobel Prize for Literature in 1998. In 2008, the noted critic Harold Bloom called him "the greatest novelist alive in the world today." Saramago wrote his first novel *The Land of Sin* in 1947 when he was 25. He was not recognized as a brilliant writer until he was 60. Some readers see some of his novels as allegories, others as satires. The Nobel Prize Committee described his books as "modern skepticism about official truths." He was an atheist and communist, and mocked religion in such books as his 1991 *The Gospel According to Jesus Christ*, which I for one enjoyed, but the Catholic Church understandably scorned and ridiculed the book.

UNIQUE WRITING STYLE

Saramago has a unique writing style. His sentences are unusually long, frequently a page long. He often mixes the novel's characters' thoughts with those of the book's narrator, but clearly differentiating the two. He does not use quotation marks. He places conversations between people in a single sentence and distinguishes each person's remarks by ending it with a comma and beginning the next person's statement with a capital letter. One might think that this style makes the book hard to read, however, this is not so. This structure adds to the velocity of the conversation and our understanding that this is a single chat.

CAIN

Saramago's last book *Cain* is a delightful, frequently funny, heretical, mocking, feverishly anti-God, retelling of the early books of the Hebrew Bible.[1] His book prompts us to think.

---

1. Jose Saramego, *Cain*, trans. Margaret Jull Costa (Boston: Houghton, Mifflin Harcourt, 2011).

According to Saramago's book, no snake spoke to Eve in Eden and persuaded her to eat the forbidden apple; snakes can't talk. It was a dream, and she followed her dream, and enticed Adam to do so as well. Adam felt guilty soon after he bit the apple and couldn't swallow or regurgitate the apple; so, it remained in his and his male descendant's neck and is called Adam's apple.

Adam and Eve's son Cain killed his brother Abel after God accepted the latter's sacrifice and ignored Cain's, despite Cain's piety. Cain was the child of the angel that God set in front of the Garden of Eden to prevent Adam and Eve from reentering it to gain food after God had expelled them for disobeying him. Eve granted the angel sexual favors for reentry to avoid starving.

God criticized Cain for Abel's murder and Cain, in turn, charged God with complicity; he shouldn't have shown undeserved favoritism to his brother. The two agree on a compromise of Cain's sentence based on the shared responsibility for Abel's death. Cain escaped capital punishment but got a disfiguring mark on his forehead and was banished to wander, like an illegal alien without a country.

Contrary to what seems to be recorded in the Bible, there were other people present on earth at that time, many living in organized cities. Adam and Eve and their descendants were a special divine project, an experiment that didn't work.

Cain drifts from place to place, like a protagonist in a sci-fi movie. He finds himself in one episode after another, moved by some force, not God, who doesn't keep track of him. The new place might be the present or the future. He is plucked back and forth, as in a roller coaster time-driven ride. He finds himself in a town called Nod where its queen takes a fancy to him and they engage in sexual escapades until the queen's husband becomes tired of the affair, is embarrassed, and tries to have Cain killed.

After this adventure, Cain finds himself following Abraham on a mission to sacrifice his son Isaac and intervenes by seizing Abraham's hand. An angel, sent by God to stop Abraham, arrives late due to a problem he has with one of his wings. Cain is then hurled back in time to watch the Tower of Babel incident, then shunted forwards in time to when God and two angels visit Abraham and Sarah and foretell Isaac's birth. This is followed by a slight shift to Lot's house and the destruction of Sodom, then to the Israelites' worship of the golden calf, Joshua at Jericho (where we are told, contrary to reports, the sun didn't stand still), Job and his afflictions where God is complicit with Satan, and Noah and the flood.

The book is jammed with Cain's disgust at the countless murders committed by God at Sodom, the Tower of Babel, the golden calf, and the flood, among others. Why, he wonders, was God disturbed at his single murder when he commits so many? He decides to take revenge against God.

The book is also packed with irreverent humor. Cain, for example, disputes with God whether Noah's vessel containing so many animals can float. Saramago describes the horrendous unsanitary conditions in Noah's ark. And he reveals that, "Among themselves, the angels were happy to acknowledge that life in heaven was the most boring thing ever invented, with the chorus of angels constantly proclaiming to the four winds the lord's greatness, generosity and even his beauty."

Science Fiction Can Teach Us to Think

Science fiction stories are fascinating and often instructive because many of the writers have highly advanced imaginations, and they develop ideas that make us think and reevaluate what we thought previously about what is important in life. Ray Bradbury's book *Fahrenheit 451* is a good example.[1]

RAY BRADBURY

Ray Bradbury (1920–2012), winner of many awards, wrote books in many genres: science fiction, fantasy, horror, and mysteries. He is known for many quotes, such as: "If you hide your ignorance, no one will hurt you, and you'll never learn." His first collection of short stories was published in 1947. *Fahrenheit 451* is his most famous novel.

The Martian Chronicles is another novel for which he is remembered. While known as a novel, it is actually a collection of short stories, some of which were published separately before being combined into the collection. Most of the stories prompt us to think about ourselves and our culture and how the present attitudes on earth may lead to its destruction as a planet and culture, and the stunting of individuals. Although written in the mid-twentieth century, it starts in the year 1999 when a second rocket was sent by America to Mars. (The space crafts are called rockets throughout the book.) The crew does not know what happened to the men that arrived on Mars in the first rocket. They discover that the Martians generally avoid them, send them to a certain doctor, and then imprison them in an insane asylum.

The third expedition included a man who realized that the earth explorers,

---

1. Ray Bradbury, *Fahrenheit 451* (New York: Ballantine, 1968).

like the Spaniards who visited South America, will destroy the highly advanced
Martian culture, and to save the Martians, he decides to kill the members of the
rocket crew. Soon, as occurred with the Spaniards, virtually all the Martians died
from a disease the earthlings brought to Mars.

In *Usher II*, another work by Bradbury, we read how by 2005, the earthlings
on Mars developed a "Moral Code" to burn all books, including fairy tales that
made people think what they should not think, and then they closed libraries.

FAHRENHEIT 451

This book is a classic that should be reread from time to time and pondered. It
is interesting and its message, like *Usher II*, is significant. It is a sermon that few
clergy men and women (who emphasize that one should spend time reading holy
books), would dare make.

I read the story as a parable that denounces the ancient but still existing
wrong-headed notion that it is better, far better, for people to be ignorant.

Governmental leaders and thinkers have known since the beginning of time
that most people are constitutionally unable to understand many truths. Several
ways were developed to manage the masses. One, discussed even by Plato in the
fourth century BCE, was to reveal complex real truths only to intellectuals, but to
teach the general population only "noble lies," what Maimonides called "essential
truths" – essential to keep them safe, but not true.

An example is the false notion that God becomes angry when he sees people
acting improperly. This is wrong. A superior dispassionate all-knowing God
would never become angry. Anger is a human not a divine emotion. God has no
emotions. But clerics teach their congregants that God becomes angry because it
helps control the otherwise uncontrollable masses who, if they did not fear God's
anger and punishment, would rob, steal, kill and commit other wrongs.

A second way of handling these people is stop them from learning the truths
about the world. For instance, the ancient Roman Catholic Church kept people
from knowing the Bible, and fought against translations other than in Latin from
the original Hebrew and Greek, which non-clergy did not understand, but which
the clergy understood.

The leadership of the future world in *Fahrenheit 451* went a step further. They
believed that people would be able to live a better life without any books because

books, they were convinced, caused wrong ideas, disharmony, confusion, and unhappiness.

Guy Montag was a government fireman whose job was to burn books. He didn't need to stop fires because homes were fireproof. Burning books seemed right to Montag. It seemed natural and rational. He knew nothing else. This is what he was taught by those who were much smarter than him.

But one day a girl woke him up. She was like the child in another parable who was able to see that the king was naked. She told him that people once read books, learnt from them and improved themselves and society. She told him that people could think for themselves and did not need others to tell them what to think.

Is the book outdated? Have people finally learned that they are closing their minds? Unfortunately, people still need the message of *Fahrenheit 451*. Most people are still convinced that God becomes angry and, what is worse, far worse, they are still burning books today when they ignore new ideas.

ISAAC ASIMOV

Isaac Asimov (1920–1992), winner of many awards for his writings, who wrote or edited more than five hundred books, is considered one of the top three science fiction writers. Although his parents were Orthodox Jews, he called himself a non-observant Jew. One of his many books is *Asimov's Guide to the Bible*, reflecting his interest in the Bible. This interest can also be seen in the 1956 short story "The Last Question" about which he wrote: "This is by far my favorite story of all those I have written." The story is very thought-provoking, and many people have offered their interpretations of it. This is mine.

THE LAST QUESTION

One may read a PDF copy before reading my interpretation by using this link: https://www.physics.princeton.edu/ph115/LQ.pdf.

The story can be summarized as follows: In 2061, humans developed an extremely powerful computer called Multivac and AC. The computer was given the ability to improve itself over the years. During six of seven historic periods over trillions of years beginning in 2061, different people were concerned about the future of the world and asked the computer the same question, "how can the world be saved from entropy," meaning, how can the world be saved from being extinguished, such as when the sun ceases to shine? Each time that the question was asked, the computer responded: "Insufficient data for a meaningful answer" or, more specifically, after the question was asked the first time, "There is yet insufficient data for a meaningful answer."

In the seventh scene, the last scene, trillions of years in the future, the descendants of humanity are separated from their bodies and live as intellect. They exist in hyperspace beyond the bounds of gravity or time. AC is also no longer physical, and it too exists in hyperspace not bound by any physical laws. The question is asked a final seventh time. AC is still unable to answer. The last humans merge with AC and disappear. Although AC is still unable to respond, it continues to ponder the question even after humans, space, and time cease to exist, and AC suddenly understands, and answers the age-old question by a demonstration. AC says: "Let there be light," and there was light.

MY UNDERSTANDING

I understand that Isaac Asimov is suggesting the origin of God and the eternity of the universe. He seems to be relying on some Jewish and other ideas.

Many people say that God did not create humans, but that humans created God. In this tale, Asimov takes the latter approach. The computer turns into what humans call God. The computer was made by humans to help humans in order to create what they need, and many people think of God as having this function. This is what AC does: it creates a new world after a former one ended.

Asimov uses the number seven, which is not connected directly with creation in his story, but it could remind readers of the biblical six days of creation with divine rest on the seventh.

Why was AC unable to answer the question about the end of the world for trillions of years? It realized that nothing in this world disappears. It may change into another state but does not leave the universe. Yet, AC could not know if in the future when humanity and all physical beings ended by humans merging with AC this rule that nothing in the world disappears would still apply. It was only at the end, when AC saw that the rule still applied, because humans merged with it, that it knew that the rule continued, and the world would not cease.

MAIMONIDES

Maimonides and others taught that the world will never cease to exist, and there are Jewish legends and legends in other cultures that worlds ended and were followed, as in Asimov's tale with another world.

The notion that the intelligence of humans would merge with something else after the body dies is also Maimonides's idea. He said that the intelligence joined the Active Intellect, a force ancient cultures believed surrounded the earth. We will not know if Asimov drew the name AC from Active Intellect since the two beings are similar, both being sources of intelligence, and active Intellect begins with AC. But it seems that he did so.

So, I see Asimov describing God as a powerful intelligent force created by humans assuring that humans will inhabit the world that will never cease.

A Story by Alexander Pushkin

The idea developed in most cultures that a person is punished for his misdeed in the same way that he committed the misdeed. Slap someone and you will be slapped. Insult another and you will be insulted. In English, the notion is called "tit for tat." In Hebrew it is *midah keneged midah* (measure for measure). It is discussed in the Babylonian Talmud *Sotah* 8b, 9a; *Megillah* 12b; and *Sanhedrin* 90a, b, and 100a, b. Many call the notion superstition: it rarely happens, and when it does it is simply happenstance. Some insist that the punishment is inflicted by God. Others that it is a part of nature. People can cite many examples of it, such as the life and death of the Russian Alexander Sergeyevich Pushkin (1799–1837).

WHO WAS ALEXANDER PUSHKIN?

Pushkin was a highly respected, poet, playwright, and novelist who lived during the Romantic Era. Many, even today, consider him the greatest Russian poet and call him the founder of modern Russian literature. His great-grandfather Ibrahim Gannibal (1696–1781) was kidnapped as a child from Africa and was raised by Peter the Great. Ibrahim became the godson of Peter the Great and was made a Russian prince. He was considered Europe's first black intellectual and rose to be a general in the Russian army. One who wants to read about him can read *The Stolen Prince* by Hugh Barnes.

PUSHKIN'S GREAT-GRANDFATHER IN FICTION

Pushkin fictionalized Ibrahim's life in "The Moor of Peter the Great," in the book *Novels, Tales, Journeys*[1] and other translations of the tale. The translators call this

---

1. Alexander Sergeyevich Pushkin, *Novels, Tales, Journeys: The Complete Prose of Alexander Pushkin* (New York: Random House, 2016).

story and the other stories in *Novels, Tales, Journeys* masterpieces. "The Moor of Peter the Great" describes Peter the Great as a hands-on, very intelligent leader, working to improve Russia side by side with his workmen. It pictures the very intelligent "Moor" preferring to stay in France because he had a sexual relationship with the wife of another man. But despite his strong affection for the woman, he gave way to Peter's call to return to Russia. This short story shows the customs of the time in Russia, the backwardness of the country, illicit sexual relationships, and the prejudices against blacks.

PUSHKIN EXEMPLIFIES THE JEWISH IDEA OF *MIDAH KENEGED MIDAH*

Pushkin, like his great-grandfather Ibrahim, enjoyed the extremes of pleasure and peril, including having sex with the wives of other men. But he could not accept that his wife loved another man, a French officer, and enjoyed being with him, even though neither he nor historians could find proof that his wife committed adultery. He was killed in a duel with the French officer because of the alleged adultery, the very crime that Pushkin committed. It was *midah keneged midah*, tit for tat: he committed adultery and died because of it.

Shakespeare's *Merchant of Venice*

> Shakespeare's *Merchant of Venice* written in 1596 seems to me to be a nonsensical play filled with actions that are irrational, and it is extremely anti-Semitic.

WHAT IS THE PLAY ABOUT?

Contrary to what most people think, that it is only Shylock's demand that the merchant of Venice, Antonio, fulfill his vow that he made to give Shylock a pound of his flesh near his heart if he is unable to repay his loan of three thousand ducats that shows a Jew to be evil, since taking this much flesh would kill the man. Yes, this is more than outrageous. But this is not all. Every time Shylock is mentioned – yes, every time – whether he is present or not, a very derogatory statement is made about Jews. The play even has Shylock's daughter's suitor telling her that she will be sent to Hell for her ancestor's killing Jesus unless she converts to Christianity. True, Shakespeare's knowledge of Jews would have been based entirely on hear-say since neither he nor his audience would have met a Jew, since Jews had been banned by law from Britain in the fourteenth century. But this is no excuse for a playwright to publicly insult other human beings.

In the play, Antonio is unable to repay the loan and is called before the Vancian Duke to pay the pound of flesh, a payment he promised to give if he could not pay with money. Portia, a very rich woman, wife of the merchant's friend, disguises herself as a man, travels to Shylock's trial with her waiting-maid, and makes three arguments to save the merchant Antonio. The last argument is based on a Vancian law: if an alien (and Shylock is an alien solely because he is a Jew) seeks to kill a citizen, the Duke can at his discretion have that alien killed. Shylock refused to show mercy to Antonio, so why should the Duke show mercy to him? However, if he converts and becomes a Christian, the duke will not kill him, only take away his fortune. Isn't this almost as bad as Shylock's demand? The law in effect kills Shylock.

EXAMPLES OF SEVERAL OTHER NONSENSICAL ITEMS IN THE PLAY

(1) Shylock's daughter is described repeatedly as a fine person because she falls in love with a Christian and converts to Christianity, yet she is praised for stealing many jewels from her father Shylock because he is a Jew when she runs away with her suitor, and she wastes much of it.

(2) Portia agrees to marry a man who can pick the right casket of three placed in front of him, one that contains her picture. He must swear that if he fails to pick the correct one, he will never marry. Does it make sense for Portia to base her marriage on a chance gamble and for a man to base his ability to marry in the future on the same gamble?

(3) Portia and her maid each give their husbands a ring with the condition that if they ever lose the ring, the marriage is over. The husbands swear to never give up the rings. After Shylock's trial, the two wives disguised as men, whom their husbands do not recognize, demand that their husbands give them the rings as payment for saving Antonio, and their husbands give the rings to the two women, forcing them to violate their oath never to give up the rings. Is this the way spouses should act?

(4) More significantly, keeping an oath is a central theme in the play. Portia demands that her suitors swear that if they fail to pick the correct casket, they will never marry. Shylock obtains Antonio's oath which he does not try to disavow that he will give a pound of flesh if he has no money to repay the three thousand ducats. Why then do Portia and her maid compel their husbands to violate their oath never to give up the rings the wives are giving them? True, this is a joke on their part, to fool their husbands; but the fact remains that they got their husbands to violate their oath. Why couldn't Antonio also violate his oath?

(5) Portia argues in one of her three arguments that Shylock cannot cut a pound of flesh from Antonio because all that he is entitled to is flesh not blood, and he cannot cut out flesh without taking blood and this is a violation. Isn't this sophistry? Surely when one bargains for a pound of flesh it includes the blood associated with it.

(6) Antonio would only fail to keep his promise to pay if he has no money, and he doesn't have any. His friend offers to pay Shylock twice what Antonio owes, six thousand ducats, but Shylock refuses payments from him. The situation could have been resolved simply by Antonio's friend giving three thousand ducats to Antonio. Antonio would then have the money to pay, would pay it, and would not have to gift him with a pound of his flesh.

In short, a close reading of Shakespeare's *Merchant of Venice* raises the question: is the play an embarrassment?

MIDRASH

What is the Value of Midrash?

Rabbi Dr. Wilfred Shuchat wrote several books in which he translates the Midrash called *Midrash Rabba*, offers his explanation of the text, gives what he calls "seed thought" applying the midrashic idea to current times, and additional commentary which supplements the idea in the first explanation of the text. His goal is to make the "psychological and philosophical perspectives in *Midrash Rabba* accessible to laymen and clergy alike." He is successful. His latest volume is *Abraham and the Challenge of Faith According to the Midrash Rabbah*.[1] What is Midrash? What is *Midrash Rabba*? Are the stories in Midrashim true? What are some items that Rabbi Shuchat mentions?

WHAT IS MIDRASH?

The root of the word Midrash is *derash*, meaning to search, investigate, and look for deeper meaning that is not explicit in the biblical words. The early and medieval rabbis used the biblical text as a springboard to teach halakha, Jewish law that is not in the Bible, or which they saw hinted at in the Bible. They also used midrashic books to teach proper ethical behavior by means of sermons, parables, allegories, legends, speculations, and fantastic stories.

Many rabbis use Midrash in their sermons today to give authenticity to and emphasize whatever point they want to make, but usually mislead their congregants when they do so.

Many rabbis in their sermons mispronounce Midrash and call the collection "medrish." There is no such thing as "medrish." The rabbis heard their teachers

---

1. Rabbi Dr. Wilfred Shuchat, *Abraham and the Challenge of Faith According to the Midrash Rabbah* (Jerusalem: Urim Publications, 2018).

mispronounce Midrash and continue the error. More importantly, they usually incorrectly say, "The medrish says," without revealing to the congregants (1) which of many different Midrashim contains what they are saying, for there are most likely other Midrashim that address the issue involved in the rabbi's sermon that have an idea or solution totally different than the idea the rabbi is expounding, and (2) that even in the one Midrash that the rabbi is addressing there is frequently not only one opinion in the Midrash, but others as well, and the others are by ancient rabbis with a different view than the one the sermon is extolling. Thus, when the rabbi says "The medrish says," he is misleading his audience to believe that what he quotes is the sole ancient opinion on the subject.

WHAT IS *MIDRASH RABBA*?

The title *Midrash Rabba* means the great Midrash. *Midrash Rabba* is a collection of sermonic material on ten books of the Bible. The ten books are the Five books of Moses and the five books that are read in synagogues on certain holidays: Ruth, Esther, Lamentations, Ecclesiastes, and Song of Songs. The ten Midrashim were composed by different authors during different times, with different agendas, and in different styles. The earliest of the ten was probably composed or compiled from various sources around the sixth century. This is the one on the book of Genesis which Rabbi Shuchat addresses in this book. The last one is on Exodus which may have been composed or compiled around the twelfth century. Although each is diverse in style, each contains halakha, legal items, and sermonic material.

ARE THE SERMONIC STORIES IN THE MIDRASHIM TRUE?

In his essay called *Chelek*, Maimonides explains that people who think that the stories in the Midrashim are true are fools, those who reject Midrashim altogether because they are not true are also fools, because while untrue, the stories are parables designed to teach people lessons.

SOME ITEMS THAT RABBI SHUCHAT MENTIONS

The Midrash, but not the Torah, asserts that Abraham converted people of his generation to the idea that there is a single God.

While comparing Abraham to Esther, the Midrash states that the rabbis calculated that Esther was seventy-five-years old when she married Ahashverosh.

God ordered Abraham to sacrifice his son Isaac because: "God wanted the world to know about Abraham, to know that such a person could exist, and others may possibly follow."

The Midrash states that Abraham's son Ishmael loved his father and would visit him from time to time.

The Bible uses the phrase "the third day" almost two dozen times, and it has meaning.

Isaac was willing to be sacrificed by his father since God ordered it, and he gave his father advice on how to do it properly.

Abraham called the site of the near sacrifice of Isaac "Adonai-jireh." Malchizedek, which the Midrash identifies as Noah's son Shem, called the place "Shalem." God did not want to give preference to either of the two, so God combined the names: jirehshalem, Jerusalem.

SUMMARY

Rabbi Dr. Wilfred Shuchat has done a great service by informing readers what one of the many Midrashim says about Abraham and, thereby, he introduces us to parables that prompt readers to think. He offers many ideas that readers can derive from the Midrashim, and therefore readers will be prompted to derive additional ones.

JEWISH PRACTICES

Is This Funny?

My teacher made the following remark, and while I do not think that he intended it to be funny, I do think that he was trying to convey a lot. I am often reminded of it when I see people who do not study the Torah kiss it when it is brought from the ark to the podium to be read on Shabbat.

THE JOKE

When I finished high school at Talmudical Academy in Baltimore, Maryland, I attended Yeshiva University for a year and a half and then returned to Baltimore where I went to Ner Israel Rabbinical College during the day and Johns Hopkins University at night.

While I was sitting in a class studying Talmud at Yeshiva University, a student opened the door and arrived late. He reached up his right hand, touched the mezuzah, and then kissed his fingers that touched the mezuzah.

The rebbe turned to him and asked, "Why did you kiss the mezuzah?"

The student replied, "Because it is a mitzvah."

The rebbe said, "Circumcision is also a mitzvah."

* * *

I told the true story to a rabbinical friend. He said he heard a variation of my story:

A rebbe saw his student walking with his tzitzit hanging out.

"Why are you hanging out your tzitzit?" asked the rebbe.

"Because it's a mitzvah," answered the student.

"I know a greater mitzvah," said the rebbe.

"What's that?" asked the student.

"Circumcision," he replied.

Another Joke, but Is It Funny?

The following could be understood as mocking the study of the Talmud, but perhaps it is stating the truth.

THE JOKE

A young man knocks on the door of a great Talmudic scholar.

"Rabbi, I wish to study Talmud."

"Do you know Aramaic?"

"No."

"Hebrew?"

"No."

"Have you ever studied Torah?"

"No, Rabbi, but I graduated from Harvard summa cum laude in philosophy and received a PhD from Yale. I'd like to round out my education with a bit of Talmud."

"I doubt that you are ready for Talmud. It is the broadest and deepest of books. If you wish, however, I will examine you in logic, and if you pass the test I will teach you Talmud."

"Good. I'm well versed in logic."

"First question. Two burglars come down a chimney. One emerges with a clean face, the other with a dirty face. Which one washes his face?"

"The burglar with the dirty face."

"Wrong. The one with the clean face. Examine the logic. The burglar with a dirty face looks at the one with a clean face and thinks his face is clean. The one with a clean face looks at the burglar with a dirty face and thinks his face is dirty. So the one with the clean face washes."

"Very clever. Another question please."

"Two burglars come down a chimney. One emerges with a clean face, the other with a dirty face. Which one washes his face?"

"We established that. The burglar with the clean face washes."

"Wrong. Both wash. Examine the logic. The one with a dirty face thinks his face is clean. The one with a clean face thinks his face is dirty. So the burglar with a clean face washes. When the one with a dirty face sees him washing, however, he realizes his face must be dirty too. Thus, both wash."

"I didn't think of that. Please ask me another."

"Two burglars come down a chimney. One emerges with a clean face, the other with a dirty face. Which one washes his face?"

"Well, we know both wash."

"Wrong. Neither washes. Examine the logic. The one with the dirty face thinks his face is clean. The one with the clean face thinks his face is dirty. But when clean-face sees that dirty-face doesn't bother to wash, he also doesn't bother. So, neither washes. As you can see, you are not ready for Talmud."

"Rabbi, please, give me one more test."

"Two burglars come down a chimney. One emerges with a clean face, the other with a dirty face. Which one washes his face?"

"Neither!"

"Wrong. And perhaps now you will see why Harvard and Yale cannot prepare you for Talmud. Tell me, how is it possible that two men come down the same chimney, and one emerges with a clean face, while the other has a dirty face?"

"But you've just given me four contradictory answers to the same question! That's impossible!"

"No, my son, that's Talmud."

Should One Kiss Holy Objects?

Most people are unable to differentiate a rational religious practice from a superstition, especially when the superstitious practice has been done by many people over a long period of time, and their religious leaders observe such practices. They feel good about doing it, and gives them a spiritual uplift.

KISSING ITEMS TO SHOW LOVE OF AN OBJECT.

One example of many such practices is the widespread custom of kissing items such as the tzitzit, tefillin, mezuzah, and the Torah scroll. The rabbis criticized these well-meaning behaviors when they first began. They are not Jewish in origin, and contrary to Judaism that stresses proper behavior, not adoration. It is better to use these items as they were intended to be used than showing love by kissing them. For example, people should study Torah, not rush to kiss the scroll on Shabbat when it is brought from the ark to the table where it is read. The purpose of the Torah, as Maimonides taught, is to teach some truths and aid people in improving themselves and society. This is not accomplished by a kiss.

Although he was a mystic, even the codifier Joseph Karo (1488–1575) criticized this practice in his *Bet Yosef, Orach Chayim* 24. He wrote that one should not handle the tzitzit during prayer, as many Jews do. By prohibiting touching, he may have meant kissing, but if touching is prohibited because it misses the point of the tzitzit command to see it and be reminded to observe all the Torah dictates, then kissing it is surely wrong. He writes that this prohibition of touching was also the view of the eighth century Natronai Gaon and the ninth century Moses Gaon. The Geonim (plural of Gaon) were Babylonian religious and educational leaders of Jewry from the late sixth century to 1038. Karo states he fears that the way the tzitzit were handled may lead to doing the same with the mezuzah, which it did.

The Impact of Encountering Other Cultures

There are two broad approaches to Orthodox Judaism, each taking an opposite view as to what Judaism requires, and feeling certain that they know what God wants them to do. Modern Orthodox Judaism is convinced that Jews must learn secular knowledge. It is as Maimonides, Judaism's greatest thinker taught, "the truth is the truth no matter what its source." In contrast, the ultra-Orthodox are certain that Jews must isolate themselves from non-Jews. They feel that God does not want them to enjoy what God has made available in this world; it is just there to entice them, to lead them astray. They are confident that the only thing that God wants them to do is study the Talmud and its commentaries. They advise their children not to study the Bible, for just as the Catholics taught in the Middle Ages, people must not know the Bible because it raises too many unanswerable questions and will lead to apostasy. So, the Catholics refused for centuries to translate the Bible and the ultra-Orthodox, who taught that Jews must not copy non-Jews, followed this thinking and did not teach Bible to their children.

SUPPORT FOR THE MAIMONIDEAN VIEW

The book *Judaism's Encounter with Other Cultures*, edited by Rabbi Jacob J. Schacter,[1] contains four essays by highly respected Jewish scholars, all professors. The four show that the ultra-Orthodox are wrong when they contend that God wants

1. Aharon Lichtenstein, David Berger, Gerald J. Blidstein, Shnayer Z. Leiman. *Judaism's Encounter with Other Cultures: Rejection of Integration*, ed. Jacob Schacter (Jerusalem: Maggid Press 2018).

Jews to isolate themselves, spend their life studying Talmud, leave the acquisition of their livelihood to their wives or social welfare, and close their minds to science and the opinions of non-Jews. Rabbi Schacter describes the four contributors: "They are each recognized authorities in their fields and collectively have made a great contribution to Jewish learning and scholarship." All four have PhDs: David Berger, Gerald J. Blidstein, Shnayer Z. Leiman, and Aharon Lichtenstein.

Three of the essays are historical, showing that Jews have learnt from non-Jews since the beginning of time, and that the contention of the ultra-Orthodox is not only wrong, but not the traditional Jewish understanding of the mandates of life. The writers focus on the early period of Rabbinic Judaism, the medieval period and early modern times, and on the modern period. The fourth takes an overall approach. He examines the issue from practical, philosophical, traditional, and halakhic aspects. All four authors present fresh insights. They show, among much else, that the rabbis of the talmudic period were not hostile to non-Jewish culture. Philo, one of Judaism's first philosophers, in the early years of the common era drew material from the Greek non-Jew Plato. Maimonides in the twelfth century acquired many of his ideas from Plato's student Aristotle. Spanish Jewry thrived in the early medieval period primarily because of the extensive involvement by Spanish Jews in Islamic culture. Rabbi Abraham Kook, the first chief rabbi of Palestine and Rabbi Joseph B. Soloveitchik did similarly in the modern period.

RABBI LICHTENSTEIN

Rabbi Lichtenstein adduces support for his view from several dozen sources, Jewish and non-Jewish, rationalists such as Maimonides, mystics like Nachmanides and Shnayer Zalman of Lyady, poets like Halevi, writers of halakha such as Joseph Karo and Moses Isserles, and many non-Jews, including Tennyson, Byron, Keats, C.S. Lewis, and many more.

Rabbi Lichtenstein writes: "Nor shall we be deterred by the illusion that we can find all we need within our own tradition. As [Mathew] Arnold insisted, one must seek 'the best that has been thought and said in the world,' and if, in many areas, much of that best is of foreign origin, we shall expand our horizons rather than exclude it.... Who can fail to be inspired by the ethical idealism of Plato, the passionate fervor of Augustine, or the visionary grandeur of Milton. Who can remain unenlightened by the lucidity of Aristotle, the profundity of Shakespeare, or the incisiveness of Newman. There is *chochma bagoyim* (wisdom among non-Jews), and we ignore it at our loss. Many of the issues which concern us have faced Gentile writers as well."

SUMMARY

In short, this book shows that secular studies have a significant even vital place in Jewish life, and that to argue that God wants Jews to reject what is true is wrong. So, too, is the view that there is insufficient time to spend on both Torah and secular studies. Also, the fear that secular culture will dilute religious commitment must not restrain Jews from studying all that God made available. Additionally, once Jews study secular subjects they will realize that they cannot really understand religious studies without knowing what science teaches.

Social Change and Halakhic Evolution in American Orthodoxy

Professor Chaim Waxman, a prominent and highly respected sociologist of contemporary Orthodoxy, has made a superb assessment of the history, development, and current and future situation of Orthodoxy in his relatively short but comprehensive 178-page book, *Social Change and Halakhic Evolution in American Orthodoxy*,[1] with 48 additional pages of bibliography and index. Readers will receive a wealth of information from the book and much in it will surprise them, especially the finding that Orthodoxy is changing, and different styles of Orthodoxy exist in different countries. The following is a summary of a few of the many insights that he offers in his insightful book.

A FEW STATISTICS OF JEWS IN THE US

Waxman quotes the Pew Center Survey that estimates that 1.5 percent of US citizens, about 3,638,000, are Jews by religion. Pew also estimates that about 12 percent of this number, 437,000, are Orthodox. Of these 12 percent, 66 percent, (about 291,000) are ultra-Orthodox, and half of this number, 33 percent, (approximately 146,000), are Modern Orthodox. Orthodox Jews have an average income lower than non-Orthodox Jews, and ultra-Orthodox have a lower income than Modern Orthodox. Pew found that the percentage of divorced or separated Orthodox Jews, 9 percent, is lower than that of Mainline Protestants, 12 percent, and Catholics, 10 percent. Pew also found that among Jews with no denominational affiliation,

1. Chaim I. Waxman, *Social Change and Halakhic Evolution in American Orthodoxy* (Liverpool: Liverpool Univerity Press, Littman Library of Jewish Civilization, 2017).

only 31 percent had a Jewish spouse, while the figure for Orthodox was 98 percent. Surprisingly, while 79 percent of ultra-Orthodox are married, only 52 percent of Modern Orthodox are married, a slightly lower rate than that of Conservative Jews.

THE ORIGIN OF ORTHODOXY

The term Orthodox did not exist before the nineteenth century. It was invented by Reform Jews in eastern Europe who used it to disparage what they considered backward, old style, more observant Jews. Soon thereafter, the more observant Jews accepted the title as a badge of honor. The term Orthodox is based on Greek words: *ortho* meaning right or true, and *dox* meaning belief or opinion. Despite what Orthodox means, many Orthodox Jews in the past and today are not literally people who agree with the traditional "beliefs and opinions." They are Orthopractic, Jews who have decided to continue all or many of the traditional "practices" of Judaism. They accept many ancient Jewish laws and traditions "but not meticulously or rigidly so."

Among Ashkenazi Orthodox Jews, those descendant from Europe, there are two main groups today, each divided into sub-groups: Ultra-Orthodox and Modern Orthodox. The former is subdivided into *yeshivish* who contend that Jewish males should separate themselves from modernity as much as possible and spend their life studying Talmud, and *hassidish* who follow the demands of Hassidic leaders called Rebbes. Modern Orthodox is subdivided into Centrist Orthodox and Open Orthodox, with the last adopting less restrictions and are more open to the involvement of women in the synagogue.

The Orthodox in America have a stronger attachment to Israel than do non-Orthodox American Jews. Orthodox Jews place greater emphasis on the law focusing on humans, *bein adam ladam,* while the ultra-Orthodox emphasize laws that focus on God, *bein adam lamakom*, generally ignoring the former. Thus, for example, 56.9 percent of Modern Orthodox feel that homosexuality should be accepted by society, but only 35.6 percent of ultra-Orthodox agree.

RABBIS

Contrary to what people suppose, ancient rabbis did not have a significant role in synagogues, they were "viewed as talmudic scholars and halakhic experts.

Particularly in the area of *isur veheter* (ritual law), which includes kashrut, sexual conduct, Sabbath observance, and so on. However, when it came to questions relating to broader matters, such as issues of communal policy, most people gave no special weight to the rabbis' opinions and did not consult with them." Rabbis "did not reign supreme" as they do today. The current notion that rabbis are elite individuals whose views must be followed did not exist in America until the twentieth century, is not a traditional teaching, but a copy by Orthodox Jews of the Hassidim and the Hassidic Rebbe.

ORIGIN OF CUSTOMS

Also contrary to what many think, "customs start with the masses, and go from the bottom up, sometimes to the point where they become actual laws." Thus, despite the recent powers given to rabbis, we can expect that the more educated Orthodox Jews of today will bring about changes in laws and behavior. Many Orthodox Jews are dissatisfied with how Orthodoxy is practiced today, and this will prompt change. "The 1990 National Jewish population survey indicated that 'among those raised Orthodox, just 24 percent are still Orthodox.'"

In the recently published *Megillat Esther Mesorat Harav*, Rabbi Joseph B. Soloveitchik recognized this phenomenon. He is reported as recognizing that Purim was instituted as a holiday by common people, not rabbis nor Jewish leaders, and it was only after the people instituted the practice that the rabbis accepted it. He is right. This is how the book of Esther portrays what happened.

TURNING TO THE RIGHT

Just as the Orthodox swerved to the right in copying the Hassidic view concerning rabbis, they did the same regarding education. While Rabbi Joseph B. Soloveitchik is highly respected in Modern Orthodox circles, and despite his co-educational classes in his Maimonides School in Boston, many Modern Orthodox day schools today separate boys and girls in different classes. Similarly, because the ultra-Orthodox insist on their own "higher" standards for the laws of kashrut, many certifying agencies require food sellers to bow to their requests to obtain their certification resulting in much higher prices for kosher foods, often twice the price of non-kosher foods. Still another radical change was pioneered by ArtScroll and Mesorah Publications which publish many books on Judaism and Jewish history, "Critics have argued that ArtScroll censors its books to present only Orthodox accounts and Perspectives."

Also, lamentably, many Orthodox synagogues have recently rejected the teaching of Maimonides, who quoted the Greek non-Jew Aristotle in his writings, and who explained that "The truth is the truth no matter what its source," and replaced the highly respected *Pentateuch* by Chief Rabbi J.H. Hertz with the censored ultra-Orthodox ArtScroll Chumash because Rabbi Hertz included explanations of the Torah from non-Jewish scholars. Many other examples of mistaken turnings to the right can be cited, such as the new stringencies that the Chief Rabbinate in Israel have placed on conversions.

Waxman states: "The 'turn to the right' in American Orthodoxy was in large measure, a reflection of the broader turn to the right and the rise of fundamentalism in a variety of different countries and continents." This seems to put the lie to the claim of many Orthodox Jews that they are not affected by non-Jews. "Much as many might deny it, Orthodoxy is affected by and does respond to its social environment. Therefore, American Orthodoxy today is different from what it was a century ago, and it is different from Orthodoxy in the United Kingdom, Europe, and even Israel."

TORAH FROM HEAVEN

As late as fifty years ago, Orthodox Jews were united in believing that both the Written and Oral Torah were given by God to Moses at Sinai, with some, "such as Joseph B. Soloveitchik and Moshe Tendler, [who] went so far as to axiomatically assert a literal version of both parts of the credo, while others simply expressed a general allegiance to the credo itself without discussing the detailed implications." But, "Today the situation is dramatically different." Orthodox Jews in America, and even more so in Israel, are accepting many critical views about the Torah, as can be seen on the website TheTorah.com. Waxman attributes the change to "the emergence of a generation of college-educated Jews" in the second half of the twentieth century. Orthodox schools, including yeshivas, in the past were like the Catholics of the Middle Ages who prohibited the translation of the Bible because they felt that when the masses read the Bible, they could be misled away from Catholicism. Orthodox schools in the same manner taught only Talmud, not Torah, and selected books on ethical behavior in the past. But now, there is an "increase in the [study of the] Bible within the religious and traditional communities since the 1960s."

Similarly, while Orthodoxy rejected the idea of evolution and even called it heresy, most Orthodox Jews today accept it as a fact: "in 2005, even the [Orthodox] Rabbinical Council of America issued an, admittedly very guarded, pro-evolution position."

CONCLUSION

Waxman concludes: "As has been shown throughout this book, American Orthodoxy is anything but static. It has changed and will continue to do so.... Although we cannot know precisely what the group will be like in the future, one thing is certain: it will not be the same as it is now."

Conversion Is Not
Required in the Bible

The Israeli Chief Rabbinate insists that conversions must be done their way, implying that the Torah tells us how it must be done. These rabbis black-balled dozens of rabbis by name who they charge did not convert people using their method. There are good reasons to think that the concept of conversion did not exist in biblical times and was only introduced into Judaism around 125 BCE. Until then, the Israelites thought of themselves as a nation, not a religion. People could join the Israelite nation simply by marrying an Israelite or deciding to be an Israelite and live with the nation. It was much like the naturalization process today, except far easier; there was no paperwork or legal requirements. The following from my book *Unusual Bible Interpretations: Ruth, Esther, and Judith* supports this conclusion. It is reprinted here because it helps confirm the next essay.

THE FACTS

- The Torah does not call the Israelites a religion. In fact, the Bible contains no word for religion.[1] Israel is a nation obligated to do what God commands. There is no procedure mentioned in Scripture for joining the Israelites. The concept of conversion, so important to Judaism today, is not mentioned. If it existed, the Torah would have said so.

- There is no reference to a convert in the Hebrew Bible. The word used today for a convert, *ger*, means "stranger" in the Bible. When Scripture states that the

---

1. The Hebrew word used today for religion, *dat*, means "law" in the Bible, not religion.

Israelites were *gerim* in Egypt (the plural form), it did not mean that they were converts but strangers in Egypt. The term appears thirty-six times in the Torah, teaching Israelites to treat non-Israelites well. When the idea of converts was established, the rabbis wanted to emphasize that Jews should treat converts well, just as they treat Jews who were born Jewish. Since the Torah repeatedly emphasizes that the Israelites should love the *ger*, the rabbis decided to use *ger* to mean "convert": one should love converts.

- The term *prosēlytos* is used in the third-century BCE Greek translation of the Hebrew Bible, called the Septuagint, as the translation of *ger*. The meaning of the Greek word is "stranger," as is the Hebrew word, and it is only later that it came into the English language to signify a proselyte, a person who converted to another religion.

- Many important Israelites married non-Israelites and the Torah never says that the women had to undergo conversion or any procedure. For example, the patriarch Abraham married Keturah,[2] Judah the son of the patriarch Jacob married a Canaanite,[3] his brother Joseph and Moses married daughters of pagan priests, the judge Samson married a Philistine, and King David and King Solomon had wives from many nations.

- Genesis 12:5 states that Abram and Sarai took with them "the souls they had gotten in Haran." *Genesis Rabba* 39:14 and 84:4 and the Babylonian Talmud, *Sanhedrin* 99b, interpret the phrase as a reference to converts; however, this interpretation is sermonic. The term *nefesh* is translated today as "soul," but it means "person" in the Torah, so the verse is saying that the couple took along the people (slaves) they had acquired in Haran.

- Some rabbis misinterpreted Deuteronomy 17:15, which states: "One from among your brothers shall you set as king over you, you may not put a foreigner over you who is not your brother." They understood the command to exclude converts from serving as a king in Israel.[4] Actually, Deuteronomy 17:15 does not mention a convert, but a foreigner. A convert is a person who ceases being a foreigner and becomes a full-fledged Jew. The Torah means what it says. Verse

---

2. Genesis 25:1. One can also add the non-Israelite concubines, such as Abraham's concubine Hagar and Jacob's two concubines, Bilhah and Zilpah.

3. Genesis 38.

4. Mentioned amid a legend in the Babylonian Talmud, *Bava Batra* 3b.

17:14 speaks about the entry of the Israelites into Canaan. In verse 15 the Israelites are told that they should not appoint a foreigner, meaning a Canaanite or any other foreigner, as their king. This rule is reasonable. In verse 18, the Torah instructs the king to follow the Torah laws. Thus, the purpose for excluding a non-Israelite was to assure that the people would observe the divine laws and not worship idols. Having a foreign king with his own agenda would frustrate the divine plan. Furthermore, the word "foreigner" is an inappropriate if not insulting description of a person who voluntarily converted to Judaism.

• Mishnah *Sotah* 7:8 supports the view that the sages felt that a convert and a descendant of a convert may serve as a king of Israel. It reports that King Agrippas (c. 10 BCE–44 CE) was a descendant of Herod, whose ancestor was converted to Judaism by John Hyrcanus.[5] Agrippas, relates the Mishnah, was crying because he understood that Deuteronomy 17:15 made him ineligible to serve as king. But the sages replied emphatically: "Fear not, Agrippas! Thou art our brother! Thou art our brother! Thou art our brother!"

• Some people argue that Moses's father-in-law Jethro converted to Judaism. They draw on Exodus 18:10–12, which narrates that Jethro was impressed with all that God did and offered sacrifices to God. However, this narrative proves nothing. It does not state that Jethro converted; it doesn't even say he gave up his pagan priesthood and joined the Israelites. Jews always accepted sacrifices from pagans without the pagans needing to accept the Lord as their sole God. Additionally, Jethro seemingly does not reject the existence of other gods; he says, "the Lord is greater than all gods."

• The Talmud states that the prophet Samuel wrote the book of Ruth in order to show the people of his time that his choice of David to succeed King Saul was proper: despite the fact that David was a descendant of a Moabite, his ancestress was legally permitted to enter the Jewish fold.[6] Whether this statement

---

5. William Whiston, trans., *Antiquities* 8:1, in *The Life and Works of Flavius Josephus* (Philadelphia: John Winston, 1957). See note with a full discussion on page 394. Because these conversions were forced, and since King Herod was born from these people, some Judeans never accepted Herod and his descendants as Jews. This reluctance by some Jews to consider the Herodians as proper kings may have been because of the force used to make them Jews, not because they were converts.

6. Babylonian Talmud, *Bava Batra* 14b.

is true or not, this view of the book's purpose is significant. If conversion was necessary at the time, the Talmud should have stated that Ruth was accepted and that she converted. This would have better demonstrated the Talmud's point.

- There is no explicit statement in Ruth that she or her sister-in-law Orpah converted, and even the rabbis who feel they, or at least Ruth converted differ on how to read the text. Rashi felt that only Ruth converted and did so during the trip to Judea. Ibn Ezra opined that both converted prior to their marriage to Mahlon and Chilion.

- The book of Ruth not only does not indicate that Ruth converted, it states seven times that she remained a Moabite – including twice in the final chapter where Boaz calls her a Moabite when he speaks about marrying her. The number seven is significant since Scripture very frequently mentions something seven times to emphasize a point. The number seven is repeated in 4:15 when the people say that Ruth is better for Naomi than seven sons; the city of Bethlehem appears seven times, as does the field of Moab and the words *el* and *natan*. This repeated use of seven emphasizes that we should pay attention to this number in Ruth.

- In 2:10, Ruth calls herself a *nokhria*, a "foreigner," in a conversation with Boaz. If she had converted, she would not be a foreigner.

- Some rabbis base their notion that Ruth converted on her statement to Naomi, "Your God is my God." This statement alone was never considered efficacious in making a person a convert. A ceremony of some sort was probably necessary.[7] There is no ceremony here and significantly, Naomi does not say to Ruth, "Now you are a Jew." Even more significant, Ruth does not declare that she will obey Torah laws. *Ruth Rabba* and other Midrashim recognize this lacuna and declare that she did promise to obey the Torah laws, but this is not recorded in the book of Ruth.

- What was Ruth saying when she said, "Your God is my God"? She was responding to what Naomi had said: "Look, your sister-in-law returned to her people

---

7. It appears that no formal ceremony existed for the acceptance of a proselyte until the second century CE. There were still discussions at that time whether circumcision was necessary (Babylonian Talmud, *Yevamot* 46a). However, even if no formal ceremony existed, we would expect at least an informal one.

and her god; you should return after your sister-in-law." Ruth answered: "No, I will go where you go, and your God will be my God."

- Additionally, many ancients, and apparently also Ruth, believed that each nation had its own god who protected his or her own land. Ruth's statement "Your God is my God" was another way of saying, "Your land will be my land."[8]
- Ezra and Nehemiah felt very strongly that the Judeans should not be married to non-Judeans. As leaders of the people at that time, they ordered Judeans to send away their non-Judean wives and children.[9] This draconian measure would not have been necessary if conversion existed.[10]
- The first mention of conversion is when the Hasmonean king John Hyrcanus forcibly converted Edomites around 125 BCE.[11]

---

8. Nachmanides, for example, was convinced that God only exercises divine power in Israel. See Charles Ber Chavel, ed., *Sefer Hamitzvot l'Harambam im Hasagot Haramban* (Jerusalem: Mossad Harav Kook, 1981), 359: "There is in this matter a secret relating to that which the rabbis have said: 'He who dwells outside of the land of Israel is like one who has no God.'" Nachmanides understood that the Talmud is stating that people who live outside of Israel are under the influence and power of these other supernatural beings and even if they try to worship God it is as if they have no God.

9. See Ezra 9 and Nehemiah 13.

10. Nehemiah tells us that he fought with the men who married non-Judeans, cursed them, smote them, and plucked out their hair. He wrote that Solomon whom God loved sinned in this way. This point is quoted by Klein in *Megillot, Olam Hatanakh* (Divrei Hayamim, 1999).

11. William Whiston, *Antiquities* 8:1, in *The Life and Works of Flavius Josephus* (Thomas Nelson, 1957), 394.

The Torah Did Not Prohibit
All Intermarriages

Jews are no longer Bible Jews. They are Rabbinical Jews. The Torah only forbids intermarriages with certain non-Israelites, not all of them. But at least since the days of Ezra and Nehemiah, Judaism has forbidden intermarriages with non-Jews who have not converted. Jews today follow the latter rule, not the biblical one.

BIBLICAL MARRIAGE CEREMONY

There was apparently no special ceremony for marriage in biblical days. Marriages were consummated by the man taking a woman to his house and having sex with her with the intention of making her his wife. The procedure for marriage and for divorce is described in Deuteronomy 24:1. "When a man takes a wife and has sex with her, and it happens that she loses his favor because he has found something indecent or unacceptable about her, he writes her a certificate of divorce, puts it in her hand and sends her out of his house." Later the rabbis felt that using the sexual act to begin marriage was not very decent, since they felt that marriage should be confirmed by the presence of two witness (which was not required in biblical times), they introduced two other methods, giving the woman something of value, such as a ring, or giving her a contract (Babylonian Talmud, *Kiddushin* 2a). I believe that the current practice of having the marriage ceremony under a canopy and the practice of the couple going into isolation in a room after the ceremony long enough to have had sex, called in Hebrew *yichud*, is a Jewish practice that recalls the ancient marriage ceremony. The wedding under the canopy symbolizes the ancient wedding in the groom's house, and the *yichud* symbolizes both the taking to the house and the sex.

184

INTERMARRIAGE PROHIBITION

There are many verses that proscribe marriages with non-Israelites, but the prohibitions only pertained to marriage with idolaters. Deuteronomy 9:3, for example, has Moses warn the Israelites who are about to enter Canaan and encounter idol-worshiping Canaanites that the Israelites must completely destroy the Canaanites. Moses also said: "Do not give your daughters to their sons or take their daughters for your sons." What is significant is that the Torah could have prohibited all intermarriage at that time as well as in the other books of the Five Books of Moses, but it only restricted intermarriage with the Canaanite idolaters.[1] There are similar restrictive prohibitions in Genesis 24:3, Exodus 34:16, Joshua 23:12, Judges 3:6 and 14:3, and 1 Kings 11:2, which do not prohibit all intermarriage.

It is possibly that the first blanket prohibition against intermarriage came from Ezra and Nehemiah. Ezra addressed intermarriage in 9:2, 12, and 10:3, and Nehemiah did so in 13:23–27.[2] However, this is not certain. It is possible that Ezra and Nehemiah were also only concerned about intermarriages that resulted in idol worship.

In Ezra 9, we are told that when Ezra came to Judea, the name Israel had at that time, he heard that all the Judeans, including the priests and Levites "have not separated from the peoples of the land, performing their abominations.... For they have taken of their daughters for themselves and for their sons; so that the holy seed have mingled themselves with the peoples of the land.... Now therefore give not your daughters to their sons, nor take their daughters for your sons." Ezra then in 10:3, instructed the people to "put away" these women. Nehemiah 13 is similar.

If Ezra and Nehemiah were only focusing on intermarriages that led to idolatry, we do not know when the blanket prohibition was promulgated.

MULTIPLE ISRAELITE INTERMARRIAGES

Not only is there no biblical prohibition before the time of Ezra and Nehemiah, many of the early Israelites, including their leaders, including Moses himself, mar-

---

1. The Torah had a strong inexplicable dislike of Canaanites. The dislike is first mentioned when in Genesis 9:20–27, Noah's son "Ham, the father of Canaan, saw the nakedness of his [drunk] father, and told his two brothers" who covered him. When "Noah awoke from his wine and knew what his youngest son [presumably Ham] had done to him, he said 'Cursed be Canaan!'" The Torah gives no reason why he cursed his grandson instead of his son Ham.
2. We do not know the dates for Ezra and Nehemiah. It is generally presumed that they lived in the mid-fifth century BCE.

ried non-Israelites. Moses married the daughter of a Midianite priest. According to the Talmud, Moses's successor Joshua married the Canaanite woman who saved the two spies that Joshua sent to Canaan and the descendants of that union made great contributions to Judaism.

All the patriarchs, except for Isaac, intermarried. Abraham married Sarai, later called Sarah, but when it appeared that she was barren, Sarai gave her Egyptian handmaid to Abram, as he was called at that time, "to be his wife."[3] She bore him Ishmael. Later, after Sarah's death, Abraham took a third wife Keturah, and had six sons with her.[4] Jacob married Leah and Rachel, who were related to him, daughters of his mother's brother, but he also married their two maids who were not related.[5] Joseph, son of Jacob, married the daughter of an Egyptian priest.

Jacob's son Judah, the ancestor of King David and the messiah, married a Canaanite. Boaz, another ancestor of King David, married Ruth a Moabite. King Solomon, David's son, married the daughter of the Pharaoh of Egypt and many more non-Israelite women, and the Bible does not criticize him for the intermarriages, but that in his old age, his wives turned him towards other gods.[6] Rehoboam, son of King Solomon who followed him as king, was the son of Solomon and married a non-Israelite woman. The judge Samson married a Philistine. And there are many others who did likewise.

All of this is interesting, but it does not dilute the current prohibition against intermarriage in any way. It emphasizes that Jews today are Rabbinical, not Biblical Jews.

---

3. Genesis 16:3.
4. Genesis 25:1–2.
5. They were concubines, but the Talmud states that concubine was a type of marriage and most importantly, their children were the leaders of several of the twelve tribes.
6. 1 Kings 11:4.

MYSTICISM AND ATHEISM

The Famed Mystical Book
Zohar May Be a Fraud

Many mystics insist that the *Zohar* was composed by Rabbi Simeon bar Yochai, called Rashbi, around the year 130 CE. They claim that the *Zohar* reveals secrets contained in God's Torah, which God did not reveal explicitly, but wants Jews to know. They say that Jews should arrange their lives and thoughts as instructed in this book. They treat it as an almost divine book. However, scholars recognize that Moses de Leon (1240–1305), a Spaniard living in Granada, wrote it around 1286 with parts of the book added by others after his death, and that the work is a pious forgery.

WHAT IS THE *ZOHAR*?

Zohar means "luminous" and alludes to the notion that God illuminates people through mysticism, which is the truth, for it reveals much about God,[1] the world, and proper behavior. But while ostensibly dealing with enlightenment, the *Zohar* is usually very difficult to understand, many of its ideas are not rational, and it is difficult to translate.

The *Zohar's* basic teaching is the doctrine of the *sefirot*, "numbers," ten divine entities that function in ten different ways. The lowest entity is Shekhina, also called *malkhut*, which mystics see as the anthropomorphic feminine part of God that interacts with humans.

The mystics are convinced that God was once whole, all of the ten divine parts

---

1. Maimonides stated in his *Guide of the Perplexed* that we are unable to know anything about God. The most we can know are negatives, such as God has no body and no emotions. He said that although the rabbis listed adjectives about God, we can say them despite their not being true.

were combined, but they became disjointed and are no longer attached. They say that humans can help God and even have a duty to perform certain acts to aid God become one again with all the ten disjointed parts reassembled, like putting Humpty Dumpty together again. When this is done, the messianic age will arrive.

SCHOLARLY VIEW

Many scholars view the notion of ten separated divine parts each acting differently as polytheism, an idea contrary to basic Judaism. Many mocked the actions that mystics claim will aid God to be made whole as unrealistic sympathetic magic, a subject discussed later in this book.[2]

They have also assembled a host of proofs showing that the *Zohar* was not an ancient document. The highly respected Rabbi Jacob Emden (1697–1776), for example, who was himself a mystic, recorded 280 contradictions, anachronisms and incorrect statements and concluded that the book is a forgery of the thirteenth-century with some later additions.[3]

THE FOLLOWING ARE SOME OF THE MANY PROOFS.

1. A renowned person visited Moses de Leon to see the ancient documents that de Leon claimed he used to copy the *Zohar*. Moses de Leon kept putting him off and later asserted that the documents had strangely disappeared. After his death, de Leon's wife admitted that the documents never existed.
2. The ideas in the *Zohar* are a later development of earlier mystical notions, showing that they were composed after these earlier works, and not in 130, as de Leon claimed.
3. Neither the rabbis nor anyone else knew anything about the *Zohar* until de Leon introduced it.

---

2. See, for example, Gershom Scholem, *Major Trends in Jewish Mysticism* (New York: Schocken Press, 2011).
3. Mortimer J. Cohen, *Jacob Emden: A Man of Controversy* (Philadelphia: Dropsie College, 1937); Jacob Emden, Sidney B. Leperer, Meir H. Wise, *Megillat Sefer: The Autobiography of Rabbi Jacob Emden* (Baltimore, MD: Shaftek Enterprises LLC 2016). Many other prominent rabbis questioned the authenticity of the *Zohar*, including: Rabbi Yitzchak d'min Acco (1194–1270) who spoke with de Leon; Rabbi Eliyahu del Medigo (c. 1458–1493), Rabbi Yahiya Kapach (1850–1931); and Rabbi Leon da Modena (1571–1648) who wrote *Ari Nohem* debunking the *Zohar*.

4. He mixed together later rabbis with those who lived long before them, people from different centuries, latter *amoraim* with earlier *tannaim*.

5. Rabbis are named in the *Zohar* who lived long after Rashbi, who he could not have known.

6. The *Zohar* author knew of the existence of vowels and accent marks used in the Torah books and gave them mystical interpretations. However, these items were not invented until the ninth century, seven centuries after the alleged composition date.

7. The terms "master of *dikduk* (grammar)" and "*tenuah gedola*" (long vowel) are used in the *Zohar* even though they were not coined until the tenth and eleventh centuries, respectively.

8. In contrast, the author used the Aramaic language improperly, mistakes Rashbi would not have made.

9. He included words of Spanish origin, words Rashbi would not have known.

10. He inserted terms from Jewish philosophy of the Middle Ages.

11. The book contains ideas copied from the eleventh-century *Kuzari* of Judah Halevi.

12. The author introduces Maimonides's twelfth-century concept about physics.

13. The volume mentions putting on two pairs of tefillin, a practice that arose in the twelfth century.

14. The *Zohar* discusses the Kol Nidre prayer of Yom Kippur, a ceremony that began in the eleventh century.

15. The language of the *Zohar* is later than its alleged date of composition.

16. There are many incorrect quotations from the Bible and the Talmud. The latter did not exist in 130.

17. Prophecies in the volume inform the reader that the *Zohar* will be revealed around 1300 CE, a blatant attempt to justify its late appearance.

18. There are parallel passages between the *Zohar* and other books that were indisputably composed by Moses de Leon, including mistakes in the original books that de Leon copied into his *Zohar*.

19. There is no mention in the Talmud or Midrashim that the alleged author of the *Zohar*, Rabbi Simeon bar Yochai, was interested in mysticism. Thus, de Leon took the wrong hero for his work.

20. There are many errors, many of which Rashbi could not have made, such as:

the Babylonian Talmud states that Pinchas ben Yair was Rashbi's son-in-law; de Leon mistakenly calls him Rashbi's father-in-law.

21. Gershom Scholem states that the *Zohar* was influenced by Christian beliefs and sites as one of many examples the description of demons.

SUMMARY

In summary, the *Zohar* is the most prominent book of Jewish mysticism and is considered holy by many people. It contains a lot of the most important notions of modern Jewish mysticism. However, the book is not what it claims to be, its ideas are at best obscure and incomprehensible, its concept of God is curious and polytheistic, it gives people wrong ideas about Judaism, and it encourage a passivity that stifles people from intellectual and emotional growth.

The Spiritual Revolution of Rav Kook

We can and should learn from all sources. Even rationalists like me can read, enjoy, and learn from the writings of mystics. We do not have to accept everything they say as being true, but there are things they say which are true.

RABBI AVRAHAM YITZCHAK HAKOHEN KOOK

Rabbi Kook was born in Latvia in 1865 and died in Jerusalem in 1935. His father was a Mitnagid, opposed to mysticism. His mother was a descendant of Chabad, a Hassidic group. When asked "What will you be?" he answered, "I will be both." In 1920, at the age of fifty-five, he moved to Jerusalem and became its chief rabbi.

Rabbi Kook's writings are generally, but not always very mystical and difficult to understand. However, Rabbi Ari Ze'ev Schwartz's book *The Spiritual Revolution of Rav Kook* unravels the writings with a new translation, with each chapter being divided into clearly stated topic headings added by Rabbi Schwartz, such as the individual, Torah, God, *teshuva*, prayer, creativity, Zionism, science, and vegetarianism.[1] Rabbi Schwartz also introduces each section with a clear explanation of what Rabbi Kook is saying.

Rabbi Kook became chief rabbi long before the State of Israel was reestablished in 1948. He lived during a period when most pioneers who sacrificed their lives and came to Israel faced difficulties in their attempts to build up the land of Israel, were irreligious Jews, and were often men and women antagonistic to religion. He is properly credited and even commended for working to draw all people close, even those who rebelled against religion. He taught that each person should want

---

1. Rabbi Ari Ze'ev Schwartz, *The Spiritual Revolution of Rav Kook* (Jerusalem: Gefen Publishing House, 2018).

to influence friends and be influenced by them for the increase of the greater good. It is through the combining of different talents within each individual that a society is formed. He also taught that everyone should find a personal Torah and realize that there is not just one type of Torah, but an endless variety that can speak to countless individuals in different ways.

The following are some other of Rabbi Kook's ideas:

- The highest type of thinking is never rejecting any idea in the world. No one has a monopoly on truth. There is truth in other religions.
- Secular knowledge is important. We must teach our children what is necessary for them to know how to confront the trials of life.
- I walk around with an overwhelming jealousy of the secular world. It is a jealousy that consumes me. For is it possible that the power of creativity has ceased within the religious world?
- Atheists may be on the right track. They may be denying an immature and distorted image of God. In other words, their denial of God is really a deeper quest for a higher, more sophisticated understanding. Atheism comes to purify the dirt, the embarrassments that have stuck to a religion that lacks any comprehension. Religious people should understand this and pay attention to what is bothering them.
- One should not only study a religious text to receive a new idea; it should serve as a tool toward understanding oneself.
- The role of an author of any book is to begin the discussion of an idea, yet it is the reader's responsibility to respond by searching for their own personal meaning.
- The ideal perfection of a person can only be accomplished by focusing one's energy on improving one's own individual self as much as possible. Yet at the same time a person should keep in mind that one's own individual perfection will never be completed until the Jewish people have successfully reached national perfection.
- People should realize that being totally perfect is unattainable and should understand that a person's true greatness is found in the journey of constantly striving to become a little better.
- More than asking God to forgive our misdeeds, we should learn to forgive ourselves and work to assure that we do not repeat our mistakes.

- Personal growth requires us to first clarify the character trait we want to assume, and only after knowing this to try to embody it.
- A person who thinks that prayer changes God's will is blaspheming.
- The demand for physical activity is enormous. We need healthy bodies. But we have focused on our souls and have forgotten the holiness of the body.
- We must agree with Maimonides who taught that the stories of creation told in the Torah should not be understood literally; rather, they have a deeper lesson to teach.
- It is hard to believe that God created a world that Genesis 1:31 calls "very good," and yet made it impossible for humankind to survive without distorting its moral sensitivity by murdering animals.

A Mystical View of Rabbi Aryeh Kaplan

Rabbi Aryeh Kaplan (1934–1983), the author of the mystical book *Immortality, Resurrection, and the Age of the Universe, A Kabbalistic View*, was an American Orthodox rabbi who was acclaimed for his many books, about fifty in all, his knowledge of physics, and Jewish mysticism.[1] He worked initially as a physicist, but in 1965, when he was around thirty years old, he changed careers and began to practice as a rabbi. He secured his rabbinical ordination from rabbis in Israel. He stressed the mystical harmony of science and religion in his writings. His book is only sixty-four pages long. It is followed in this volume by a long sermon by the mystic Rabbi Israel Lipschitz (1782–1860), delivered by him in 1842, sixty-seven pages long. It addresses most of the same subjects and defends the assertions with essentially the same supports and opinions as those by Rabbi Kaplan.

RABBI KAPLAN'S UNDERSTANDING OF THE ISSUES

Rabbi Aryeh Kaplan's book was published in 1993, a decade after his death, by people who respected the rabbi and his ideas greatly. The volume contains his mystical views about the age of the universe, the reasons for the long lives of many early biblical figures before the flood, which was only slightly reduced after the flood and then reduced even further, immortality in Judaic sources, resurrection, astrology, the effect of stars on humans, angels, and the reason for the religious differences between men and women. He felt that women are inferior to men and the exclusion of women from many Jewish practices is proper.[2]

---

1. Rabbi Aryeh Kaplan, Yaakov Elman, Israel Lipschutz, *Immortality, Resurrection and the Age of the Universe, A Kabbalistic View* (New York: Ktav Publishing House, 1993).
2. Rabbi Kaplan was not alone in holding this erroneous view, nor were mystics the only group

None of these subjects are explicitly mentioned in the Torah, and arguably not even hinted at.[3] Yet, today many Jews believe in all of them, even some rationally thinking Jews. Rabbi Kaplan offers his views on each from mystical sources. He starts with the notion that whatever the ancients said is true, even the somewhat absurd narratives in Midrashim, which others, such as Maimonides assert should not be taken literally for they are only parables designed to teach moral lessons.[4] Kaplan also asserts that every statement made by an ancient rabbi is true even if the majority of rabbis, even those far smarter than he, disagreed with what the rabbi said.[5] With these two ideas as his base of his thinking, Rabbi Kaplan contends that he can prove the truthfulness of each of the ideas he is discussing.

ADAM AND EVE WERE NOT THE FIRST HUMANS

Relying on a kabbalistic book, *Sefer ha-Temunah* (*Book of the Figure*), traditionally composed in the first century but written around 1270, a book rejected by other mystics, Rabbi Kaplan asserts that there were other worlds before Adam and Eve were created. These worlds were populated by people who were still alive when Adam and Eve were born.[6]

THE AGE OF THE UNIVERSE

Thus, because of the information in this mystical book, even if we accept the biblical chronology which seems to assert that the world existed only about six

---

that held this mistaken notion, an idea that has hurt women greatly. The famed generally rational Bible commentator Gersonides argued that women are a breed between animals and men. Seymour Feldman, *Gersonides: Judaism within the Limits of Reason* (Liverpool: Littman Library of Jewish Civilization, Liverpool University Press, 2010).

3. Some scholars assert that the late book Daniel, in chapter 12, speaks about resurrection, but others contend that Daniel is not speaking about individuals but the nation of Israel.

4. In his essay called *Chelek*, Maimonides stated that anyone who accepts the notion that what Midrashim say is the truth is a fool and so are those who dismiss the Midrashim entirely since they are not true, because the rabbis wrote the fables as parables to teach lessons.

5. Many Jews held this view, even Rabbi J.B. Soloveitchik. Some went so far as to say that the intelligence of the ancients was far superior to that of moderns because the level of intelligence has been declining. They use this argument to support their insistence that we must do what the ancients said we should do without change. Menachem Kellner shows that Maimonides rejected this notion. Menachem Kellner, *Maimonides on the "Decline of the Generations" and the Nature of Rabbinic Authority*, (New York: SUNY Press, 1996).

6. Around 1550, the famed Rabbis Moses Cordovero and Isaac Luria, known as the Holy Ari, rejected this view. Kaplan notes the disagreement.

thousand years since Adam and Eve, Judaism can accept the scientific finding that the world is millions of years old.

LENGTH OF ANCIENT LIVES

Rabbi Kaplan explains that originally the descendants of Adam and Eve were meant to live a long life, but they began to intermarry with the pre-Adam primitive humans and this explains why early humans lived long lives, but the intermarriages caused a reduction in their lifespan.[7]

RESURRECTION

He argues that science proves that resurrection is possible, for we see that we can clone animals, which is the bringing the former being back to life. He adds that humans can be cloned by using the DNA of the dead person and when the DNA is not available "it will be restored prophetically," but "the soul and its memories would have to be supplied by God Himself."

ASTROLOGY

Like many mystics, he believed in the efficacy and truthfulness of astrology and writes that it is "a combination of science and the supernatural." He describes stars as divine creations that have angels associated with them, and the stars and their angels influence humans, which can be verified "as we probe into our classical texts."

WOMEN

The rabbi asserts that Jewish law is different for men and women because Eve and her female descendants' ability to think was reduced when Eve ate from the forbidden tree. Men, he asserts, can learn from past experiences, an ability he states that women lack.

---

7. Based on the Midrash *Genesis Rabba* 26:5.

The Strange Story of Moshe Chaim Luzzatto

One of the most important books on Jewish ethics is *Mesillat Yesharim*, translated as *The Path of the Upright* or *The Path of the Just*. Amazon describes the book as: "Of all creatures, only the human being was created incomplete in the sense that one must pay conscientious attention over the course of a lifetime to develop and refine one's character and personality. In the Jewish tradition, this development takes on a sacred dimension, and one of the classic guides to outline a clear, progressive path toward spiritual perfection is *The Path of the Just*. Beginning with an essential essay on Man's Duty in this World, the author methodically charts a course of personal growth like climbing the rungs of a spiritual ladder that ultimately leads to true humility and holiness." The following is the strange story about the author of this very popular book, Moshe Chaim Luzzatto.

LUZZATTO'S VIEW ABOUT THE MESSIAH

While the concept of a messiah sent to miraculously reorganize civilization and bring peace is not in the Hebrew Bible, it began to be accepted by Jews around the fourth or third century BCE, and later by Christianity. There is no single view as to how the messianic age will occur, or when, and many notions, along a wide spectrum of beliefs have been developed, including the radical mystical proposal of Moshe Chaim Luzzatto (b. 1707 in Padua, d. 1746 in Acre, Israel), known by the Hebrew acronym Ramchal, an Italian rabbi and kabbalist. Luzzatto is more respected today, long after his death, than when he was alive. Rational thinkers reject his kabbalistic opinion about the messiah.

THE SUPERNATURAL SOURCE OF HIS BELIEF

When Luzzatto was twenty years old, he began to claim that he heard the voice of a divine being, which he called a *maggid* (one who communicates). He said that the *maggid* revealed mystical secrets to him. He was not alone in making this claim. Joseph Karo, the author of the *Shulchan Arukh* (*The Code of Jewish Law*), also said that he spoke with a maggid, an angelic narrator and wrote a book about it.

Luzzatto also wrote about his encounter with the *maggid*. He wrote that before his first encounter, he "fell into a trance, awoke, heard a voice saying, 'I came to you to reveal the hidden secrets of God.' He revealed to me that he was a *maggid* sent from heaven, and he gave me certain incantations that I was to perform to cause him to come to me in the future. I never saw him but heard his voice. The prophet Elijah also came to me and told me secrets. I was also visited by the angel Metatron and souls whose identity I did not know. Every day, I write down the revelations each of them imparts to me."

Luzzatto also wrote his views about the messiah and how Jews can hasten his coming in books such as *Maamar Hageulah*. Unfortunately for Luzzatto, leading Italian rabbinical authorities were highly suspicious of him, thought that he might have non-traditional Jewish beliefs, and threatened to excommunicate him.

They recalled that one hundred years earlier another young mystic, Shabbtai Tzvi (1626–1676), had claimed that he was the expected messiah, captured the attention of hundreds of thousands of Jews and caused devastating dissention. Tzvi taught that Jews must give up certain religious practices and ideas. He ended up recanting his teachings and converting to Islam. Luzzatto admitted that he agreed with some of Tzvi's views, and the rabbis were therefore concerned that Luzzatto's writings were dangerous and heretical.

OTHER LUZZATTO BELIEFS

Luzzatto accepted the views of the sixteenth century Lurianic Kabbalah that God is made up of ten parts, the lowest part being feminine, called *malkhut* and Shekhina. He believed that the ten divine parts became disassembled and if humans can help God reassemble, the reassembled God would bring the messiah. He married in 1731 and felt that his marriage was an act of sympathetic magic. He believed that he could perform an act on earth that could affect heaven. As he, a male joined with his wife, a female, it could cause the union of the male and female parts of

God. He felt he had the duty to perform this sex because he believed that he was the reincarnation of the biblical Moses and felt that he was created, like Moses, to rescue the Jewish people.

HIS FINAL YEARS

Persecuted and mocked in Padua, in 1743, Luzzatto and his family traveled to Israel and lived there until he and his family died in 1746 in a plague, when he was thirty-nine.

HIS PLACE IN HISTORY

Despite his radical views and his persecution during his lifetime, many Hassidim today consider him a saintly kabbalist and accept many of his kabbalistic notions. Many yeshivot, rabbinical schools, even those which are not mystically-minded, encourage their students to study his ethical treatise *Mesillat Yesharim* (*The Path of the Upright*).

MESILLAT YESHARIM

The Jewish Publication Society published an excellent volume of *Mesillat Yesharim*.[1] The publisher states that this "is a classic of Jewish ethical literature. Written by one of the leading kabbalists of the late Middle Ages, it is also a window into the kabbalist's understanding of the connection between ethics and mystical vision."

Luzzatto discusses the steps, or path, that people need to take to reach the level of holiness. These are as follows: 1) the developments of the trait of watchfulness, 2) the trait of zeal, 3) cleanliness, 4) separation, 5) purity, 6) *hassidut* (meaning, to Luzzatto, combining rational and intellectual principles with proper behavior, "An ignoramus cannot be a hassid"), 7) humility, 8) fear of sin, and 9) the goal, holiness.

Stressing the mystical concept that one can cling to God, Luzzatto states that "the purpose for which man was created is realized not in this world, but in the world to come." "One who is holy," he writes, "clings constantly to his God, his soul traveling in channels of truth, amidst the love and fear of his Creator – such

---

1. Rabbi Moshe Chaim Luzzatto, *Mesillat Yesharim* (*Path of the Just* [*Upright*], trans. Mordecai M. Kaplan (Philadelphia: JPS, 2010). The 509-page volume also includes Luzzatto's original Hebrew.

a person is one walking before God in the land of the living, here in this world. Such a person is himself considered a tabernacle, a sanctuary, an altar."

THE RESULTS OF SUCH A LIFE

The results that he describes are mystical. He writes, "the things that will help a man in the quest after holiness are solitude and abstinence, for when there are no distractions, the soul is able to gather strength and to commune with the Creator." A person who conquers his corporeal desires will "cleave to the holiness of God, blessed be he, and thus be rendered perfect...be endowed with the holy spirit... his power of comprehension [will] exceed mortal limitations. In his communion with God he will attain such excellence that he will be entrusted with the power of resurrection, as were Elijah and Elishah," (which the Bible states were able to resurrect dead bodies).

Secular Jewish Culture

Secular Jewish Culture, edited by Yaakov Malkin, is an important, indeed valuable book, a book that will prompt people to think.[1] While focusing on Judaism, the book will open the minds of people of all religions. As previously mentioned, the first Chief Rabbi in Israel, Rabbi Kook, wrote: religious people can learn much from atheists. Religious people may be living an immature and distorted image of religion and God. In contrast, the denial by atheists of God is really a deeper quest for a higher, more sophisticated understanding of life and human responsibility. Rabbi Kook wrote that atheism comes to purify the dirt, the embarrassments, that have stuck to a religion that fails to understand the absurdity of some of its teachings and practices. Religious people should understand this, and pay attention to what is bothering the atheists, learn from them, and improve.

SECULAR CULTURE

The philosopher Blaise Pascal[2] (1623–1662) argued the opposite, that people should not act like atheists, but should bet their lives on whether God exists. This idea is called Pascal's wager. He argued that practicing religion does no harm, but the failure to be religious could result in eternal punishment by God. Taking both possibilities into consideration, since being religious causes no harm, but being an atheist could cause an eternity in Hell, it is a good bet to be religious and foolish to act otherwise.

---

1. Yaakov Malkin, *Secular Jewish Culture* (Library of Secular Judaism, 2017); Hebrew version, Jerusalem: Keter Books, 2005.
2. Blaise Pascal, *Pensees*, trans. W.F. Trotter (New York: Dover Publications, 2013).

There are obvious problems with Pascal's wager. First and foremost, feigning belief will not fool God. Second, since there are so many different concepts of god, there is a high probability that the wager will choose the wrong god and thereby eliminate the advantage of Pascal's bet. Third, similarly, what one religion considers proper behavior another rules blasphemy. Additionally, Pascal's wager ignores the benefits of atheism pointed out by Rabbi Kook. Many religious people live a passive life ignoring the good things that God made available, and ignoring what Maimonides, atheists, and most other thinkers recognize as a human obligation, to work to improve themselves and society.

YAAKOV MALKIN AND OTHERS

The editor of this excellent collection of articles, Yaakov Malkin, is a world-recognized scholar, professor, award-winner, and expert on secular Judaism. What he and the assembled thinkers in this book say is eye-opening. Malkin introduces his book informing readers of the many contributions that secular Jews made to Judaism. He also lists five common elements shared by religious and secular Jews. The book follows with close to three-dozen essays from well-informed thinkers.

Among the many are famous Jewish novelists such as Amos Oz, A.B. Yehoshua, S. Yizhar, Haim Be'er; politicians like Shulamit Aloni; professors such as Amos Funkenstein, Yeshayahu Leibovitz, Arye S. Assar, Rachel Elior; Justice of the Israeli Supreme Court Haim Cohn; and many others.

We discover in reading this book that Secular Jewish Culture is the culture of the majority, not the minority, of Jews around the world. We are told what secular Jews think and believe and what they consider important. Many questions are addressed. Why do so many Jews reject many religious ideas and practices? What are the origins of Jewish theology? What is the significance to Jewish Culture of Hebrew, the Jewish state, the definition of what is a Jew, and prophetical traditions? What part did Spinoza, Maimonides and others play regarding secular Judaism? Should secular Jewish culture or some parts of it be taught in Israeli schools? What change has secular Judaism made to Bible study? What impact has been made on Judaism because of new ideas about the role of women in Judaism and the current more sophisticated understanding of God? Does it make sense to want to be Jewish but not want to obey rabbinical laws? Shouldn't we strive for human happiness and well-being, dignity, justice, and the dignity of man? Was Einstein correct when he said the belief in a personal god is an "expression of human weakness"? What is Zionism? What makes the state of Israel a Jewish state?

The book, in short, is very enlightening. Readers will finish the book with a new understanding of life and the purpose of religion.

Amos Oz Considers Religion Irrational, but Makes Good Points

Amos Oz (1939–2018) was the author of many books and the winner of multiple awards. Many considered him to be Israel's most famous author of his time. He was a proponent of the two-state solution to the Israel-Palestinian conflict and was outspoken on the subject, He considered religion irrational. His last published book *Dear Zealots*,[1] should make us think.

THE BOOK

Dear Zealots is a short book of 140 large-print pages, which was translated expertly from the Hebrew by Jessica Cohen. It is broken into three parts: Dear Zealots; Many Lights, Not One Light; and Dreams Israel Should Let Go of Soon.

THE FOLLOWING ARE SOME OF OZ'S THOUGHTS IN "DEAR ZEALOTS"

- Fanaticism dates back much earlier than Islam, earlier than Christianity and Judaism. It is an elemental fixture of human nature, a "bad gene."
- Fanatics of all kinds, in all places at all times, loath and fear change, suspecting that it is nothing less than a betrayal resulting from dark, base motives.
- It is not the volume of your voice that defines you as a fanatic, but rather, primarily, your tolerance – or lack thereof – for your opponent's voices.
- Fanatics tend to live in a black-and-white world, with a simplistic view of good against evil. The fanatic is in fact a person who can only count to one.

---

1. Amos Oz, *Dear Zealots: Letters from a Divided Land*, trans. Jessica Cohen (Boston: Houghton Mifflin, Harcourt, 2018).

- The urge to follow the crowd and the passion to belong to the majority are fertile ground for fanatics.
- One of the distinct hallmarks of the fanatic is his fervent desire to change you so that you will be like him.
- An example is ultra-Orthodox fanaticism, which secludes itself inside a walled ghetto and defends itself against anything different.
- I, for one, have never met a fanatic with a sense of humor. Nor have I ever known anyone capable of making a joke at his own expense become a fanatic.
- To remove the fanaticism that hides inside our souls means ridiculing, just a little, our own convictions; being curious; and trying to take a peek, from time to time, not only through our neighbor's window but, more important, at the reality from that window, which will necessarily be different from the one seen through our own.

OZ'S THOUGHTS IN "MANY LIGHTS, NOT ONE LIGHT"

- Judaism is a culture, rather than just a religion or a nationality.
- Jewish culture is analogous to the musical concept of counterpoint, as well as to the notion of human polyphony, whereby the community is viewed as a chorus of different voices, or different instruments orchestrated by an agreed set of rules.
- Jewish culture has been one of ever-expanding ripples, as though a giant meteor fell into an ocean and the effects are still rippling in an ever-wider circle around the revelation at Sinai.
- Some people maintain that the secular pioneers that helped the establishment of Israel were no more than unwitting instruments of divine supervision, and that everything they believed in, their entire self-determination, made no difference. They were nothing more than "the Messiah's donkey." Such an insult is intolerable.
- I sometime reduce all the commandments into one: Cause no pain. I am sometimes willing to narrow down humanism and pluralism into one simple formula: Recognize the equal right of all human beings to be different.
- Disagreement is not a troubling state of weakness, but a vital climate for the growth of a creative life.

OZ'S IDEAS IN "DREAMS ISRAEL SHOULD LET GO OF SOON"

- If there are not two states in Israel very soon, there will be one. It will be an Arab state that stretches from the Mediterranean to the Jordan River.
- Jews and Arabs can and should live together, but I insist on the right of Israeli Jews, like other people, to be the majority, if only on a tiny strip of land.

Fascinating Ideas of Arnold Ehrlich on Noah and Abraham

The great scholar Arnold Ehrlich (1848–1919) authored *Mikra Ki-Pheshuto* (*The Bible According to Its Literal Meaning*), in three Hebrew volumes.[1] His ideas are frequently unconventional, even untraditional – for example, he denied that Kings David and Solomon ever existed – yet his ideas are generally very intelligent and thought provoking. The following are some of his ideas on the Noah flood story and the introductory biblical statements about the patriarch Abraham in Genesis 6:9–11:32. We may not agree with what he says, but what is most important is that he makes us think.

EHRLICH'S IDEAS

1. How should we translate Genesis 6:12: *ki hishchit khol basar et darkho al haaretz?* The Jewish Publication Society *Holy Scriptures* translates it "[God decided to destroy the world with a flood] for all flesh corrupted their way upon the earth." How did humans and animals corrupt their ways? Ehrlich offers a novel approach: humans and animals began to eat meat and even became cannibals. This, Ehrlich writes, is contrary to the biblical spirit. We read in the story of the Garden of Eden that Adam and Eve were only allowed to eat fruits and vegetables. The prophet Isaiah foresaw that in the ideal world of the future the lion would lie with the lamb because humans and animals would no longer consume flesh. However, realizing that human nature desires meat, God allowed Noah and humanity to consume meat, but only under

---

1. Ehrlich, *Mikra Ki-Pheshuto*.

certain conditions. (Ehrlich also writes that the flood obviously didn't destroy fish who survive in water. However, we may ask why God didn't kill fish as well, for they also eat living beings such as worms and other fish.)

2. There is a marked difference between the flood stories of the ancients and the biblical report. The former are filled with miraculous events, such as the saved humans needing to throw stones to create people to repopulate the world, but the biblical version is generally told as a natural event. Noah is given time to construct the ark and gather animals, the ark's rooms are arranged to accommodate its inhabitants. Men and women slept separately so that only two rooms were necessary instead of four for the four families.

3. Verse 8:21 should not be translated "The inclination (*yetzer*) of man is evil from birth," which fits the Christian notion that we need Jesus to save humans from their evil nature. The true translation is "The human inclination today is more evil than it was in earlier times." People were getting worse and worse.

4. Why does the Torah mention that Noah cursed his grandson Canaan that he would be the lowest level slave? Why do we need to know this? This tale justifies the Israelite conquest of the land of Canaan. Slaves own nothing, so the Israelites did not hurt them by taking their property.

5. Why are some of the names mentioned in the Five Books of Moses different when reported in the book of Chronicles? The author(s) of Chronicles was not careful in recording names.

6. Scripture states in 11:5 and 18:19 that God came down from heaven to examine what was occurring on earth. This is contrary to our current notion of God not being restricted to a single place. However, the ancients thought that God dwelt in Heaven. The Greeks had a similar notion. Interestingly, after the story of the revelation of the Decalogue at Mount Sinai, this primitive notion does not reappear in the Hebrew Bible.

7. One of the purposes for the Bible telling us the story of Abraham's nephew Lot is to help us understand Abraham better. To fully understand something, we need to understand its opposite.

8. The Bible states that Abraham's father died to inform us that Abraham didn't heartlessly abandon his father when he left his homeland, traveled to Canaan, and settled there. Since his father died, he had no need to care for him.

9. The Bible frequently explains the origin of names in a poetic and sermonic

but not linguistic manner, even though it claims that it is giving a linguistic reason. Babylon was not called by this name because God had mixed up the languages of the people at the tower of Babel. The Hebrew word for "mix" is *b-l-l*, while the root of Babylon is *b-b-l*. These words are not related. Babylon may have been named after the word for god, Baal.

10. One may not agree with all of Arnold Ehrlich's interpretations, but one must recognize that they provoke us to think.

Meditation Works

Although I am a rationalist, and encourage thinking and common sense in all of my books, (insisting that Aristotle was correct when he said people who do not think are no better than animals and plants because what distinguishes humans from animals and plants is their ability to think), I still find that meditation – stopping the thought process for a while – works, and it does so in a very beneficial manner. I will give three examples.

HOW MEDITATION COULD WORK

I enjoy reading a variety of books, and most especially the narrative parts of the Hebrew Bible. I find that the stories raise many questions, which I find fascinating. Sometimes, I am unable to unravel and understand an event immediately. Many years ago on a Sabbath evening, I was lying on the couch and wasn't thinking about my inability to decipher a tale. I did not think about it at all. Suddenly, the answer came to me. I felt at the time that it was almost like a prophetic revelation. It wasn't a revelation, of course, but it felt like there was divine intervention. I understood that if one stops thinking about a subject consciously, the subconscious continues to work out the problem, and eventually brings the solution to the conscious mind. Yes, humans need to think, but they can also think subconsciously without realizing it.

Another example: I worked in the US Army in the Pentagon first as a colonel and later as a brigadier general. The army seemed to think that I was smart and gave me all kinds of difficult tasks. Sometimes, I was unable to resolve the difficulty immediately, but since I was allowed to leave the building whenever I wanted, morning or afternoon, I would go for a jog. I ran six miles every day while working at the Pentagon, and whenever I could not find the solution to a problem immediately, I would leave my desk and go for a run. While running, I did not think of the problem that I faced while inside the building. Yet, remarkably, in what seemed like every time, when I returned, I knew the solution. And the solutions were good. Perhaps this was why I was promoted to the rank of brigadier general.

One final example: I find that when I close my mind as I am about to go to sleep, good ideas come to me on a subject that I am writing about. Again, my subconscious worked out the idea. I am not talking about ideas that come when I am sleeping. These are not usually good. But the ones that come before sleep, when the conscious mind is empty, are good.

Ntathu Allen published an easy to read informative book on meditation which is called *Meditation for Beginners: How to Meditate for People who Hate to Sit Still.*[1]

As far as I can see, this works. But what she does not mention is that it can cause subconscious understandings to rise to the consciousness.

1. Ntathu Allen, *Meditation for Beginners: How to Meditate for People Who Hate to Sit Still* (TCK Publishing, 2014).

MORE ON MAIMONIDES

Maimonides's Unknown Personality

Too many people, including rabbis and scholars focus on just two of Maimonides's books to help them decide Maimonides's frame of mind: his philosophical *Guide of the Perplexed* and his code of law which he called *Mishneh Torah*, which means the Second Torah.[1] Focusing on these two books, many are unable, or unwilling to think that the same man wrote a philosophy book that they feel is not wholly consonant with traditional thinking, and a book that outlines traditional Jewish thinking. Some people are therefore convinced that Maimonides did not write the *Guide of the Perplexed*. Others are simply confused and do not know how to deal with what they see as a problem. There are several mistakes that these people make.

CONTRARY TO WHAT SOME PEOPLE THINK, *MISHNEH TORAH* HAS PHILOSOPHY

Mishneh Torah also contains many philosophical ideas, especially in the first of the fourteen books, ideas which are also in Maimonides's *Guide of the Perplexed*, such as his discussion about what we can know about God.

MAIMONIDES DISCUSSED THE 613 COMMANDMENTS TO HELP PEOPLE

Most ancient rabbis recognized that the first report that the Torah contains 613 commandments dates to the third century CE, when Rabbi Simlai mentioned

---

1. Feeling that the title degrades the divine Torah, many gave it the title *Yad*, whose letters denote fourteen and refer to the fourteen parts of *Mishneh Torah*, while the word itself means hand and refers to the aid that Maimonides gives to the Jewish population by listing the 613 commandments that the rabbis thought were explicit or implicit in the Torah.

this concept in a sermon that is recorded in the Babylonian Talmud, *Makkot* 23b. The Talmud states: "Rabbi Simlai gave as a sermon (*darash Rabi Simlai*): 613 commandments were communicated to Moses – 365 negative commands, corresponding to the number of solar days [in a year], and 248 positive commands, corresponding to the number of the members [bones covered with flesh] of a man's body." Rabbi Simlai invented the number 613 because it fit his sermon: A person should observe the Torah with all his body parts (248) every day (365). The two numbers total 613.

As far as we know, no one thought that there were 613 biblical commandments before Rabbi Simlai delivered his sermon. In fact, 150 years before Rabbi Simlai, ben Azzai is quoted as saying that there were three hundred biblical commands.[2] E.E. Urbach wrote: "In the Tannaitic sources this number [613] is unknown."[3]

Maimonides certainly knew that the notion of 613 biblical commands is only sermonic, but also knew that the general population accepted the notion, and he knew that they wanted information about what Judaism required and what it prohibited, so he wrote *Mishneh Torah* to meet the need of the general population. He included commands that he felt the rabbis considered either explicit or implicit in the Torah, or, to state this differently, he helped fellow Jews by listing and explaining what he thought the rabbis considered Jews are required to do and not do.

MAIMONIDES ADDRESSED THE NEEDS OF THE UNEDUCATED PUBLIC IN HIS *GUIDE OF THE PERPLEXED*

Many people who do not understand Maimonides's personality, are not aware of his sensitivity to the needs of the general population, how he wanted to help them, (as seen in his *Mishneh Torah*), or that he wrote his *Guide of the Perplexed* for two audiences, the intellectual and learned reader and those who were unlearned and had traditional but unsophisticated views. Doing so, he did not follow the practice of most writers of philosophy who write their books at a high level and address it to intellectuals.

---

2. Midrash, *Sifrei Devarim* 76.
3. Ephraim E. Urbach, *The Sages: Their Concepts and Beliefs* trans. Israel Abrahams (Cambridge, MA: Harvard University Press, 1987). See my book *Mysteries of Judaism II* (Jerusalem: Gefen Publishing House, 2017) chapter 23, "There are not 613 biblical commands," for more information on this subject, including the views of sages agreeing the 613 is sermonic, not real.

Menachem Kellner[4] writes, for example, that Don Isaac Abarbanel (in his *Rosh Amanah*), and many others recognize that Maimonides composed his thirteen principles of Judaism for the less educated public to strengthen their feelings about Judaism. Abarbanel faults those who take "Maimonides's words at face value."

Leo Strauss, Shlomo Pines,[5] Yeshayahu Leibowitz[6] and other scholars also explain that there is an "exoteric and esoteric Maimonides." Exoteric statements are ideas that Maimonides writes which he felt were untrue, but necessary to teach and help the less educated people, most of them Jews, because he recognized that they will feel threatened if they are told their long-held ideas are untrue. He called these "essential truths." The esoteric statements are hints that Maimonides does not state explicitly, but which he expects the learned Jew, who knows both Jewish and non-Jewish studies, to draw from his writings and understand.

This exoteric-esoteric approach to understanding Maimonides is supported by Maimonides's own writings. In his *Guide of the Perplexed* 3:28, he explains that there are two kinds of truths: true truths and essential truths. "True truths" are statements that express a truth that can help one understand an idea and grow intellectually. These are what Strauss, Pines, Leibowitz, and others called esoteric teachings.

An "essential truth" is a tradition, a mistaken or wrong notion. These truths are not taught because they are correct, but to fulfill a social purpose like instilling obedience to the Torah, regulating social relations, improving humanity or society, and alleviating fears.

Maimonides was not the first person to recognize the importance of teaching "essential [but untrue] truths." The Greek philosopher Plato writes in his *Republic* and other works that the masses need to be taught untruthful myths – which he called "noble lies" – to survive.

Maimonides gives many examples of "essential truths." He states, for instance, that the Torah teaches that God becomes angry with those who disobey God, even though this is only an "essential truth." God does not really become angry.

---

4. Menachem Kellner, *Principles of Faith (Rosh Amanah)*. (Liverpool: Littman Library Of Jewish Civilization; Revised ed., 2004).

5. In two introductory essays to the *Guide of the Perplexed*, 1963.

6. Yeshayahu Leibowitz, *Conversations with Yeshayahu Leibowitz* (Jerusalem: Mira Ofran, several volumes 1995–2003).

The Torah transmitted the idea that God becomes angry because it is necessary for the masses to believe that God becomes angry if they disobey God in order that they control and improve their behavior.[7]

HIS LETTER TO THE JEWS OF YEMEN

All too many writers about Maimonides also ignore his writings other than the *Guide of the Perplexed* and *Mishneh Torah* where he shows his concern for the needs and feelings of fellow Jews. He used the concept of essential truths when he wrote to the persecuted Jews of Yemen. In his *Letter to Yemen*, he assures the Yemenite Jews that the messiah will be coming soon to relieve their suffering, even though he was convinced that this matter was impossible to predict. The Yemenites never forgot Maimonides's consolation, and to this day they thank and praise him daily many times when they recite their Kaddish prayer.

HELPING PEOPLE DAILY

Another of the many instances showing Maimonides's feelings towards the need to help other people can be seen in his letter to Samuel ibn Tibbon who translated the *Guide of the Perplexed* into Hebrew and wanted to visit Maimonides.

In the letter, Maimonides tells somethings about his daily activities. He tells how, as the Sultan's physician, he must travel every day[8] from his home in Fostat to Cairo to check on the Sultan's health and to care for his harem. When he returns to Fostat, half the day is gone, and he is exhausted and hungry. Many people are in his home, from the government to common people, wanting to see him. He asks to be excused until he has eaten the one meal he eats each day. Then he sees the petitioners who generally do not leave until early morning. The last ones he can only see while lying down. When the last one leaves, he is so exhausted he is unable to speak. On Shabbat, he is also busy, teaching the people. In view of this constant involvement in official and community affairs, he tells ibn Tibbon that he will have little time to speak with him.

---

7. Interestingly, although the situation is different, many doctors advise families to sometimes lie to dementia patients, such as when a patient forgot that his wife was dead and asked why she hasn't visited him. One should not hurt him by telling him each time he asks that she is dead, say, instead, she is shopping and will visit later.

8. Presumably, except for Shabbat.

HIS REACTION TO HIS BROTHER'S DEATH

Maimonides's deep feelings for others can be seen in his reaction when he heard of the death of his younger brother. Maimonides mourned his brother's death and was ill for a year, perhaps due to depression. However, in 1166 he recovered and decided to support himself and his brother's family by practicing medicine. He ultimately became a court physician and treated the Sultan.

COMPASSION TO ANIMALS

Maimonides empathized with the pain of animals and had compassion for them, and disagreed with Nachmanides. Deuteronomy 22:6 commands: "If you chance upon a bird's nest along the road, in any tree or on the ground, with fledglings or eggs, and the mother is sitting over the fledglings or the eggs, do not take the mother together with her young." Leviticus 22:28 is similar: "No animal from the herd or from the flock should be slaughtered on the same day with its young."

In the *Guide of the Perplexed*,[9] Maimonides explains that animals, like humans, have feelings and the Torah prohibits people from tormenting them.

> [Regarding the slaughtering of animals] the Law enjoins that the death of the animal should be the easiest. It is not allowed to torment the animal by cutting the throat in a clumsy manner, by poleaxing, or by cutting off a limb whilst the animal is alive.
>
> It is also prohibited to kill an animal with its young on the same day, in order that people should be restrained and prevented from killing the two together in such a manner that the young is slain in the sight of the mother; for the pain of the animals under such circumstances is very great. There is no difference in this case between the pain of man and the pain of other living beings, since the love and tenderness of the mother for her young ones is not produced by reasoning, but by imagination, and this faculty exists not only in man but in most living beings.

Maimonides gives three reasons for the prohibition against taking the dam and its young: (1) the animal's feelings, (2) assuring that humans eat healthy food, and (3) training people to be similarly sensitive to the feelings of other humans.

---

9. Moses Maimonides, *Guide of the Perplexed* 3:48, trans. M. Friedlander (New York: Dover, 1956), 371.

The same reason applies to the law which enjoins that we should let the mother fly away when we take the young.... When the mother is sent away, she does not see the taking of her young ones and does not feel any pain. In most cases, however, this commandment will cause man to leave the whole nest untouched, because [the young or the eggs], which he can take, are, as a rule, unfit for food. If the Law provides that such grief should not be caused to cattle or birds, how much more careful must we be to not cause grief to our fellow men.

Nachmanides disagrees. He contends:

...that it was not a matter of God's mercy extending to the bird's nest or the dam and its young, since His mercies did not extend so far with them, for, if so, He would have forbidden slaughter altogether. But the reason for the prohibition [against taking the dam with its nest, or against killing the dam with its young in one day] is [only] to teach us the trait of compassion and that we should not be cruel, for cruelty proliferates in man's soul.[10]

Nachmanides concludes by stating that there is also a mystical reason for the command, but he does not elaborate, and his commentators differ in suggesting interpretations of his intention.

SUMMARY

Once we know that Maimonides helped people, how he was kind, considerate, compassionate, sensitive to the needs of others, and that he acted based on these feelings, we can recognize that this selfless altruistic personality motivated him to write the varied books that he did. The *Guide of the Perplexed*, the *Mishneh Torah*, his many medical books, his correspondences with many people and groups, can be read with the understanding of his motives and derive a deeper comprehension of what and why he is writing.

---

10. Moshe ben Nachman (Nachmanides), *Commentary to Deuteronomy* 22:6, trans. C.B. Chavel, in *Ramban, Commentary on the Torah, Deuteronomy* (Woodburn, OR: Shiloh Publishing House, 1976), 271.

Does God Punish Even
after a Person Repents?

In the September 9, 2018 TheTorah.com, Dr. Rabbi Zev Farber[1] offers a
very thoughtful essay "Does YHWH Remit Punishment." He asks if God
inflicts punishment even after a person repents. He cites several Torah
statements that seem to indicate that even after people repent, they and
their innocent descendants are punished for several generations. The rabbi
finds this troubling since the Bible tells us that God is compassionate, and
he offers a solution to the problem. The following is my solution.

THE PROBLEM VERSES

Exodus 34:5 to the middle of verse 7 states that God is compassionate, gracious,
slow to anger, very kind, faithful, showing kindness to the seventh generation,
forgiving iniquity, transgressions, and errors. However, the last part of verse 7
states what appears to be a contradiction of the prior statement: "and that by no
means clears the guilty; visiting the iniquity of the fathers upon the children, and
upon the children's children, unto the third and fourth generation."[2]

Besides the apparent contradiction, the verse seems to punish guiltless descendants for an ancestor's misdeeds. Dr. Rabbi Farber does not address this problem,
which also exists in the Decalogue, in Exodus 20:2–5, and Deuteronomy 5:7–10.
My solution answers both difficulties.

---

1. The general practice today is to place the rabbinical title before the doctorate, but TheTorah.
com prefers to reverse the order.
2. Because of this apparent contradiction, the rabbis included the words of Exodus 34:5–7 as
an integral part of synagogue services, including Yom Kippur, with the final wording deleted.

CLASSICAL SOLUTION

The issue is discussed in the Babylonian Talmud *Rosh Hashanah* 17a, *Sanhedrin* 102a, and *Yoma* 86a where the Bible and Talmud commentator Rashi (1040–1105) explains that the verses are speaking of two circumstances: God is gracious to people who repent but punishes those who fail to do so. This solution resolves the first problem, not the second, but the resolution that the verse is speaking of two types of people is not even hinted at in the verse.

DR. RABBI FARBER'S SOLUTION

Dr. Rabbi Farber relies on the view that the Torah was changed from time to time by various editors with divergent world views. He suggests that the verses start with the opinion of an editor who felt that God is always merciful and forgiving, while the ending of the verses reflects the contrary notion that God will punish people who misbehave even if they repent. This solution contains the same problem as Rashi's: there is no hint in the verses that that they were composed by two editors.

MY UNDERSTANDING

I understand the passages in accordance with Maimonides's teaching in his *Guide of the Perplexed* 2:48 that God created the laws of nature and does not interfere with them or change them.[3] The verse is telling us that God is compassionate, but people need to realize that in nature actions have consequences that not only affect the actor, but also the actor's family, friends, and often an entire community, and the after affects may last for generations.

Repentance is good if done properly. People are not forgiven by attending a synagogue and praying to God to remove their misdeed. When a man mistreats his wife, rushes to the synagogue and begs God to forgive him, returns home and finds his wife angry, he should not be surprised that his wife is not satisfied when he claims, "I don't know why you are still mad; I went to shul and asked God to forgive me."

---

3. God is not like the plumber who fixed a sink and needs to return to re-fix it. Many scholars are convinced that Maimonides did not believe that God performed miracles; there was no need to do so. What appeared to be miracles was the laws of nature in action.

Maimonides explained that the process of repentance is just common sense. True repentance is when individuals recognize that they did wrong, decide not to commit the wrong again, do all they can to correct the wrong – such as apologizing to the wronged individual, repairing what was broken, and paying reparations if appropriate – and develop habits of behavior to assure that the wrong will not be repeated. This solves a lot. It may even prompt the person who was hurt to forgive the wrongdoer. But it does not address and remove the natural consequences of the misdeed. Every act has consequences which generally cannot be avoided by words, prayers, or even the best of intentions.

I described an example of this in my book *The Tragedies of King David*. David's act of adultery and the murder of Bat Sheba's husband and his military unit affected his children and grandchildren who copied his unlawful sexual behavior and murders. In fact, all of King David's tragedies – the rape by one of his sons of his half-sister, her full-brother Absalom's murder of the rapist, the agony David felt when he punished Absalom, Absalom's rebellion, Absalom's rape of his father David's mistresses, David's grief over Absalom's death, and more – were consequences of his act despite begging God to forgive him.

The sole exception of the multiple disasters that David suffered that was not a consequence of the Bat Sheba affair were the tens of thousands of deaths that followed his counting of his troops. And even these deaths were a natural consequence of his counting, as I explain in the book. David foolishly ordered his officers to draft soldiers for a secret attack against an Israelite enemy, to count the men who were mobilized, and report the count to him. Since he foolishly had the mustering and counting done publicly, the enemy learnt of the impending attack, mustered its forces, and were able to butcher many of David's soldiers. David realized his mistake and pleaded with God to forgive him, but his repentance did not stop the massacre of his troops by enemy forces and the plague that followed because of the multitude of dead bodies.

The Solution is Simple

In an excellent and informative article, Professor Rabbi Marty Lockshin of York University examined the difficulty raised by Deuteronomy 13:2–4, and tells of the solutions offered in a Midrash, and by several medieval Jewish commentators.[1] I will add another solution.

THE PROBLEM

Deuteronomy states: "If there appears among you a prophet or a dream-diviner – and he gives you a sign or potent, and the sign or potent that he named to you comes true – saying, 'Let us follow other gods – whom you have not known – and worship them,' do not heed the words of the prophet or the dream-diviner."[2] The verse concludes by saying that God is testing you in regard to this matter. Since the term "a sign or potent" in the Pentateuch is used to indicate a miracle, the question arises "can a false prophet perform miracles?" Or, Does God give false prophets the ability to create a miracle, especially one that could mislead the people.[3] Professor Lockshin gives us the solutions offered by various rabbis and scholars.

A MIDRASH

Midrash Sifrei Devarim 84:3 has the opinion of R. Yossi, an opinion held by many, but not all ancient rabbis. He contended that the idolaters were given control over the sun, moon, stars, and constellations, who were semi-gods who could

---

1. TheTorah.com, *A Historical and Contextual Approach*, August 2018, "Can a False Prophet Perform Miracles?"
2. Professor Lockshin's translation. The term "potent" can also be translated "wonder."
3. The term "sign and wonder" is also used to describe Moses's activities in Deuteronomy 34:11, "the signs and wonders which the Lord sent him to do in the land of Egypt."

help people, and can use their power to accomplish what they want. Jews were forbidden to use these semi-gods. Those who held R. Yossi's opinion believed that people using these semi-gods could perform miracles.

RASHBAM

Rashbam (about 1080–about 1165) is like R. Yossi in the Midrash. He felt that, with the proper tools, all humans can foretell the future. They can do so by using sorcery or other magic. It works, but God prohibited the Israelites from using this natural phenomenon as well as the sun and other heavenly spheres in Deuteronomy 18:9–22, a section that also speaks about false prophets, as does Deuteronomy 13, described above.

IBN EZRA

Abraham ibn Ezra (1089–1167) offered three possible solutions: (1) The false prophet stole (plagiarized) the prophecy of a true prophet. (2) Ignoring how a false prophet can perform a miracle, the verse is telling us that we should never rely on miracles. People must rely on reason. This verse is hypothetical, even if a man should be able to perform a miracle, you should not react based on his act. When he states that one should worship idols and proves it by a miracle, reject it because reason must trump miracles, and reason states that idol worship is absurd. (3) The solution preferred by ibn Ezra is that "a sign or potent" does not mean a supernatural miracle, it is some symbolical act performed by the false prophet, such as Isaiah walking naked and barefoot in Isaiah 20:3 was not a miracle, but a symbolic act to call the people's attention to Isaiah's message.[4] The question of how a false prophet can perform a miracle disappears. The false prophet did not perform a miracle.

---

4. This explanation is an excellent example of ibn Ezra's rational approach to the Bible, and it makes sense. Professor Lockshin sees ibn Ezra's view as problematical because the biblical text states that whether to follow the false prophet or not is a test, "But if the false prophet simply performed a symbolic action, what is the test?" I understand ibn Ezra to say that a man tries to persuade people to act unreasonably and uses some symbols to prove the rationality of his view. The test is whether the people will see through the trick, use their minds, their ability to reason, and not abandon God for hand-made idols.

228 · MYSTERIES OF JUDAISM III

MAIMONIDES

A similar response to the question is the view of Maimonides about prophecy, a view that Professor Lockshin does not discuss. In his *Guide of the Perplexed* 2:32–48, Maimonides explains that prophecy is not a miraculous experience and it is not a communication from God. Prophecy is a natural experience. Prophets are individuals with higher than average intelligence that makes it possible for them to understand events better than others. Understanding problems facing people that do not understand the difficulties, prophets explain them to the people. The prophets also have a far better imagination than the average person, which enhances their understandings, and which makes it easy for prophets to communicate their understanding to others. A third requirement is that prophets be virtuous and principled so that they look to improve and benefit society. In 2:48, Maimonides states that when the Bible says that God is testing the people, it means that nature is testing them. If people heed false prophets, the natural result will be that they will be harmed. Maimonides says that the Torah ascribes this natural event of harm (coming to the people) to God because God created the laws of nature.

In contrast, a false prophet is an intelligent person who is either not altogether smart, lacks enough imagination, is immoral, and who communicates his unreasonable views to the people. The Torah is saying you must use your intelligence and evaluate what people say to you; do not be persuaded by any signs and wonders, or any tricks of sophistry, oratory, convoluted arguments, demonstrations, or half-truths.

The Gay Science by Friedrich Nietzsche

Friedrich Nietzsche (1844–1900) offers three main ideas in *The Gay Science*, written in 1882 with additions in 1887,[1] a book called "One of His Most Beautiful, Most Idea Rich Books,"[2] whose title is also translated as *The Joyful Wisdom*. First, God is dead or, as I understand it, the reliance on God should cease. He is saying that we should act as if there is no God. There are similarities between Nietzsche and Maimonides.

NIETZSCHE'S VIEWS

Nietzsche contended that the character and motives of Christianity were unnatural, mendacious, and injurious, and that true happiness cannot be obtained until people cease relying on religion. The best human, he wrote, was the *Übermensch*, the "overman," "superman," or "ideal man," who ceased living in accordance with the traditional theological and moral conceptions of God as the source of existence and of moral values. The *Übermensch* lives and thinks outside the norms and values of society. He recognizes that morality is a system developed for average unthinking people who need a generally inflexible and absolute code of conduct that tells the masses how to act for every situation they encounter for what is "good" and what is "evil."

The *Übermenschen* are people who go "beyond good and evil" and rely instead on their intellect, on what is "true" and "false." They realize that morality does not always give individuals the proper way of acting in every situation. It does not tend to create the ideal result, it fosters an unthinking system, and it often prompts people to be passive and not exert themselves. Morality further does

---

1. Fredrich Nietzsche, *The Gay Science*, trans. Thomas Common (Barnes & Noble, 2008).
2. Ibid., vii.

not encourage creativity, and does not promote concern for the safety of society. The *Übermensch* realizes that he or she must do his or her best and not act like the herd. There are different codes of morality for Catholics, Protestants, Muslims, Jews, etc., each designed to further the ideology of the religion, and each insists that the adherents of the religion accept and act according to the morality they are teaching without deviating from that morality since the morality, they say, is what God dictated. Each disparages the *Übermensch* because the *Übermensch* does not make decisions and act according to the religion's view of morality, that they insist is the behavior that God requires.

MAIMONIDES AGREES WITH THIS IDEA

Maimonides expressed Nietzsche's first idea about morality in the first two chapters of his *Guide of the Perplexed.* He was convinced that this idea of using one's intelligence vs. morality is taught in the opening chapters of the Bible. Maimonides notes that the Bible states in Genesis 1:26 that God proclaimed, "Let us make man in our image." This, Maimonides explained, certainly does not refer to humans looking like God. It refers to the intellect. Humans were created with a mind, with the ability to think. This ability to think, as the Greek Aristotle (384–322 BCE) taught, distinguishes humans from animals and plants. People who do not use their intellect are no better than animals and plants. Maimonides viewed the following chapters in Genesis about the Garden of Eden as a parable. He noted that the forbidden fruit was not from a tree "of truth and falsehood," but "good and evil": Adam and Eve, representing all people in the parable, are told not to eat from "the tree of good and evil," meaning living their lives according to the rules made for the masses, the laws of morality as to what is good and what is evil, but eat (that is, live) according to "the tree of truth and falsehood," by using their intellect throughout their lives.

NIETZSCHE'S SECOND IDEA

Nietzsche's second idea in this book is like the first. It is "the eternal recurrence of the same." By these words he distinguishes between people who disparage the natural world and this life and focus all of their thoughts and actions on what they consider a promise of an award in the afterlife, and in contrast, the ideal people who enjoy life and want their moments of joy to recur eternally.

MAIMONIDES AGREES

Maimonides focus in the third part of his *Guide of the Perplexed*, where he explains the biblical commandments, is that the commands teach some truths and are designed to help people be all they can be and to improve society.

NIETZSCHE'S THIRD IDEA

The third idea is "the love of fate," the realization that what seems harmful or difficult is good. It can make a person stronger, more creative, and more responsible. Those things in life that are easy will not help people grow.

MAIMONIDES AGREES

Maimonides has the same teaching in his *Guide of the Perplexed* 3:24 where he states that the "sole object of all the [six] trials mentioned in Scripture is to teach man what he ought to do or believe; so that the event which forms the actual trial is not the end desired; but is an example for our instruction and guidance." In other words, when people experience trials – that is, natural difficulties, not pain delivered by God – they learn from their experience, apply what they learned to other situations, and grow.

Maimonides's Political Thought

In Howard Kreisel's 1999 scholarly study of Maimonides's philosophy, *Maimonides' Political Thought*,[1] Dr. Kreisel points out that Maimonides reflected the "Aristotelian tradition" that "investigated the world with the impartial tools of reason." Reason is a tool, the goal of which is "the creation of a social environment most conducive to the individual's pursuit of perfection."

KREISEL'S VIEWS

Kreisel's book is filled with interesting information. For example, he reminds readers that Maimonides wrote for two audiences; he combines ideas that would satisfy the unlearned general community with correct ideas that would inform the intellectual. A reader needs to learn how to read Maimonides's *Guide of the Perplexed* to distinguish the two and accept only the latter, and it is worth the effort to do so. He explains that it "was primarily fear of persecution that led Maimonides to resort to the art of esoteric writing, but [also] fear of the social destruction would result if he did not."

According to Kreisel, the "picture of God's 'personal' involvement in revealing the Law and in reward and punishment [for instance] remains the public teaching" of Maimonides, but not his true view. "God," according to Kreisel's understanding of Maimonides's teaching, "exercises no direct involvement in human affairs."

Kreisel explains that when Maimonides stressed in *Guide* 1:2[2] the need to acquire knowledge, and criticized using generally accepted moral principles when

---

1. Howard Kreisel, *Maimonides' Political Thought: Studies in Ethics, Law and the Human Ideal* (New York: SUNY Press, 1999).
2. In his discussion of the fruit of the tree of good and evil.

making decision, this was not "a rejection of the value of this [moral] knowledge. His purpose is to stress its inferior value in comparison to knowledge of 'true and false' – that is knowledge of the sciences." In essence, Maimonides stressed that people should not make decisions based only on traditional moral teachings, but should develop an understanding of the world and how it functions, and make decisions based on this knowledge. The reasoned decisions may be far better for the individual and society in a particular situation than the traditional moral lesson.

These are some of the many ideas that Kreisel discusses in his book.

Is the Concept of "Faith" Sensible?

My answer is no. Ever since I was a child, I heard about faith and understood that it makes no sense. One day when I was still young my father Rabbi Dr. Nathan Drazin took me to hear a lecture by the famous Rabbi Abraham Joshua Heschel. Heschel said that faith is not a Jewish concept and that if we want to use the word, we should understand it as "faithful," meaning: we should faithfully *do* what the Torah teaches us to do. It is good *behavior* that the Torah demands, not misguided ideas. (Heschel's lecture inspired me so much that I asked him for his autograph and bought his book.)

WHAT IS FAITH?

Faith is the acceptance by a person that an idea is true even though the person's reasoning is unable to support its truthfulness. It is that which science and one's senses say is untrue. The American satirist Ambrose Bierce (1842–c. 1913) defined faith in his humorous *The Devil's Dictionary* as, "belief without evidence in what is told by one who speaks without knowledge of things without parallel." Bierce defined religion based on faith sarcastically as, "A daughter of hope or fear, explaining to ignorance the nature of the unknowable."

An unknown source wrote similarly, "Faith is believing what you know ain't so."

The Mishnah *Pirkei Avot* 2:6, reports that Hillel said that an individual who acts without reason is not pious.

One can find other cynical comments in other sources. Each highlights the absence of any reasonable basis to faith and the difficulty that a person of faith has in making an informed decision. Unfortunately, most people seem to resolve the difficult decision by not thinking at all, and by relying instead on the opinion of others.

FAITH NOT MENTIONED IN THE HEBREW BIBLE

The term "faith" does not appear in the Hebrew Bible. Instead, the Bible frequently encourages one to think and to act reasonably. The biblical word that some mistakenly translate as "faith," *emunah*, means "steadfast" or "steady." It refers to behavior, not thinking. Thus, Moses held up his hands "steadily," without letting them fall. The current meaning of *emunah* as "faith" is a new idea.

MAIMONIDES

Maimonides repeatedly stressed that people should not accept ideas that other people tell them if they are unverifiable, even if the person is an authority, but they should use their own reasoning. In his medical book *Aphorisms*, he wrote: If anyone tells you that he has an idea that he wants you to accept and claims that he has proof from his own personal experience that confirms his idea, do not accept it just because he is so anxious for you to believe his notion. This applies even though he is recognized as a man of great authority and truthfulness – religious, sincere, and moral. Do not allow yourself to be swayed by the novelties that he tells you. Examine his theory and belief carefully.... Look into the matter. Don't let yourself be persuaded.

It is true that in his essay called *Chelek*, Maimonides offers thirteen principles of Judaism, which to most people means that there are thirteen basic beliefs in Judaism. But this is not correct. Scholars know that in his Introduction to his *Guide of the Perplexed*, Maimonides alerted his readers that he will write for two audiences, each will find in his writings what they need to see. He will write ideas that will satisfy the public, ideas they feel are important. He will also write for the more intelligent reader, those with a good background in the sciences. The first are only "essential truths." These are not real truths, but rather ideas that the public needs to know to live a better life for themselves and society. The second are the real truths. Many scholars place the thirteen principles among the essential truths.

Maimonides did not think that one can mandate beliefs. Therefore, he began his *Mishneh Torah*, his fourteen books on Jewish law, with the law that one should "know God." How do people come to know God? By studying the laws of nature that God created or formed. He taught that it is impossible to know about the nature of God. All we can know is what God has done. This, he explains, is the meaning of the conversation between Moses and God in Exodus 33:18–23. Moses begs God to let him see "your glory." God replies that this is impossible. But God will pass by Moses, and after God is gone, "you will see my back, but my face will not be seen."

SOME QUOTES ABOUT THE RELIANCE ON FAITH

"Faith may be defined briefly as an illogical belief in the occurrence of the impossible." (H.L. Mencken, *Prejudices*: series III)

"In the affairs of this world, men are not saved by faith, but by avoiding and surpassing it." (Benjamin Franklin, *Poor Richard's Almanac*)

"He wears his faith, but as the fashion of his hat." (Shakespeare, *Much Ado About Nothing* 1:1)

"Faith must have adequate evidence; else it is mere superstition." (Archibald Alexander Hodge)

"Faith can stifle all science." (Henri Frederic Amiel, *Journal*)

THE CLASSIC STORY ABOUT RELYING ON FAITH

The synagogue officials were united. Even the rabbi agreed. They had all seen that the poor man was suffering. So, they gathered at the east wing of the Synagogue and prayed in unison, "Please God, please allow the poor man to win the lottery so that he can eat!" When Wednesday came, and his name was not announced, the group gathered again at the east wing.

Again, they prayed, full of faith, "Please God, please let this poor man win the lottery so that he can eat!" When the next Wednesday came and they saw the same result, they prayed again. After the third failure, the rabbi addressed God, "Why Lord, why didn't he win?" A voice came from heaven, "He never bought a ticket."

The Big Book of AA

Stationed in the Pentagon between 1980 and 1984, I was tasked to handle legal cases where soldiers were attacked because of their religious practices, and on other matters involving the connection between the law and religion. This was in addition to my main job, which was to work out a defense against the legal challenge that the military chaplaincy was in violation of the First Amendment to the US Constitution. A case we won. Among the hundreds of cases, there was an interesting one where I helped to write a MASH episode involving Chaplain Mulcahy trying (in the wrong way) to give a soldier sanctuary. Another case addressed the Army's desire to aid soldiers who abused alcohol.

GIVING SOLDIERS A SECOND CHANCE

The Army developed a procedure where soldiers would be given a second chance after they were found to have abused alcohol. Among other requirements, the soldier had to agree to stop drinking alcohol and had to attend AA sessions. I objected to the latter requirement and it was changed to read that the soldier had to join the AA program or a similar one.

AA's philosophy, as spelled out in the program's Big Book is a philosophy that is contrary to my own.[1] The Big Book belittles human will. It states that human will is not enough to overcome alcoholism and alcoholics need to realize this, renounce self-control, and turn their lives over to a "higher power," their term for God. AA applied its philosophy to all aspects of life. It states: "Any life run on self-will can hardly be a success." The problem, according to AA is not alcohol or

---

1. Alcoholic Anonymous World Services, Inc. 2002.

the physical constitution of the alcoholic, but in the wrong-headed concept that humans can and must control their lives. People need to realize, they claim, that they are powerless; they are anonymous. Once a person surrenders to and relies on the "higher power," there is a huge benefit, a "release from care, boredom and worry.... Your imagination will be fired. Life will mean something at last."

AA instructs addicts that they need a cure where the tyrant of one addiction, alcohol, is traded to mindless obedience, to be a puppet to God.

As previously stated, this is not my view of human responsibility. Failure to use one's intelligence makes the person no better than an animal and plant. I objected to the regulation and it was changed.

Difficulties with the Akeidah
Story Explained

The thrust of Soren Kierkegaard's 1843 influential book *Fear and Trembling* is long reflections on Abraham's near sacrifice of his son Isaac, a story told in Genesis 22.[1] Kierkegaard concludes from his analysis that Abraham represents the prototype of faith, for he showed faith when he was willing to obey God's command to sacrifice his beloved son Isaac. Ethics, Kierkegaard stresses clearly demands that a father not kill his son. But faith, he continues, is something higher than ethics and demands the "teleological suspension of the ethical," with "teleological" meaning "purposeful" and "suspension" implying "a temporary pause." He states that that the story teaches that morality must give way to faith, which is a higher level. The concept of a "leap of faith" attributed to Kierkegaard is derived from this analysis. One must leap over morality to the higher level "faith," although the words do not appear in his book.

KIERKEGAARD WAS NOT ALONE

Rabbi J.B. Soloveitchik cited Kierkegaard in many of his writings and agreed with him. He taught on many occasions that the human duty is to "surrender oneself" to God, the quote is from the rabbi's many writings. Many other religious leaders of all religions agree with Kierkegaard.

PROBLEMS WITH THE BIBLICAL STORY

The story in chapter 22 is called the Akeidah, a word meaning "binding," referring

---

1. Soren Kierkegarrd, *Kierkegaard: Fear and Trembling* (Cambridge University Press, 2006).

to Abraham's binding of Isaac before starting to kill him. A careful reading reveals many difficulties, such as: Why did God need to test Abraham? Didn't the all-wise deity already know that Abraham was dependable and loyal? Didn't God know what the outcome would be before the test? What is a test? If the purpose was to use Abraham as an example for others, couldn't God have done this without causing Abraham huge worries before and after a three-day journey to where the sacrifice was supposed to be made?[2] Why did Abraham have to travel three days to get to the sacrifice site? Why didn't God tell him where he should sacrifice Isaac? Why was Isaac so silent during the three-day trip other than to ask simple questions? Why didn't Abraham inform Sarah where he was going and why he was doing it, even if he had to lie? Why doesn't the Bible tell us Sarah's and Isaac's reactions when the event was concluded? Why was it necessary to bind Isaac? Was Isaac willing to be sacrificed? Why do Midrashim amplify the story by contending that God tested Abraham because Satan argued that Abraham would not obey a command to sacrifice his son? Why do the Midrashim compare the Abraham story to that of Job where God and Satan have this conversation? What is the same and what is different between the two stories? Why do Midrashim add that Satan tried to stop Abraham on his three-day journey? These are only a few of the questions.

IS KIERKEGAARD CORRECT?

Once it is realized that Kierkegaard's analysis fails to answer most of these questions, it should be clear that his analysis of the Abraham story of Genesis 22 to extoll "faith" is wrong. The story has nothing to do with "faith."

There are two possible ways to understand the story. The first takes the story literally. Abraham heard God speak to him and demand that he kill Isaac. Abraham agreed to do so for how could a human who heard God's command disobey the command? Abraham obeyed God not because of "faith" but out of fear to disobey the all-powerful deity. The story shows that Abraham obeyed God even when God demanded an act that caused him great pain.

---

2. Abraham ibn Ezra explains that the number seven indicates a complete act, while three, being about half of seven symbolizes a somewhat long but not very long endeavor.

A MAIMONIDEAN APPROACH

The second way clarifies the story by using Maimonidean insights from his *Guide of the Perplexed*.

Maimonides tells us that trials are not divine inflictions. They are natural human struggles in which God is not involved. In *Guide of the Perplexed* 3:24, Maimonides writes: "The sole object of all the trials mentioned in Scripture is to teach man what he ought to do or believe.... This is the way how we have to understand the accounts of trials; we must not think that God desires to examine us and to try us to know what He did not know before. Far is this from Him; He is far above that which ignorant and foolish people imagine concerning Him, in the evil of their thoughts." In 2:48, Maimonides explains that while scripture states that God did something, it happened according to the laws of nature, and Scripture states that the deity did it only to remind us that God was the ultimate, although not immediate cause, because God created the laws of nature.

The second way to understand the story is that God did not actually speak to Abraham. It reflects Abraham's thinking. If so, again, his act has nothing to do with "faith." Abraham looked at the pagans of his generation and saw that they showed their love of God by sacrificing to God what was dearest to them. Either in a dream or day-time thinking, he wondered whether he should do the same. At first, he thought the pagans were right and God wanted the sacrifice of Isaac, but he then realized that God is not cruel and would not require that he murder his son to in order to show love. This interpretation sees chapter 22 showing how Abraham rose higher in his understanding of God than his neighbors.

By realizing that the story reflects Abraham's thinking about himself, and how he should show his love of God, we can understand why there is no mention of Sarah, why there is only a little focus on Isaac, and that the internal struggle took time (symbolized by three days). These and other problems are similarly answered.

Buddhist Ideas Maimonides Would Like

Dr. Oliver Kent wrote two fascinating educational books called *Inspirational Buddhist Quotations: Meditations and Reflections* books one and two.[1] He quotes 200 Buddhist teachings and adds his own brief reflections on each of them.

MAIMONIDES

Maimonides wrote that people should realize that "The truth is the truth no matter what its source." Although Jewish, he saw no problem with drawing his philosophy from the Greek pagan Aristotle (384–322 BCE).[2] He taught that reason is primary, above all else, and that people need to improve themselves, develop good habits, and help others and society develop. He states that the purpose of the Torah is three-fold: it teaches some truths, and helps people improve, and advance society.[3] The following are a sample of many quotes that Maimonides could agree with without the insightful comments that Dr. Kent appends to them.

BUDDHISM

"You are searching the world for treasures, but the real treasure is yourself."

"You will not be punished for your anger, you will be punished by your anger."

"We become what we think."

---

1. Dr. Oliver Kent, *Inspirational Buddhist Quotations: Meditations and Reflections I, II* (Amazon Digital Services LLC, 2017).
2. Needless to say, many rabbis who were not nearly as smart as he, berated him for doing so.
3. Maimonides, *Guide of the Perplexed* 3:28.

"Your pain can become your greatest ally in your life's search for love and wisdom."

"No one saves us but ourselves."

"Beauty surrounds us, but usually we need to be walking in a garden to know it."

"To keep the body in good health is a duty...otherwise we shall not be able to keep our mind strong and clear."

"However many holy words you read, however many you speak, what good will they do if you do not act upon them."

"There are only two mistakes one can make along the road to truth; not going all the way, and not starting."

"The lamps are different, but the light is the same."

"You were born with wings. Why prefer to crawl through life?"

"Do not be satisfied with stories that come before you. Unfold your own myth."

"Listen to the secret sound, the real sound, which is within you."

"A diamond was laying in the street covered with dirt. Many fools passed by. Someone who knew diamonds picked it up."

Gersonides, Somewhat
like Maimonides

In *Judaism within the Limits of Reason*,[1] Seymour Feldman describes the
views of Gersonides. Since people are unable to fully understand a subject
if they do not understand its opposite, and since Gersonides had ideas
that are somewhat but not exactly like those of Maimonides, it is worth
knowing what Gersonides thought.

WHO WAS GERSONIDES?

Levi ben Gershom, Gersonides in Latin, (1288–1344), was one of several great
Jewish rationalistic philosophers. He lived in Provence, France, and wrote books
on philosophy, science, and Bible commentary. He wasn't as deep a thinker as
Maimonides and Abraham ibn Ezra, who preceded him, but far more intellectual
and innovative than most people. All three had unconventional opinions that
either the public doesn't know, or misunderstands: ideas about God, creation,
miracles, prophecy, life, death, the functioning of the world, and human respon-
sibilities. Seymour Feldman gives readers an excellent introduction to Gersonides, describes his thoughts in language appropriate for scholars and the general
community, and compares his views with those of other thinkers. The following
are some of these ideas.

REASON

The three great rationalistic philosophers stressed the use of reason. Human perfection, they wrote, is based on an improved and effective use of reason, not tradition

---

1. Feldman, *Gersonides: Judaism Within the Limits of Reason*.

or beliefs. Individuals must study the sciences and how the world functions. The Torah begins by teaching about creation to emphasize the importance of understanding science. Reason even supersedes the literal meaning of the Bible: "For when the Torah, interpreted literally, seems to conflict with doctrines that have been proved [to be true] by reason, it is proper to interpret these passages according to philosophical understanding" and not accept the biblical words literally.

THE BIBLE

Gersonides was convinced that the Bible teaches philosophy, not only history and laws. But while Maimonides and most ancient thinkers, Jewish and non-Jewish recognized that most people lack the education and intellect to understand philosophy, Gersonides felt that they could and should understand it. Maimonides composed his writings so that the intellectual would see what he intended and understand what he wrote in one way, the true way, but the masses would only see their mistaken notions reflected in his writings and think that the Great Eagle, as Maimonides was called, thought as they thought. But Gersonides wrote his philosophy and philosophical interpretations of Scripture openly, convinced that everyone would understand his views.

CREATION

Feldman does not read Maimonides in this dual – one might call it elitist – manner. He feels, as many scholars, that Maimonides was hiding nothing. He reads Maimonides repeating the conventional belief that God created the world out of nothing. Other scholars, such as Straus and Pines[2] and this reviewer, contend that Maimonides could be saying that God created the world out of preexisting matter, which he formed into the currently existing universe. In any event, Gersonides takes the latter view and states it clearly.

END OF THE WORLD

Both, but not ibn Ezra, agree that the world will last forever. Ibn Ezra accepted the notion in the Babylonian Talmud, *Sanhedrin* 97a, that the world would last only six thousand years in his commentaries on *Genesis* 1:5, 8:22, and *Leviticus* 25:2.[3]

---

2. Maimonides, *The Guide of the Perplexed*.

3. Maimonides wrote that one may rebuff rabbinical opinions about non-legal matters. He

MIRACLES

Since scholars read Maimonides differently, some say he thought miracles occur and others the opposite. Gersonides and ibn Ezra are also unclear. Yet, even those who are convinced that miracles happen say that they are rare, and that the world generally (or always) functions according to the laws of nature. The scholarly understanding that the three were convinced that miracles do not occur seems correct because it is consistent with the three thinkers' feelings about God's knowledge.

DIVINE KNOWLEDGE, REWARD AND PUNISHMENT

As startling as it may appear, all three of these rationalistic philosophers were convinced that God doesn't know details about people; God only knows the general rules of the laws of nature – what could possibly occur – and that people can subvert the laws of nature. Since God does not know the details of human activities, the idea that God punishes people for their misdeeds and rewards them for proper acts, is impossible. Therefore, the three reject this common conception, focus on this world, and contend that people should use their intellect and act properly because it is better for them and society.

PROPHECY

Since God has no specific idea of what is happening, it would be illogical to say that God speaks to people and sends them messages on how to behave. Thus, the three define prophecy as a higher level of intelligence, not a divine communication. Prophets are intelligent people of high moral integrity with imaginative skills that stimulate their minds and give them the ability to communicate. Prophets are people who understand events and share their understanding with others because they realize that this is their moral duty. Thus, many scholars contend that the three would say that the pagan Aristotle who had these qualities was a prophet.

DREAMS, DIVINATION, AND ASTROLOGY

Nevertheless, seemingly inconsistently, Gersonides and ibn Ezra were convinced that some people receive a kind of mental experience that enables them to avoid

---

rejected the rabbis' superstitious notions. Gersonides felt the same, but he accepted many of them. He also accepted as true many biblical tales that are contrary to reason, tales that Maimonides said were untrue, just parables or dreams.

danger or obtain a benefit. This occurs through dreams, divination, and astrology. They were not alone. Most ancient people, including rabbis, believed this, but not Maimonides.

IMMORTALITY

Maimonides and Gersonides reject the generally held view that a person's soul survives the body's death. The two felt that only people's intellect lives after them. Like other philosophers who had this opinion, Maimonides is unclear whether this surviving intellect can recall the person's prior life. Most likely, Maimonides felt that this was a subject that he had better not reveal to people. Some scholars are certain that Maimonides thought that the surviving intellect has no recollection of the past, but this is mere conjecture. However, Gersonides writes openly that the surviving intellect could recall its pre-death thoughts. The intellect spends eternity contemplating these thoughts, but learns nothing new, since the intellect now lacks the five senses that are used to acquire knowledge. (Some readers might call this hell.)

RESURRECTION

According to the scholars who read Maimonides taking a dual tract in his writings, one for intellectuals and one for the general population, Maimonides did not think that people would be resurrected after death. He states clearly this clearly in the beginning of his essay *Chelek* but says the opposite at the end of *Chelek* when he lists the thirteen principles of faith; a list he wrote for the general public.

THE MESSIAH

All scholars recognize that he said that the messiah will be human, and the messianic age will be like current times except that Jews will no longer be persecuted. However, Gersonides believed in resurrection and wrote that the messianic age would be one that is filled with "marvelous miracles that will be seen by all the earth." (This seems inconsistent with his general view about miracles, but Gersonides is not known for pure consistency.)

SUMMARY

Most rabbis and scholars recognize and respect the vast and deep learning of Gersonides but they cannot accept his radical heterodox conclusions concerning the creation of the earth out of preexisting matter; that miracles don't occur; God doesn't know the details of human behavior, only the laws of nature; neither the soul nor personality of people survive their death, only their intellect; when the Torah differs with scientific proofs the Torah must be interpreted according to science; people who study Torah and Talmud, even daily, haven't fulfilled their human duty, which is to study and understand the sciences and use the knowledge to improve themselves and society; and similar unorthodox stances.

Readers may prefer the conservative positions. They may be bothered by the fact that there is no fixed agreement on how to interpret Gersonides and Maimonides and be annoyed at what seems to be Gersonides' inconsistencies. But they will find that these bothersome thoughts will remind them of great mysteries of Judaism; there is no clear mandate on what they should believe, great sages had contrary views, and they should begin to develop their own ideas.

Afterword

It is hard for some Jews to accept. But, although I am an observant Jew and I keep Jewish laws and customs as an Orthodox Jew, I have no problem with saying the following.

If we think about it, we must acknowledge that Judaism today is totally unlike the Judaism as understood and practiced in biblical days. Neither Abraham nor Moses nor King David wore yarmulkes. They did not attend a synagogue, pray three times a day, or wear tefillin. They practiced holidays different from how we do so today, and there were many other differences. Judaism today is not biblical Judaism although it is built on and inspired by biblical Judaism, which lays the groundwork. It is rabbinical Judaism.

As shown in the first volume of *Mysteries of Judaism*, all the biblical holidays, without any exception, are not practiced today as required by the Torah. In the second volume, the practices of Judaism today are different than those in ancient time. And in this volume, Jewish ideas have also changed.

Change is a natural phenomenon. Hopefully, the changes in the future will bring all people to strive to be all they can be and to respect one another.

References

Alcoholics Anonymous. *The Big Book*. Alcoholic Anonymous World Services, Inc. 2002.

Abarbanel, Rabbi Don Isaac. *Rosh Ammanah*. Warsaw: 1884.

———, *Perush Abarbanel* (Abarbanel's commentary). New York: Seforim Torah Vada'at, 1955.

Allen, Ntathu. *Meditation for Beginners: How to Meditate for People Who Hate to Sit Still*. TCK Publishing, 2014.

American Heritage Dictionaries editors. *100 Words Almost Everyone Confuses & Misuses*. Boston: Houghton Mifflin Harcourt, 2004.

Angel, Rabbi Hayyim. *Keys to the Palace, Exploring the Religious Value of Reading Tanakh*. Kodesh Press, 2017.

Aristotle. *Physics*.

ArtScroll. *Chumash*.

ArtScroll. *The Prophets, I–II Kings*. New York: Mesorah Publications Ltd., 2006.

Asimov, Isaac. "The Last Question." *Science Fiction Quarterly*, 1956.

Asimov, Isaac. *Asimov's Guide to the Bible*. Random House, 2000.

Augustine. *The City of God*.

Babylonian Talmud tractates: *Bava Batra, Hagigah, Kiddushin, Makkot, Megillah, Moed Katan, Niddah, Rosh Hashanah, Sanhedrin, Shabbat, Sota, Yoma*.

Barnes, Hugh. *The Stolen Prince*. Ecco, 2006.

ben Gershom, Levi (Gersonides). *Sefer Milhamot Hashem*.

Ben Nachman, Moses (Nachmanides). *Ramban Commentary on the Torah: Deuteronomy*. Translated by C.B. Chavel. Woodburn, OR: Shiloh Publishing House, 1976.

ben Sira, Yeshua ben Eleazar. *Apocrypha Ecclesiasticus* (The Wisdom of Ben Sira).

Bradbury, Ray. *Fahrenheit 451*. New York: Ballantine, 1968.

———. *The Martian Chronicles*. New York: Doubleday, 1950.

Cardozo, Rabbi Dr. Nathan Lopes. *Jewish Law as Rebellion, A Plea for Religious Authenticity and Halachic Courage*. Jerusalem: Urim Publications, 2018.

Chavel, Charles Ber, ed. *Sefer HaMitzvot l'haRamban in Hasagot haRamban*. Jerusalem: Mossad HaRav Kook, 1981.

Cohen, Mortimer Joseph. *Jacob Emden: A Man of Controversy*. Philadelphia: Dropsie College for Hebrew and Cognate Learning, 1937.

Cohen, Rabbi Yehoshua. *Siddur Eizur Eliyahu K'minhag Rabbenu Hagra*. Jerusalem: Machon Kerem Eliyahu, 5771.

da Modena, Rabbi Leon. *Ari Nohem*, Venice, 1639.

de Leon, Moshe. *Zohar*.

Diamond, James Arthur. *Maimonides and the Hermeneutics of Concealment: Deciphering Scripture and Midrash in the Guide of the Perplexed*. New York: Suny Press, 2002.

Drazin, Rabbi Dr. Israel. *Mysteries of Judaism I*. Jerusalem: Gefen Publishing House, 2014.

———. *Mysteries of Judaism II*. Jerusalem: Gefen Publishing House, 2017.

———. *Nachmanides: An Unusual Thinker*. Jerusalem: Gefen Publishing House, 2017.

———. *Onkelos on the Torah*. 6 vols. Jerusalem: Ktav Publishing House.

———. *The Authentic King Solomon*. Jerusalem: Gefen Publishing House, 2018.

———. *The Tragedies of King David*. Jerusalem: Gefen Publishing House, 2018.

———. *Unusual Bible Interpretations: Hosea*. Jerusalem: Gefen Publishing House, 2017.

———. *Unusual Bible Interpretations: Judges*. Jerusalem: Gefen Publishing House, 2015.

———. *Unusual Bible Interpretations: Ruth, Esther, and Judith*. Gefen Publishing House, 2016.

———. and Rabbi Dr. Stanley Wagner. *Onkelos on the Torah, Genesis*. Jerusalem: Gefen Publishing House, 2006.

Drazin, Nathan. *History of Jewish Education from 515 B.C.E. to 200 C.E.* Baltimore: The Johns Hopkins Press, 1940.

Ehrlich, Arnold Bogumil. *Mikra Ki-Pheschuto*. (*The Bible According to Its Literal Meaning*). Edited by Harry M. Orlinsky. New York: Ktav, 1901, 1969.

Emden, Jacob, Sidney B. Leperer, Meir H. Wise. *Megillat Sefer: The Autobiography of Rabbi Jacob Emden*. Shaftek Enterprises LLC, 2016.

Encyclopedia Talmudit (*Talmudic Encyclopedia*) Jerusalem: Yad Harav Herzog, 1982.

Farber, Dr. Rabbi Zev. *Does YHWH Remit Punishment*, essay, TheTorah.com.

Feldman, Seymour. *Gersonides: Judaism Within the Limits of Reason*. Liverpool: Littman Library of Jewish Civilization, Liverpool University Press, 2010.

Fredriksen, Paula. *Sin: The Early History of an Idea*. Princeton: Princeton University Press, 2012.

Gaon, Saadiah. *The Book of Beliefs and Opinions*. Yale Judaica Series, book 1. Newhaven: Yale University Press, 1989.

Ginzberg, Louis. *The Legends of the Jews – Volume IV: Bible Times and Characters from Joshua to Esther*. Cosimo, Inc. 2006.

Halevi, Judah. *Kuzari*.

Harari, Yuval Noah. *21 Lessons for the 21st Century*. New York: Spiegel & Grau; Penguin Random House, 2018.

———. *Sapiens: A Brief History of Humankind*. New York: Harper 1st edition, 2015.

———. *Sapiens: Homo Deus*. New York: Harper, 2017.

Harris, Jay M. *Guiding the Perplexed of the Modern Age*. New York: New York University Press, 1991.

Hartman, Rabbi Dr. David. *From Defender to Critic: The Search for a New Jewish Self*. Woodstock: Jewish Lights, 2012.

———. with Buckholtz, Charlie, *The God Who Hates Lies, Confronting & Rethinking Jewish Tradition*. Woodstock: Jewish Lights, 2011.

Hertz, Joseph H. *The Authorized Daily Prayer Book*. New York: Bloch Publishing Company, 1948.

Heschel, Abraham Joshua. *God in Search of Man: A Philosophy of Judaism*. New York: Farrar, Straus and Giroux, 1976.

———. *The Prophets*. New York: Harper Perennial Classics, 2001.

Hesse, Hermann. *Demian*. New York: Dover Publications, 2000.

———. *Magister Ludi*. New York: Bantam Books, July, 1982.

Horowitz, Rabbi Isaiah. *Sh'lah*.

Jerusalem Talmud: *Berakhot, Yoma*.

Jewish Publication Society. *Holy Scriptures.*

Josephus, Flavius. *The Antiquities of the Jews.* Translated by William Whiston. Nashville, TN: Thomas Nelson, 2003. First published 1737.

Kaplan, Aryeh, Rabbi, Yaakov Elman, Israel Lipschutz. *Immortality, Resurrection and the Age of the Universe, A Kabbalistic View.* New York: Ktav Publishing House, 1993.

Karo, Joseph ben Ephraim. *Bet Yosef, Orach Chayim.*

———. *Shulchan Arukh.*

Kellner, Menachem. *Maimonides on the "Decline of the Generations" and the Nature of Rabbinic Authority.* New York: SUNY Press, 1996.

———. *Maimonides' Confrontation with Mysticism.* Liverpool: Littman Library of Jewish Civilization, Liverpool University Press, September 2006.

———. *Principles of Faith (Rosh Amanah),* Liverpool: Littman Library of Jewish Civilization, Liverpool University Press, 2004.

Kent, Dr. Oliver. *Inspirational Buddhist Quotations: Meditations and Reflections I, II,* Amazon Digital Services LLC, 2017.

Kiel, Yehuda. *Yehoshua. Da'at Mikra.* Jerusalem: Mossad HaRav Kook, 1994.

Kierkegaard, Soren. *Kierkegaard: Fear and Trembling.* Cambridge: Cambridge University Press, 2006.

Klein, Y. *Megillot, Olam Hatankh.* Divrei Hayamim, 1999.

Kreisel, Howard. *Maimonides' Political Thought: Studies in Ethics, Law, and the Human Ideal.* New York: SUNY Press, 1999.

Krochmal, Nachman Kohen, (published posthumously by Zunz, Leopold). *Moreh nevukhe ha-zeman (The Guide of the Perplexed of the Time).* 1851.

Kugel, James L. *The Great Shift, Encountering God in Biblical Time.* Boston: Houghton Mifflin Harcourt, 2017.

Lauterbach, Jacob Z. *Rabbinic Essays.* Cincinnati: Hebrew Union College Press, 1951.

Leibowitz, Yeshayahu. *Conversations with Yeshayahu Leibowitz on the Moreh Nevukhim of Maimonides* (Hebrew). Jerusalem: Mira Ofran, 2003.

Levine, Samuel J. *Was Yosef on the Spectrum?: Understanding Joseph Through Torah, Midrash, and Classical Jewish Sources.* Jerusalem: Urim Publications, 2018.

Lichtenstein, Aharon, David Berger, Gerald J. Blidstein, Shnayer Z. Leiman. Edited by Jacob Schacter. *Judaism's Encounter with Other Cultures: Rejection of Integration*. Maggid Press, 2018.

Luzzatto, Rabbi Moshe Chaim. *Mesillat Yesharim (Path of the Just [Upright])*. Translated by Rabbi Mordecai M. Kaplan with Introduction by Ira F. Stone Philadelphia: JPS, 2010.

———, *Maamar Hageulah*.

Luzzatto, Samuel David. *Shadal on Exodus: Samuel David Luzzatto's Interpretation of the Book of Shemot*. Edited by Daniel A. Klein. Kodesh Press, 2015.

Maimonides, Moses (Rambam). *Commentary on the Mishnah*.

———. *The Guide of the Perplexed of Maimonides*. Chicago: University of Chicago Press, 1974.

———. *Guide of the Perplexed*. Hebrew translation: Alharizi, Ibn Tibbon with Hanarboni. New York: 1946. English translation: M. Friedlander. New York: Dover, 1956.

———. *Hilchot Melachim*.

———. *Mishneh Torah* (Code of Law and Ethics).

Malkin, Yaakov. *Secular Jewish Culture*. Library of Secular Judaism, 2017 (Keter 2005).

Martyr, Justin Saint. "Dialogue with Trypho."

Melamed, Rabbi Eliezer. *Laws of Prayers,* Maggid Press, 2011.

Midrashim: *Ecclesiastes, Genesis Rabba, Mekhilta, Sifrei Devarim, Tanchuma*.

Mishnaot: *Hilkhot Teshuva, Pirkei Avot*.

Moore, Carey A. ed. *Studies in the Book of Esther*. New York: Ktav Publishing House, Inc., 1982.

Moore, Carey A., trans. *The Anchor Bible Esther*. New York: Doubleday & Co, 1971.

Nietzsche, Fredrich. *The Gay Science*. Translated by Thomas Common. New York: Barnes & Noble, 2008.

Olam Hatanakh, Sifrei Chamad Yehoshua, Jerusalem: Misrad Hachinuch Veha-tarbut.

Oz, Amos. *Dear Zealots: Letters from a Divided Land,* Translated by Jessica Cohen. Boston: Houghton Mifflin Harcourt, 2018.

Pascal, Blaise. *Pensées*. Translated by W.F. Trotter with an Introduction by T.S. Elliot. New York: Dover Publications, 2013.

Pushkin, Alexander Sergeyevich. *Novels, Tales, Journeys: The Complete Prose of Alexander Pushkin*. New York: Random House, 2016.

Radon, Jeffrey. *Reconciling A Contradictory Abraham: On the Orthoprax and Anti-Theological Nature of the Hebrew Bible*. Mazo Publishers, 2017.

Samuel, Rabbi Michael Leo. *Torah from Alexandria: Philo as A Biblical Commentator, Exodus*. New York: Kodesh Press, 2014.

Saramago, Jose. *Cain*. Translated by Margaret Jull Costa. Boston: Houghton Mifflin Harcourt, 2011.

Saramago, Jose. *The Gospel According to Jesus Christ*. Penguin Vintage Classics, 1999.

———. *The Land of Sin (Terra do Pecado*, Portugese), Minerva, Lisbon, 1947.

Scholem, Gershom. *Major Trends in Jewish Mysticism*. New York: Schocken Press., 1961.

Schwartz, Rabbi Ari Ze'ev. *The Spiritual Revolution of Rav Kook*. Jerusalem: Gefen, 2018.

Scriptures, Megillot, and Apocrypha sources (Pentateuch/Prophets/Writings): II Chronicles, Daniel, Deuteronomy, Ecclesiastes (Kohelet), Ethics of the Fathers, Exodus, Ezekiel, Ezra, Genesis, Hosea, Jeremiah, Job, John, Joshua, Judges, Judith, I/II Kings, Lamentations, Leviticus, Micah, Nehemiah, Philippians, *Pirkei Avot*, Psalms, Proverbs, Romans, Ruth, I/II Samuel, *Sifrei Devarim*.

Sefer ha-Temunah (Book of the Figure).

Shakespeare, William. *Merchant of Venice*, play, c. 1596.

Shapiro, David. *Rabbi Joseph B. Soloveitchik on Pesach, Sefirat ha-Omer and Shavu'ot*. Edited by Jacob J. Schacter. Jerusalem: Urim Publications, 2005.

Shapiro, Marc B. *Changing the Immutable: How Orthodox Judaism Rewrites Its History*. Liverpool: The Littman Library of Jewish Civilization, Liverpool University Press, 2015.

Shuchat, Rabbi Dr. Wilfred. *Abraham and the Challenge of Faith According to the Midrash Rabbah*. Jerusalem: Urim Publications, 2018.

Shulchan Arukh, *Yoreh De'ah*.

Soloveitchik, Haym. *Yeinam, Principles and Pressures*. Tel Aviv: Am Oved Publishers Ltd., 2003. Jerusalem: Koren Publishers, 2018.

Soloveitchik, Joseph B. *Megillat Esther Mesorat Harav*. Jerusalem: Koren Publishers, 2018.

Sperber, Rabbi Daniel. *Minhagei Yisrael*. Jerusalem: Mossad Harav Kook, 1995.

Stollman, Aviad. *Eruvin, Chapter X*, ed. Freidman, Shamma, The Society for the Interpretation of the Talmud, 2008.

Freidman, Professor Shamma, ed. *Talmud Ha-Igud Series*. Jerusalem: Society for the Interpretation of the Talmud, 2008.

Targumim: *Neophyti, Onkelos, Pseudo-Jonathan*.

TheTorah.com

Tosephtot: *Makkot, Yevamot*.

Urbach, Ephraim E. *The Sages: Their Concepts and Beliefs*. Translated by Israel Abrahams. Cambridge, Mass: Harvard University Press 1987.

Valentinus. *The Gospel of Truth*.

Waxman, Professor Chaim I. *Social Change and Halakhic Evolution in American Orthodoxy*. Liverpool: Liverpool University Press, Littman Library of Jewish Civilization, 2017.

Whiston, William. *The Life and Works of Flavius Josephus, Antiquities*. Thomas Nelson, 1957.

Wilde, Oscar. "The Picture of Dorian Gray." *Lippincott's Monthly Magazine*, July 1890.

Winston, David. "The Wisdom of Solomon." *Anchor Bible*. New York: Doubleday, 1979.

Wolfson, Harry Austryn. *Philo, Foundations of Religious Philosophy in Judaism, Christianity, and Islam*, Cambridge, MA: Harvard University Press (London: Oxford University Press) 1947.

Zunz, Leopold. *Moreh nevukhe ha-zeman* (the Guide of the Perplexed of Our Time), posthumously published book of Nachman Krochmal, 1851.

Index

About the Author
Dr. Israel Drazin

EDUCATION: Dr. Drazin, born in 1935, received three rabbinical degrees in 1957, a BA in Theology in 1957, an MEd In Psychology in 1966, a JD in Law in 1974, a MA in Hebrew Literature in 1978 and a PhD with honors in Aramaic Literature in 1981. Thereafter, he completed two years of post-graduate study in both Philosophy and Mysticism and graduated the US Army's Command and General Staff College and its War College for generals in 1985.

MILITARY: Brigadier General Drazin entered Army Active Duty, at age 21, as the youngest US Chaplain ever to serve on active duty. He served on active duty from 1957 to 1960 in Louisiana and Germany, and then joined the active reserves and soldiered, in increasing grades, with half a dozen units. From 1978 until 1981, he lectured at the US Army Chaplains School on legal subjects. In March 1981, the Army requested that he take leave from civil service and return to active duty to handle special constitutional issues. He was responsible for preparing the defense in the trial challenging the constitutionality of the Army Chaplaincy. The military chaplaincies of all the uniformed services, active and reserve, as well as the Veteran's Administration, were attacked utilizing a constitutional rationale and could have been disbanded. The Government won the action in 1984 and Drazin was awarded the prestigious *Legion of Merit*. Drazin returned to civilian life and the active reserves in 1984 as Assistant Chief of Chaplains, the highest reserve officer position available in the Army Chaplaincy, with the rank of Brigadier General. He was the first Jewish person to serve in this capacity in the US Army. During his military career, he revolutionized the role of military chaplains making them officers responsible for the free exercise rights of all military personnel; requiring them to provide for the needs of people of all faiths as well as atheists. General

Drazin completed this four-year tour of duty with honors in March 1988, culminating a total of 31 years of military duty.

ATTORNEY: Israel Drazin graduated from law school in 1974 and immediately began a private practice. He handled virtually all manners of suits; including, domestic, criminal, bankruptcy, accident and contract cases. He joined with his son in 1993 and formed offices in Columbia and Dundalk, Maryland. Dr. Drazin stopped actively practicing law in 1997, after 23 years.

CIVIL SERVICE: Israel Drazin joined the US Civil Service in 1962 and remained a civil service employee, with occasional leave for military duty, until retirement in 1990. At retirement he accumulated 31 years of creditable service. During his US Civil Service career, he held many positions; including, being an Equal Opportunity Consultant in the 1960s (advising insurance company top executives regarding civil rights and equal employment) and the head of Medicare's Civil Litigation Staff (supervising a team of lawyers who handled suits filed by and against the government's Medicare program). He also served as the director for all Maryland's Federal Agencies' relationship with the United Fund.

RABBI: Dr. Drazin was ordained as a rabbi in 1957 at Ner Israel Rabbinical College in Baltimore, Maryland and subsequently received semichot from two other rabbis. He entered on Army active duty in 1957. He left active duty in 1960 and officiated as a weekend rabbi at several synagogues, including being the first rabbi in Columbia, Maryland. He continued the uninterrupted weekend rabbinical practice until 1974 and then officiated as a rabbi on an intermittent basis until 1987. His rabbinical career totaled 30 years.

PHILANTHROPY: Dr. Drazin served as the Executive Director of the Jim Joseph Foundation, a charitable foundation that gives money to support Jewish education, for just over four years, from September 2000 to November 2004.

AUTHOR: Israel Drazin is the author of forty-six books, more than five hundred popular and scholarly articles, and close to six thousand book and movie reviews. He wrote a book about the case he handled for the US Army, edited a book on legends, children's books, and scholarly books on the philosopher Maimonides and on the Aramaic translation of the Bible. His websites are www.booksnthoughts.com and Times of Israel. He places two essays on these sites weekly.

LECTURES: Dr. Drazin delivered lectures at Howard Community College, Lynn University, and the US Army Chaplains School.

MEMBERSHIPS AND AWARDS: Brigadier General Drazin is admitted to practice law in Maryland, the Federal Court, and before the US Supreme Court. He is a member of several attorney Bar Associations and the Rabbinical Council of America. He was honored with many military awards, the RCA 1985 Joseph Hoenig Memorial Award, and the Jewish Welfare Board 1986 Distinguished Service Award. Mayor Kurt Schmoke, of Baltimore, Maryland, named February 8, 1988 "Israel Drazin Day." A leading Baltimore Synagogue named him "Man of the Year" in 1990. He is included in the recent editions of *Who's Who in World Jewry, Who's Who in American Law, Who's Who in Biblical Studies and Archaeology*, and other *Who's Who* volumes.